# SINKING the RISING SUN

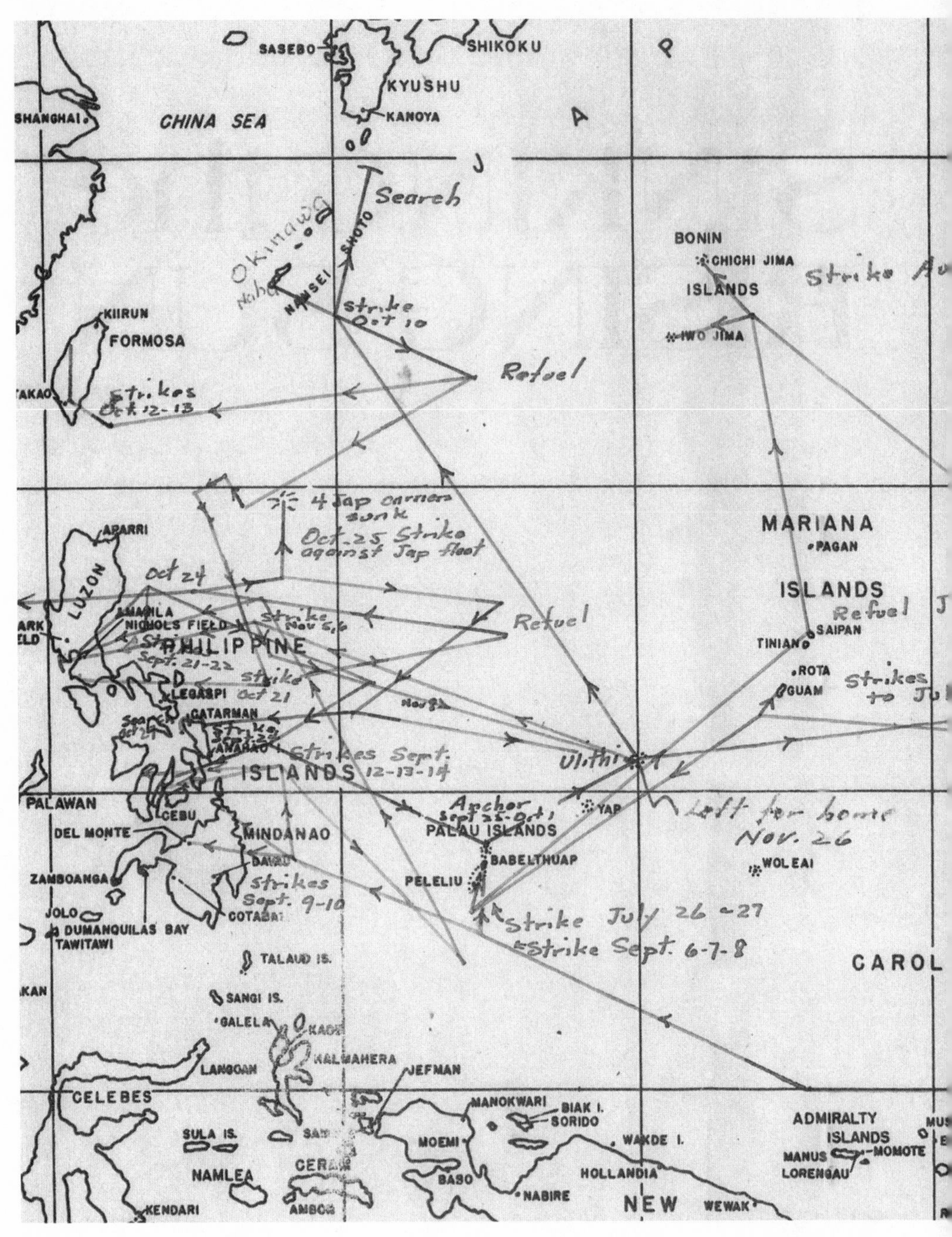


*Author campaign map*

A NAVY FIGHTER PILOT'S STORY

# SINKING the RISING SUN

## DOG FIGHTING & DIVE BOMBING IN WORLD WAR II

by William E. Davis

Foreword by Jonathan Winters

ZENITH PRESS

First published in 2007 by Zenith Press, an imprint of MBI Publishing Company LLC, Galtier Plaza, Suite 200, 380 Jackson Street, St. Paul, MN 55101 USA



Zenith Press titles are also available at discounts in bulk quantity for industrial or sales-promotional use. For details write to Special Sales Manager at MBI Publishing Company, Galtier Plaza, Suite 200, 380 Jackson Street, St. Paul, MN 55101 USA.

To find out more about our books, join us online at www.zenithpress.com.

Designer: LeAnn Kuhlmann

***On the front cover:*** The motion of its props causes an "aura" to form around this F6F on the USS *Yorktown. Department of the Navy*

***On the back cover:*** An F6F vs. the Japanese light cruiser *Oyoda*. U.S. carrier-borne aircraft from Task Force 38 sunk *Oyoda* on July 28, 1945, while it was laid up at Eta Jima. *Lonnie Ortega, artist*

Library of Congress Cataloging-in-Publication Data
Davis, William E., 1921-
Sinking the Rising Sun : dog fighting & dive bombing in World War II : a Navy fighter pilot's story / by William E. Davis.
p. cm.
ISBN-13: 978-0-7603-2946-7 (hardbound w/ jacket)
ISBN-10: 0-7603-2946-X (hardbound w/ jacket) 1. Davis, William E., 1921-
2. United States. Navy—Officers—Biography. 3. Fighter pilots—United States—Biography. 4. Dive bomber pilots—United States—Biography. 5. World War, 1939-1945—Aerial operations, American. 6. World War, 1939-1945—Naval operations, American. 7. World War, 1939-1945—Campaigns—Pacific Area.
I. Title.
V63.D38A3 2007
940.54'5973092—dc22
[B] 2006032321

Printed in the United States of America

*To Diane and Wendy, who loved the stories, and*
*Connie, without whose encouragement*
*I would never have finished it.*

Bill Davis in an F6F on the deck of the *Lexington*.

# CONTENTS

# FOREWORD

*by Jonathan Winters*

Jonathan H. Winters, III, in
Marine uniform at age 18 in 1944.

Before I tell you about my friend "Bill," better known as William E. Davis, III, let me tell you briefly about my feelings about flying and wanting to be a pilot. I was born over eighty years ago in Dayton, Ohio. My grandfather, Valentine Winters, owned the Winters National Bank. He attended school with the Wright Brothers and helped finance their development of the first airplane. I was just a very young boy when my grandfather introduced me to Orville Wright. His brother Wilbur had died many years before. Along about that time I wanted to be a pilot—a fighter pilot.

But from the first grade on I struggled with math! I was tutored, failed, and finally folded completely with Plain Geometry. I knew I would never be a pilot. And so in 1943, I enlisted in the marines, and of all places to end up, I was admiral's orderly and a gunner on the USS *Bon Homme Richard* (CV-31). I never got to land on or take off from a carrier, but I sure saw a lot of planes.

It was when I moved to Montecito, California, that I met and worked with Bill. In my fifty years in show business, like many of us, I've met some fascinating people from all walks of life. I've met Orville Wright; Jimmy Stewart, Army Air Corps; Jimmy Doolittle, Army Air Corps; Eddie Rickenbacker, World War I ace; and Neil Armstrong. But I must stop here and mention after reading this book and knowing Bill for a number of years: if you're in need of a role model, this man ranks to me with the men I've mentioned. So put the canopy forward; you're about to take off on a wild and wonderful adventure.

—Jonathan Winters

IN 1953, JONATHAN WINTERS HEADED TO NEW YORK for the "big time" with $56.46 in his pocket. Then came *The Jack Paar Show*, *The Steve Allen Show*, and *The Tonight Show*, where Jonathan was able to demonstrate his comic genius. He became a top name in American comedy. Jonathan and his wife Eileen have two children and five grandchildren. They live in Santa Barbara, where Jonathan paints and writes when he is not performing.

# ONE

# DAY OF INFAMY

December 5, 1941, was going to be the most important day of my life. I wanted to look good, and I wanted to be sharp. Trying to remain calm, I sat through what seemed like endless classes, nine till twelve, then ate a light lunch. I didn't want to be dull or sleepy as I had been so many afternoons as I slept through metallurgy class. The study of how to harden metals was boring, and the eutectoid diagrams involved were unfathomable.

This was going to be different. I brought an extra white shirt with me that morning, and went down to my locker to change for the interview. I looked at the grungy clothes in the locker that I normally changed into for foundry class, but nothing like that would suffice now. Today I had to be Mister Ivy League. I had a job interview with RCA, Radio Corporation of America, one of the largest companies in the United States. They were going to hire several engineers right out of college, and I sure as hell wanted to be one of them.

Things had changed a lot since I entered college in September of 1938. The engineering graduates the previous June were receiving few job offers, and those that were hired were getting only about ninety dollars a month. What would RCA offer, if they offered? The Depression had finally started to ease with the start of the war in Europe. In addition, the United States had started to rearm, and England would take all the armaments they could beg, borrow, or steal.

Cashing in on the good times the previous summer, I had gotten a job as a final inspector of aircraft instruments in a plant newly set up in the Philadelphia area. In the late 1920s, this plant had been the largest manufacturer of radios in the world, and Atwater Kent owned and managed it. Kent took a dim view of the candidacy of Franklin D. Roosevelt in 1932 and announced to his employees that if Roosevelt won the election, he would close the plant and go out of business. The day after the election, he did exactly that, retaining only two secretaries out of thirteen thousand employees, to handle the paper work until he closed the doors permanently. The plant had remained idle until the government took it over and leased it to Eclipse Pioneer, manufacturer of aircraft instruments.

The work was tedious, but the pay was exceptional, sixty-five cents an hour. With the work days alternating from twelve to sixteen hours, I was soon at time and a half, then double time, and the last half of the week, triple time. Sunday being a day of rest, I only worked eight hours. By the end of the summer I had over one thousand dollars in the bank and the prospect of an actual job.

Climbing the steps from the locker room, I entered the marble halls of the engineering building at the University of Pennsylvania, and proceeded to the interview room. I sensed that this was a critical moment in my life. I stopped at the door and looked at my watch: one thirty exactly, engineering students are nothing if not precise. I straightened my tie one last time and knocked. A very faint voice answered, "Come in." I was on my way.

He was anything but personable: rather aloof and removed, certainly no one you could warm up to or try to get to know on a personal basis, and definitely no one you could joke with. I put on my most serious demeanor and hoped for the best. He had a transcript of my grades in front of him. I wasn't number one in the class, although I wasn't too far behind, but as the interview continued it seemed he wasn't looking for number one, he was more interested in a broad feel for engineering. One question stuck in my mind: "Without doing any figuring, how long would it take to fill a reservoir one mile cube with water coming in at the rate of one hundred gallons a second?" he asked.

I made a wild guess, "twenty years." Right or wrong, he seemed to like it. He made me an offer.

One hundred ninety dollars a month, every month, and I would be assistant plant engineer at the Camden plant. My God! I'd arrived:

a job with big money. The struggle I'd gone through had been worth it. The summers preparing for the college board exams, the miracle of a four-year tuition scholarship, the summer jobs to make enough to keep myself in school another year, the Christmas job selling men's furnishings at a department store to pick up an extra thirty bucks, all worth it.

Camden was close enough for me to live at home for a while, then in my own, real-life apartment, so I could bring a guest home, a female guest if I got lucky. No more cramped love in the rear seat of a car. The world was opening up all for the better. Then it hit me.

"How long can you keep making radios?" I asked the interviewer with a degree of apprehension.

For the first time he smiled. "This is still company confidential, but I'm permitted to tell you since we've made you an offer. About the same time you start with us in June, we're going to start making an entirely new line. We're going into the production of television sets. It will be a revolution, and the future is unlimited."

I didn't know what a television set was, but I acted as if I did.

"I'll need an answer by next Wednesday. You can call me at this number."

I had five days to think it over, but I'd already made up my mind, however, I was going to play it cool. I didn't want him to know I was going out of my mind. I could see it all now: president of RCA, an office in Rockefeller Center. I was on my way.

Leaving the office, I realized I was walking two feet off the ground. I had a feeling of confidence I'd never known before. How good could you feel, I wondered? I'd call him Wednesday, maybe in the afternoon. After all, the future president of RCA wouldn't call in the morning.

I decided not to tell anyone right away. I wanted to savor my little secret for a while, just roll it around in my mind and smile inside. I decided not to tell my girlfriend. We were driving out to her Uncle Harry's farm that Sunday with her mother and father, but I had a feeling that the moment she knew, *plans* might be underway.

The Sunday drive to the farm was delightful. Although it was December, it wasn't one of those typical bleak, cold days that made Philadelphia so dreary in the wintertime. One odd thing did occur on the trip. Crossing a bridge near Norristown, we were startled to see soldiers stationed at both ends of it. They were in full battle gear with fixed bayonets on their rifles. We decided they must be having maneuvers in the area, but look as we might, we couldn't spot anything.

We soon forgot about the soldiers and drifted off into silence. A nagging thought crept back into my mind. It had been bugging me for over a day but I kept pushing it back. I didn't want to think about it, but it wouldn't go away. I was going to work in six months, probably for the next forty years. After the first year I'd get a week's vacation; after two years, two weeks. I would have to buy a car, and it would be a long time before I could afford to join any kind of athletic club, or anything else as far as that was concerned. This would be the beginning of what was starting to sound like a very boring life, but what other choice did I have?

Arriving at the farm almost an hour later, we'd completely forgotten about the soldiers until we saw the look on Uncle Harry's face as he raced out the door to greet us.

"What's happened?" we asked, thinking there'd been an accident.

Uncle Harry answered in the voice of doom, "The Japanese have attacked Pearl Harbor. The first reports sound disastrous."

We all sat dumbfounded for a moment. "Probably one of those hoaxes, like the one a few years ago when that boy wonder put a show on radio claiming Martians had landed in New Jersey," my girlfriend's father offered.

"This is no hoax, and you may not know it but our son Robert was in ROTC in college, and he's in the army reserve. We've been trying to reach him all morning, but so far, no luck."

Entering the house, we heard the continuous radio reports of the attack. It appeared the Japanese had sailed close to the Hawaiian Islands, unopposed, and launched an attack with planes from aircraft carriers. We waited expectantly for reports of our instant retaliation, but they were strangely silent. Rumors of large losses on our part were already being reported, but nothing factual. What was going on?

The dinner was less than a roaring success. Between reports coming in and Uncle Harry's efforts to reach his son, it was a somber party. Finally, just before we left, Robert phoned. He had already been contacted by his reserve unit and ordered to Washington the next day. I couldn't get over the idea that that morning Robert was having breakfast and reading the Sunday paper expecting to go to work the next day, but instead he was now in the U. S. Army, and no doubt going to war. After thirteen years of the doldrums called the Great Depression, this was a shock of unbelievable proportions.

Driving back to Philadelphia, I thought about the Japanese. I felt I already knew something about them. I'd taken geography and knew a little about their country, and there were the newsreels at the movies every week. Their progress in their invasion of China was reported regularly, including the massacre at Nanking, in which it was reported that the Japanese butchered three hundred thousand people, mostly women and children. This was considered so unlikely that almost no one believed it but looked on it as Chinese propaganda.

The Japanese did, however, sink an American gunboat, the USS *Panay*, in the Yangtze River with planes from an aircraft carrier. The Japanese apologized, saying they thought the ship was a pirate ship, although the *Panay* had a large American flag painted topside. The Japanese paid reparations for the sinking, but almost everyone knew this was a deliberate attack, no doubt to show the Chinese that they could expect no help from the United States.

The Japanese I thought I knew were far different. The year before I started first grade, a terrible earthquake struck Japan, leveling Tokyo, as well as many other cities. We received a request at school to bring canned goods to help alleviate the starvation in Japan. Where my mother found cans of peas that large, I'll never know, but each Monday morning I struggled with a gigantic can, barely able to carry it. It seemed that this went on for months. I don't know if the Japanese like peas or not, but I must have fed half the country by myself.

Three months later the letters came. They were in English and were obviously written by students well past the first grade. I say they were in English; they were in beautiful English. Young as I was, I recognized that these letters were exceptional like Shakespeare, with a Japanese accent. I thought of Japan as the land of the beautiful letters. Perhaps they had a dark side; we were soon to find out it was blacker than anyone could imagine.

On December 25, the "Prince of Peace" came to earth—December 25, 1926, that is. On that day, Hirohito was proclaimed emperor of Japan, and a living god. He immediately announced that he was ushering in the Showa, or Peace Era. Even the Japanese should have realized this was no god. The Greeks and Romans knew what gods looked like, bodies that put Arnold Schwarzenegger to shame, bulging muscles and long, flowing beards, not little pipsqueaks. And gods do not wear glasses. Gods have vision that can see forever; they can see over the horizon and into the future. Hirohito couldn't see beyond the head of the horse he was riding. That white horse was the most magnificent horse I'd ever seen, noble and perfect in every respect. The Japanese should have made the horse a god, as the world could have used another Pegasus. Instead, we got the little runt that was riding him. Looks can be deceiving; that little runt turned out to be one of the most brutal leaders of all time. Monday, December 8, the president addressed a joint session of Congress and asked for a declaration of war against Japan.

Roosevelt did not ask for a declaration of war against Germany. This was an interesting turn, as most people felt he had been doing everything possible to get us into a war with Germany in order to save England. Not all of my fellow students at the University of Pennsylvania favored entering the war. There was a strong feeling of pacifism on the campus. We had seen enough of European wars that seemed to break out every twenty years and settled nothing. All of this changed instantly with the Japanese attack. Bitter was hardly the word for it. They had committed a heinous act. They had attacked without a declaration of war, like an assassin in the night, and killed nearly two thousand four hundred American boys.

Japan would no longer be looked on as just the producer of inferior products that flooded U.S. markets before the war. Nor would we any longer believe stories circulated by our naval attaché in Tokyo, telling how Japanese pilots took off from carriers during naval maneuvers but had to fly to land bases in Japan because they couldn't make carrier landings. Or were the Japanese shrewd enough to stage such an operation for the benefit of Western observers? Whatever the truth, we had been lulled into a feeling of superiority with respect to Japan. In one day that disappeared, along with our Pacific Fleet.

Whatever the failings on the part of the navy in the Pacific, they were on the ball in Philadelphia. On Wednesday, only three days after the attack on Pearl Harbor, eight naval officers showed up at the engineering building, set up offices in two classrooms, and were open for business, recruiting engineers. They held interviews with one and all, offering immediate induction into the navy. Several of the officers were doctors, and they'd give you the physical right there. There were many benefits. You immediately became a naval officer and could start wearing the uniform as soon as you could get one. Your salary started immediately, and you could continue going to school until graduation. You'd then go to work in Washington, in one of the bureaus, designing ships, airplanes, and other materials of war. You would probably never get into combat, and at the same time you'd be gaining valuable work experience. My entire class signed up, with one exception.

The moment I heard about the attack on Pearl Harbor, I had but one thought in mind. I was going to volunteer for the air corps—the Naval Air Corps. I wanted to fly, and I wanted to fight against the Japanese. Although being in the navy couldn't guarantee that you'd fight in the Pacific, the odds were awfully good.

That same Wednesday, Hitler took President Roosevelt off the hook by declaring war on the United States. Roosevelt had long been trying to get us into the war, and now Hitler obliged for reasons unknown. The Germans had not attacked us, but the Japanese had, and for no reason. They were going to pay. Since I was only twenty and not yet eligible for the draft, I decided to wait until semester break in February to make my move. I phoned the man from RCA and declined their offer.

The Christmas of 1941 was the saddest I'd ever seen. There were lots of parties, but they were all farewell parties, as almost everyone I knew was heading for some branch of the service. There was more drinking than I'd ever seen before, a foreshadowing of things to come.

TWO

# AN EARLY PASSION FOR FLIGHT

The first time I saw an airplane in flight, I knew that someday I'd learn to fly. Planes were so rare when I was young that I used to run out of the house when I heard one going over. I was six when Charles Lindbergh made his solo flight over the Atlantic, and hung on every report that came over the radio. Then the long silence when there were no reports. We all held our breaths as we knew he'd gone down in the ocean . . . then the miracle. He'd not only succeeded in crossing the Atlantic but had made it all the way to Paris. Thirty-three hours flying alone without sleep. He was my hero.

A Philadelphia newspaper offered a portrait of him suitable for framing for seventy-five cents. I sent for one, had it framed, and hung it over my bed. My mother took pity on me, and together we got up at four in the morning and took the train to New York City, to see the ticker-tape parade in Lindbergh's honor. Fortunately, a man in the front row reached down and lifted me up on his shoulders just as Lindbergh went past in an open car. He was only a few feet away, and he was bigger than life. Unlike Hirohito, he had the look of a god.

Then there were the movies of aerial combat in World War I. It appeared so glamorous, especially compared with the horror of trench warfare. The one-on-one combat had a special appeal, unlike the random nature of artillery shells fired from miles away at unknown targets. My favorite books in my childhood were about King Arthur and the Knights of the Round Table, who went out and destroyed evil for no personal gain but merely because it was there. Aerial combat seemed to personify these qualities.

My friend Henry and I used to ride our bicycles out to the two airfields nearby, Wings Field and Pitcairn, and watch the airplanes take off and land. An old wreck had been pulled over to one side of the field, and after much begging on our part, the airport manager at Wings allowed Henry and me to climb in the cockpit of the wreck. I was actually sitting in the cockpit of an airplane. I could hear the imaginary roar of the engine as I worked the stick and throttle. I could almost feel the motion of the plane. I suspected this might be as close as I'd ever get to a real airplane.

Movies about aircraft carriers were rare. In fact, I can only remember one with Wallace Beery, which featured the *Saratoga*. The story took place in peacetime and wasn't very exciting. The high point was when planes from the *Saratoga* attacked a zeppelin. Wallace Beery was going to get pictures of those gas bags.

The U.S. Navy was fascinated with Zeppelins. The United States received two from Germany as part of our war reparations from World War I. These might prove to be the aircraft carriers of the future, and the navy built two, the *Akron* and the *Macon*. I watched them along the coast of New Jersey during the summers in the mid-1930s. Single-place navy fighter planes would take off from Naval Air Station Cape May and fly up the coast and rendezvous with the dirigibles. They would practice catching a trapeze from the dirigible using a hook that extended above the upper wing of the fighter. Once attached, they would be pulled up into the bag, then lowered again and released. This looked really exciting, but something happened when I was thirteen that made even more of an impression.

The local garage out on the pike had been taken over by a mechanic after the original owner murdered a customer in an argument over a bill. Greasy Dan, so named because of thirty years of grease built up under his fingernails, was an expert mechanic, and my father swore by him. He was about as close-mouthed as a man could be, perhaps because he kept an unlit cigar clenched in his mouth all day. If I took my bicycle by to get air in the tires, he'd come out and check it over and fix anything that needed fixing. He wouldn't charge me anything, but he wouldn't talk to me. I guess I was just too young.

We'd just sat down to dinner on an overcast winter night when the phone rang. Dad took the call and was back in the dining room in seconds, pulling on his coat.

"Come on, Bill." He said as I jumped up and followed him out.

"What's up?" I asked

"Greasy Dan needs us out at Sander's meadow," he answered.

"What for?"

"I have no idea," my father answered.

This did not really surprise me. My father was always there when anyone needed him, and the range of his abilities never ceased to amaze me. He was well known in town for his athletic abilities as a young man, and helped a neighbor's son that had made it into the major league as a pitcher. I caught those lessons, and my father had more stuff on the ball than the professional pitcher. His Welsh background gave him a love of music that ranged from ragtime to grand opera. He was also always there for me.

Just as he started the car, I caught the sound of an airplane above.

Sander's meadow was a cleared field surrounded by woods. I was surprised at the number of cars that were headed in the same direction. As we neared the field, Greasy was out in the road directing traffic up a narrow dirt road that led to the meadow.

"Drive in, pick a side of the field, point your car toward the center and keep your lights on," Greasy instructed as we drove past.

All of the cars turned in and took their places around the field. We recognized everyone there; they were all neighbors.

Greasy followed the last car into the meadow, but before anyone could question him, we all heard it. An airplane was circling overhead. The glow of the car headlights must have been visible from above. The pitch of the propeller changed as Greasy waved everyone off the field. He seemed to know what was going to happen even though the sound of the plane had almost disappeared.

Suddenly, there it was coming in just above the trees, in fact, almost clipping the trees. The plane settled toward the ground and started to flare for a landing. It glided some distance across the field before touching down, and none too soon. It came to a stop only a few feet short of the trees. The engine stopped. We all stood for a moment, stunned, then rushed toward the plane. It was a slick, low-wing monoplane with an open cockpit. The pilot sat there, no doubt also stunned. Finally, the pilot stood up as Greasy jumped up on the wing. The pilot pulled off his helmet. Greasy took one look, jerked the cigar out of his mouth, and slammed it into the ground.

"Jesus H. Christ," he screamed in utter disgust, "no wonder you're lost . . . it's a woman!" I was equally stunned: a woman pilot, and I'd never even been up in a plane. She wanted to thank Greasy for realizing she was lost when she cut her engine a few times over the town, but he'd already walked away in disgust.

The following morning we were all out at the meadow looking at the airplane. The pilot explained that she was trying to set a new cross-country record from Burbank, California, to New York but had become lost when the fog set in. We were about ninety miles from New York City. She took one look at the small field and shuddered.

"I can't fly out of here, it's too small." She looked at the narrow road into the field. "They'll have to take the plane apart to get it out of here."

"I'll get your plane out for you, lady."

We all turned to see Greasy standing there. "Just put five gallons of gas in her, and I'll fly it over to Pitcairn Field. Someone can drive you over," Greasy instructed.

The female pilot looked at Greasy with disdain. "I gather you're a pilot . . . well, not a very experienced one or you'd know you can't fly this plane out of this field. No one could."

"By my standards this is a large field," Greasy replied with equal disdain. "I was with Fighting Six aboard the *Saratoga*."

"You're a carrier pilot?" she asked, her manner changing completely.

"Was, until I retired, the Flying Chiefs, greatest squadron that ever existed."

There was no more argument as Greasy took over, supervising the addition of the gasoline, instructing us on how to push the plane to the far end of the field until the tail was in the woods, then how to hold the horizontal stabilizer while he started the engine. He let it warm up for a few minutes, then ran it up to full power as we hung on to the tail.

Greasy raised his arm, then dropped it, our signal to let go.

Picking up speed slowly, it rolled across the rough field. The trees at the far side came closer. Still, the plane showed no signs of taking off. It continued rushing toward the trees, still on the ground. Just as all appeared lost, Greasy pulled it off and literally clipped a few branches off the trees. He continued to Pitcairn Field with the pilot following in a car. I tried to get Greasy to tell me about flying off a carrier, but to no avail. Somehow, Greasy didn't quite fit my image of a navy pilot; he wasn't tall dark or handsome, but he could sure fly.

THREE

# VOLUNTEERING FOR THE NAVAL AIR CORPS

Finishing the semester's final exam, I walked out of the classroom, heading for downtown Philadelphia and the navy recruiting office.

"Wait up," a voice called from behind me.

I turned to see my namesake following me out of the exam. It turned out in our first day at Penn, that there were two William Davis' in mechanical engineering, William E. and William J. We became immediate fast friends and remained so through college.

"Where are you off to?"

"Down to see about enlisting in the Naval Air Corps."

"I'm going downtown. I'll give you a lift."

We headed toward downtown Philadelphia.

"Why are you doing this?" Bill asked.

"Doing what?" I answered.

"Enlisting in the air corps. Why don't you take one of the engineering positions the navy is offering?"

"I want to fight," I answered without hesitation.

"So do I," Bill answered, "but I think I owe it to my family to take the engineering duty. I'll probably do more for my country in the long run anyway."

He had a point. Engineers were in big demand, and there was a shortage.

"I'm an only child," Bill continued. "I hate to think what it would do to my family if I got killed."

He hit a nerve. I'd been having the same reservations about going into combat when I didn't have to. Was I being selfish in putting my wishes ahead of other considerations? How much does someone owe to his family? There was no dishonor in being a naval officer stuck in Washington for the duration, and it was certainly the smart thing to do.

We arrived at the fort-like building in the center of Philadelphia and made the turn into the underground garage. Bill's father was president of the Federal Reserve Bank for the Philadelphia District, and he was permitted to park in the garage. We started down the steep ramp and came to a complete stop halfway down where the ramp took a ninety-degree turn to the right. Two guards sat behind one-foot-thick bullet-proof glass with their .30-caliber tripod-mounted machine gun trained on us through a slit in the glass. They smiled and waved us on. No car was ever stolen from this garage.

Walking up the street to the naval recruiting office, I was deeply bothered by my conversation with Bill. Did I have the right to put my life in jeopardy because of my own ego or whatever? I hesitated, but only momentarily, at the entrance to the recruiting office. I went in.

The moment I entered the office I could see it was all business. A grizzled navy chief took one disdainful look at me as I walked up to his desk.

"I want to volunteer for the Naval Air Corps," I said.

"There's no point in talking to you unless you have twenty-twenty vision. Come with me."

I followed him into a room with an eye chart and took the test. I had twenty-twenty vision.

"Let's see if you're color blind."

I wasn't.

"Depth perception?" He sat me down in front of an opening through which I could see two poles. Using cords attached to them, I attempted to line them up. He didn't tell me the results, but they must have been good. He started arranging appointments for me for the following afternoon.

The requirements were quite simple. You had to be a college graduate between twenty-one and twenty-six-and-a-half years old; at least five feet four, but not over six feet two; and you could not be married or ever have been married—no divorced men need apply. The physical was something else. It had been set up in the 1930s, when the Naval Air

Corps took only seventy-five cadets a year and the object was to screen out as many as possible. For example, you couldn't have malocclusion; that is, the teeth in your upper and lower jaw had to mate perfectly. We were never told why.

The next day was easy, sort of an intelligence test, mostly math. Having gone through engineering school, I found it relatively simple. Finishing, I took my answers up to the chief.

"Not taking the test? Too tough, huh?"

"No," I replied, "I've finished."

"You couldn't."

"I did," pushing the paper forward.

Reluctantly, he looked at it and checked the answers. "Christ, they're all correct," he said with a look of awe.

The next day wasn't quite so flattering; I had an appointment with a psychiatrist. They were going to shrink my brain. If it hadn't been for seeing a recent movie featuring a psychiatrist, I wouldn't have known what he was.

They had the right man. Doctor Haberstam was a psychiatrist right out of central casting. His sloping shoulders failed to fill out his uniform. In fact, he didn't look like a naval officer at all. Thick, horn-rimmed glasses accentuated his piercing eyes, which seemed to bore right through you. His voice was a misfit, too; it was what was known at the time as a Harvard pin voice. He waited for me to speak, but this was his office, and I wasn't walking into any traps. I waited him out.

Finally, he started with a simple enough question: "Why do you want to join the Naval Air Corps?"

I gave him an equally simple answer. "I want to defend my country, and I want to avenge the Japanese attack on Pearl Harbor."

He stared at me for a long time as if I'd just pleaded innocent to a string of murders I had committed.

"I doubt that that is the real reason," he said finally.

I out waited him once more.

"You've seen the posters?" he asked.

"Posters, what posters?" I answered.

"The ones showing a navy pilot in full uniform, the dress blues, or perhaps whites . . . a stunning uniform," he continued.

What was this, I thought, a fashion show? Where is this idiot going?

"Come now, don't tell me you don't see yourself in one of those uniforms with all of those women chasing you—and the flight pay. You know the slogan, 'glamorous life, good pay.'"

Flight pay was $125 a month for putting your life on the line every day. Did he actually think that would sway me? "I've never thought of myself in one of those uniforms, but I do see myself in a flight suit." At no time did he venture into questions that might reveal any neurosis or psychosis on my part. After all, you had to be at least half crazy to fly off an aircraft carrier. He gave me one long last look as he asked again if it wasn't the uniform. I did my best to assure him it wasn't. He wrote a few notes on my application, and I was out of there. The physical took all day Saturday. I passed and was scheduled to be sworn in on Monday afternoon. The whole thing had taken a week.

I was ushered into the office of a full commander. He was an Annapolis graduate who had retired but had been called back when the war started. He had served with the fleet and gave me some advice on being a naval officer. He also mentioned that he had final approval regarding who would be accepted for training as an officer. I asked him how he made that decision on such short acquaintance.

"Easy," he answered, "I look at the man and decide if I'd like to have him as a roommate on a ship for two years."

I had an idea that diversity might not be a major consideration in his decision.

We stood. I faced him and the American flag as I took the oath. It was February 1942. I was in. When, if ever, would I get out?

FOUR

# STARTING PREFLIGHT TRAINING

In my last semester in college I went into a period of suspended animation. I could be called up at any time, but I tried to concentrate on my classes as war news, which was as bad as it could get, continued to come in. We lost the Philippines. Stories started to drift out of the Bataan Death March. American and Filipino soldiers that had been captured were marched to prisoner of war camps miles away under terrible conditions. A man I met years later was on that march. He had a large blister on one foot and stopped to try to patch it. A Japanese doctor came along and looked at it. He took the flap of skin from the blister, put a stone under it and sewed the skin back down. My friend was ordered to march on it or be bayoneted on the spot. He survived.

Everything seemed to move faster. The very heartbeat of America seemed to be running on double time. Unemployment was a thing of the past. Everyone had work, and everyone's job was important: everyone but me, that is. I was sitting in college, and time seemed to drag. Then the university made a startling announcement: graduation would be pushed up three weeks. The same day I received my orders. I would have five days off after graduation before I had to report for active duty. How many parties can you go to in five days? A lot!

Suddenly I was someone. Fathers of girls I'd dated treated me like a friend, not a threat. After all, I was no threat, I was leaving. One father told me he'd tried to get in the Army Air Corps in World War I, but failed. I could tell he'd regretted it for the rest of his life. I basked in that short-lived glow. I'd graduated from college and I was in the navy; how good could it get?

Saturday morning I watched at the dining room window as our dog Spec raced out the front door and came around to the flower garden in the back. Sliding to a stop, he put his nose in the first flower and collapsed the petals around his nose as he inhaled. Moving from flower to flower, he smelled every bloom in the garden. Later that morning I said a tearful good bye to Spec and got licks on the face in return. Mother, Dad, and my sister Bette took me to Penn Station, where a special train was waiting to take us to preflight training at the University of North Carolina. This was goodbye to everything I'd known in life. My parents seemed cheerful, but my sister was crying. The fact that they might never see me again was the furthest thing from my mind, but perhaps not theirs.

The train was filled with men who had just graduated from college like me. There were twenty of us from Penn. It was like a rolling fraternity house, full of fun and promise. When anyone asked me what type of pilot I hoped to be, I always answered, "Whatever type they assign me," but inside I knew I wanted to be a fighter pilot. I just didn't want to tempt the gods by saying so. Of course, I wasn't superstitious.

Buses met the train in North Carolina and took us to the university. We were still in civilian clothes and had been allowed to bring one bag each. Marching to the supply room, we were issued uniforms, complete with shoes, socks, and underwear. Finding my room, I changed into the uniform and packed all of my civilian clothes and shipped them home in the one bag. In one hour I'd gone from the top to the bottom, from Ivy League graduate to seaman second class. There was nothing lower.

Indoctrination classes started immediately, particularly in when and how to salute: it was often. The Navy had taken over almost all of the university, and it was filled with officers, almost all of them former coaches, both high school and college. We also had officers that were college football players who had graduated the same time I did. One of the officers was Eugene Davis, who had been captain of the Penn football team the previous year. The preflight schools were going to have the best football teams in the country, coached by former coaches from the NFL. The excuse was that it would help recruitment, but the preflight schools were set up for a different reason.

The moment the war started in the Pacific, the United States sustained a terrible beating. The Japanese had been at war in China for at least eight years, and their troops and pilots were experienced. They also had two superior pieces of equipment: the Zero fighter plane and torpedoes. The results were devastating. Despite this, the Americans quickly developed tactics that offset some of this advantage. The Japanese seemed to lack the ability to adapt to changing conditions, a critical advantage for the Americans.

Reports started to filter in to Washington, relating stories of extreme heroism and a dogged will to survive. Navy pilots were being shot down but managed to spend long periods of time in a one-man life raft under the blazing sun, catching fish if they could, and going without water for extended periods of time. One pilot landed on a Jap-held island, managed to evade the enemy, then sailed to another unoccupied island at night, making his way back to an allied base. Some of these exploits lasted as long as fifteen days.

These reports came to the attention of Commander Tom Hamilton, the naval aide to the secretary of the navy. The commander had been an All-American football player at Annapolis, and he quickly became convinced that all naval pilots would experience the same fate as the ones shot down early in the war. He instigated the preflight program, which was total immersion in athletics. We marched, ran, boxed, and swam. Professional wrestlers taught us hand-to-hand combat. We learned every known method of killing a man. I especially liked the one where you bit the carotid artery in half. This, no doubt, was the reason we couldn't have malocclusion.

It's not that the navy was perverse, they just wanted you to forget everything you thought you knew when you came in. The saying was,

"There's a right way, a wrong way, and the navy way." For example, everyone had to be vaccinated, whether you needed it or not. Following this was two weeks of boxing. Large sores formed over the vaccination on your arm. Your opponent punched you there, transferring the oozing liquid to his glove. Then he punched you in the face, eventually leaving a vaccination mark on your face as well as various other parts of your body.

Swimming was scheduled immediately after lunch, to prove you wouldn't get cramps from swimming too soon after eating. This sort of attitude pervaded everything we did. At the time, it was the toughest training in any of the services. Later, ranger and airborne training were even tougher, but ours was tough enough. We were on a 5,500-calorie-a-day diet and losing weight.

The temperature in North Carolina in the summertime was ferocious, topping one hundred degrees every day. Wednesday afternoons and Saturday mornings we went on twenty-mile hikes. Because we were in training to become officers, we weren't permitted to roll up our sleeves or loosen our ties. As a result, the only way to remove the tie at the end of the hike was to cut it off, as there was no way you could open the sweat-soaked knot.

The real fun was at the end of the Saturday hike. Approaching Chapel Hill, we went into drill formation, four across, and marched on campus. Nearing the field, we went into columns of two, then single file. Continuing, we marched between two lines of tables and rolled up our sleeves on the count. As we marched by, medical corpsmen gave us immunization shots in each arm, sometimes as many as five. They gave ten shots per needle before using a new one. The needles dulled quickly, and if you were unlucky enough to be the last shot, it was more like being hit with a blunt instrument than getting the needle. We then stood at attention until the entire cadet regiment was immunized. This could take as long as twenty minutes, during which time as many as fifty men would pass out. You were not permitted to catch them or help them; they just lay there. Those standing were then dismissed to go to lunch, after which we had the entire afternoon and evening off to do as we pleased—that is, until ten o'clock, or 2200 hours, as we were learning to call it.

The problem was, there was nothing to do. There were girls attending summer school at the university, but we had no way of meeting them. We were restricted to our area during the week, and they were holed up in their magnificent sorority houses on the weekends. Then we found our salvation. There was one male student at the university; he was 4F. Generally, 4F'ers were looked down on, but this guy was the most sought-after man on the campus. We found him in his room, and we were prepared to offer him anything if he'd arrange introductions. It turned out we didn't have to offer him anything. The girls were equally anxious to meet us, and if he set it up, he'd have a date the other six nights of the week. After all, we were only free Saturdays. Everything was arranged for that night.

We arrived at his room as polished as we could manage. He took one look at us.

"Where are they?"

"What?" we answered

"The two essentials, a six pack of coke and a blanket," he answered matter-of-factly

"You're telling us we're going to a sorority house with a six pack and a blanket, meet the house mother, and leave with one of the girls?" we asked incredulously.

"What did you think you were going to do?"

Apparently there was more to Southern hospitality than we realized.

Filled with trepidation, we approached the beautiful, Southern-style sorority house, U.S. Navy blanket under one arm and a six pack of coke in hand. Had I approached a sorority house on the campus of the University of Pennsylvania with similar items, I'd never have gotten past the front door. In fact, I'd probably be blackballed for life.

This house mother greeted us at the door, and she did greet us, almost with open arms. Everything was sweetness and light. She loved us despite the fact that we were Yankees. We were going to defend our country, and she had arranged a date for each of us. After introductions, we left, not knowing exactly where we were going, but loving who we were going with. The girls were beautiful in a very natural way and full of life. They laughed a lot and flirted like crazy. I loved it. "Where are we going?" I asked in all innocence.

"Silly boy, we're going to the stadium," my date informed me in that beautiful Southern accent.

What the hell were we going to do at the stadium? We walked across the open campus to the woods, then down into a natural bowl that formed the football stadium at the university. But we weren't going in the stands; we were going on the field itself. Once there, my date helped me spread the blanket as we stretched out under the stars and listened to classical music that was being played over the loudspeaker system. The Coke was for resuscitation. I was immediately converted to the Southern cause.

The navy was not. After two weekends, an order came to the effect that navy property, namely blankets, could not be removed from our rooms. Grass stains were unacceptable.

# FIVE

# "WILL WE EVER GET TO FIGHT?"

It was a tough transition going from college into the navy. We were on a university campus, but we were also in boot camp, almost like prison with lockdown every night. We were playing a new game with a completely new set of rules, and there were serious consequences if you violated any of those rules. This wasn't fraternity stuff. We were almost all fresh out of college—all but one. Bob Dawson had graduated four years before and happened to end up in our platoon. He just squeezed in under the age limit of twenty-six and a half. Naturally, we called him Pop.

We were housed in the university dorms, four to a room on upper and lower bunk beds. The navy contracted with local businesses for the required furniture, including mattresses and pillows. Sleeping on the mattresses would have been out of the question except for the fact that we were dog-tired each night. The pillows were another matter. Some local farmer had the contract to manufacture them, and he must have made a killing. He raked up all the feathers in the chicken coop and had someone stuff them into a pillow cloth and sew them up. The problem was, he raked up the chicken shit as well, which he no doubt included at no extra charge.

The nights were hot and there was no air conditioning; we sweat a lot. The sweat ran down our faces and onto the pillows. The odor was unbelievable. It was so bad the navy actually did something about it. They got us new pillows—I'm sure at much greater expense.

There were forty-eight of us in a platoon with two officers. Ensign Warwick had been a football coach at a small New Hampshire college while Lieutenant O'Meara had been a coach at a high school in Boston. Warwick could have passed as a naval officer anywhere, but O'Meara just wasn't cut out for the military. He was slightly older, had a visible gut, and always looked confused. Every order he gave began, "Hell, men," followed by an explanation of how he was going to get us out of the mess he'd gotten us into.

This was particularly true when we marched. He shouted out a cadence, "Hut, one, two three, four." We quickly adjusted, hopping on the hut, then marching normally on the four counts. As soon as we showed up on the drill field, the other platoons stopped and watched as we hopped across the field. One afternoon O'Meara got us trapped behind a series of soccer nets and had to work like hell to get us out of there without forcing us to climb the nets.

The entire platoon became aware of Paizano the first day of swimming. He was a tall, lean Italian from the Boston area. We lined up on one side of the largest swimming pools I'd ever seen.

An officer shouted out an order. "On the count of three, everyone jump in."

"I can't swim," Paizano shouted back.

"I didn't ask you if you thought you could swim, I said jump in, and we'll tell you if you can swim or not. One . . . two . . . three!"

Everyone jumped, including Paizano. To say he sank like a rock would be an understatement. He streaked to the bottom, so fast no one could grab him.

"What the hell," the instructor shouted, "grab the hook."

Another instructor raced to the side of the pool and took the hook out of the cradle. Too late, Paizano was already at the bottom of the deep end and the hook wasn't long enough. "God damn it," the officer moaned as he ripped off his jacket and shoes and dove in. In a few moments he surfaced with Paizano at his side as others pulled him out.

"What the hell was that?" the officer asked.

"I told you I couldn't swim," Paizano answered defiantly.

"I've seen guys that couldn't swim, but I've never seen anything like that—and I just had this uniform cleaned."

The fact that Paizano couldn't swim and never did learn did not wash him out.

We all had to pitch in to help Pop. He'd had a desk job for the four years he'd been out of college, and he wasn't in very good shape. We had to run a timed obstacle course every week, and we were supposed to improve every week. Pop couldn't make it through once on the run. We all took turns running in his place, making sure none of our platoon officers were there at the time. Carefully we improved Pop's time each week. He even received compliments on his improvement.

One cadet in the platoon stood out from all the rest, Duke de Luca. He was of Italian decent and had attended NYU. He was well built and was very close to handsome, but there was something else that set him apart. He was cocksure of himself but in a way that was not arrogant. He was always smiling and nothing could take it away. As a result, everything went his way. He expected it and he got it. Duke had spent a lot of time at jazz clubs in New York and knew his music.

We soon became good friends—good enough that one day he showed me a framed eight-by-ten glossy of a girl, autographed, "Love, Helen." I recognized Helen Wellbank immediately, as she regularly graced the covers of various women's magazines. She was a New York model and as gorgeous as a woman could be.

"Sometime during our training we'll get leave, and I want you to come to New York with me and meet her," Duke volunteered.

"Anytime," I answered. "Does she have a friend?"

Our mornings were made up of classes to which we marched dutifully. One was in aircraft recognition, where we learned to identify all of the military planes in the world. No one knew where we might be stationed, so we had to know them all, as well as all of the naval vessels. These images were flashed on a screen at one seventy-fifth of a second. It's amazing what you can see in that short a time.

We learned Morse code until we could receive thirteen words a minute. I sat an hour each day with earphones on, listening to those electrical signals. What seemed impossible at first soon became routine.

I learned to read weather maps and navigate. Dead reckoning was pretty simple; celestial navigation was somewhat harder.

They gave us courses in etiquette: which spoon and knife to use, how to conduct yourself when calling on your commanding officer socially, and how to hold a girl when dancing. You were not allowed to touch her bare skin; you had to wear gloves. Deiter, an up-country Dutchman, sent home for his work gloves. He wanted to be a proper naval officer when he took a date to the stadium.

We viewed a training film almost every day, made by a company named Jam Handy. They must have been making a fortune, as they had a film for every military activity: gunnery, both antiaircraft and aerial, and how to fire a mortar or throw a hand grenade. The best, however, were the ones warning us about venereal disease. I loved the title of one of these, "Flies Breed Germs, Keep Yours Closed," and the line in that film when the doctor examines the sailor and says, "Son, you've got a venereal disease."

"I must have gotten it in a public toilet," the sailor answers.

"That's a hell of a place to take a date," the doctor replies. We were learning something every day.

The most interesting of all was a course in naval history, taught by an Annapolis graduate who'd had to resign from active duty due to a medical problem, but was brought back when the war started for non-combat duty. He was from the South, and you could tell the navy was his life. When he told about a battle, you felt you were there.

Our feeling of invincibility was shattered, however, when he started to analyze the recent landing of American troops on Guadalcanal, on August 1, 1942. He did not feel we would be able to hold the beachhead in view of the overwhelming superiority of the Japanese forces in the area. The idea of our losing another battle to the Japanese was unacceptable. We had taken to quoting famous naval sayings, but "I have not yet begun to fight" was taking on new meaning.

Our marines were engaged in deadly combat and we were sitting here in a classroom. Our motto became, "Will we ever get to fight?"

Lying awake at night, I thought of those marines fighting for their lives against banzai attacks by masses of Japanese troops, with nothing but their courage and the Browning water-cooled machine gun to sustain them. Despite this carnage, a joke came out of that setting. It went that a platoon of marines was fighting every day against hordes of Japanese. After each battle the sergeant would debrief his troops.

"How many Japs did you kill?" he'd ask each marine.

They'd answer variously, "Two," "Five," "Seven," and so forth. But, one marine always answered, "None."

"Don't you know how to get a Jap?" the sergeant asked. "When they're near, you shout out, 'Hirohito is a horse's ass,' and that Jap will leap up to attack you, and you shoot him." That evening the sergeant debriefed the men. As usual, the one marine hadn't shot a Jap. "What happened?" the sergeant asked, mad as hell.

"Well, I done what you told me, I shouted, 'Hirohito is a horse's ass,' and sure enough this Jap leaps up and starts running at me, but before I can shoot, he shouts, 'Roosevelt is a stupid idiot,' and sarge, I couldn't shoot a fellow Republican."

We finished preflight and were scheduled to move to an E base. The E didn't stand for electronic, as in e-mail; it stood for elimination! The base where we were to learn to fly was called an elimination base. Were they trying to tell us something? The problem was, they didn't have any room for us at any flight base and wouldn't for another week. What to do with us? Someone came up with the bright idea, let's see how the army lives. We marched to Fort Bragg.

The army really didn't know what to do with us. In fact, they didn't know what we were. We were going to become officers, but what were we at this point? The first night, they decided we were officers and had us dine in the officer's mess. The next night they decided we weren't, and sent us to the enlisted men's mess. To make matters even worse, they put us in line in front of the enlisted men, who were already standing in line. To say they resented us would be putting it mildly. The cooks behind the counters got even for all of them.

As we marched past the vats of food, they instructed us to hold our metal trays at a forty-five–degree angle. Then they served us by filling a wooden ladle with the food and swinging it until the ladle hit a large block of wood they had in their other hand. The food flew and, if you were lucky, struck your tray and stuck. The deserts were at the end of the line. They placed ice cream on top of the meat and potatoes then poured chocolate sauce over everything. Delicious.

One week there and we couldn't wait to go back to Chapel Hill, where we received good news. The E bases had opened up, and they were ready for us. One hundred would go to Saint Louis, four hundred to Norman, Oklahoma, and twenty to Philadelphia. We drew our assignments from a hat. I lucked out with Philadelphia, my home town.

SIX

# FIRST SOLO FLIGHT, AND BARNSTORMING OVER LAKEHURST

Philadelphia meant the Philadelphia Navy Yard, a facility that had been there probably since the Revolution, and many of the buildings appeared to be original. There was a single, short runway that ran across the base between rows of buildings, all housing secret work. As a result, aviation cadets were not allowed to fly out of or into the facility. Our field was across the river in Camden, the home of the RCA plant.

We were housed in one cozy room, all sixty of us. Privacy would have to wait. Every morning at five thirty, the officer of the day would come in with a wake up call that resounded through out the barracks. "Let go of your cocks and grab your socks." It had a certain ring to it.

The first morning at the base I reported to the flight line, all suited up with everything including a parachute, to meet my instructor. This would be my first flight in an airplane, and I was jumping out of my skin while trying to appear calm. Would he let me handle the controls on the first flight? He had something more exciting in mind. Fortunately, I didn't know.

Lieutenant Junior Grade Keiffer approached me with a look of disdain on his face as he went over my file. The look became a sneer.

"You graduated in engineering?" he asked.

"Yes sir," I answered.

Maybe he'd done poorly in math or something, but he seemed to take an instant dislike for me. I had the sickening feeling he was going to do everything possible to wash me out. "Get in," he ordered.

I climbed up on the wing and slid into the rear cockpit, trying to fit the parachute in the metal bucket seat. The plane was Naval Aircraft Factory N3N, the navy-built version of the Stearman two-place open-cockpit biplane.

Keiffer buckled himself in the front cockpit as an enlisted man cranked the inertia starter until it screamed. With the clutch engaged, the engine turned over a few times before it caught, while at the same time spewing flames out the exhaust pipes. Another crewman started forward with a fire extinguisher, but the flames quickly disappeared as the engine roared into action. We taxied out to the one runway, weaving back and forth so that we could see in front of us.

Keiffer ran the engine up and checked the mags. They checked out, and with that he added full power, and we started rolling down the runway, picking up speed as we went. Suddenly we were airborne, and I was looking down on the navy yard and a British battleship that was tied up there for repairs. The battleship bristled with guns, most of them antiaircraft guns. Would I ever look down on an enemy battleship in combat?

I was connected to the instructor by a gosport, a hollow tube that was strapped over his mouth and went to a set of earphones I was wearing. He could talk to me, but I couldn't answer, only shake my head yes or no. He could watch me in a small rear-view mirror.

Climbing over New Jersey, we arrived at an area with open fields and few homes.

"Got your seat belt tight?" he asked.

I checked and shook my head yes.

"Well, tighten it more. We're going to do the original screaming asshole maneuver."

I knew the names of a lot of aerobatic maneuvers, but I'd never heard of this one. While I was still thinking, he pushed the nose over and went into a vertical dive. The wires between the wings began to sing as the needle on the air-speed indicator climbed toward the red line. The speed continued to increase as the needle passed the red line and approached two hundred miles an hour. It appeared I was going to die on my first flight.

The noise was horrendous. The wires no longer sang, they screamed, along with the engine, wings, and everything else. We were already thirty miles an hour above the design limitation of the airplane.

I wedged the fingers of one hand under the seat-belt release and grabbed the parachute rip cord with the other. I was ready if the wings flew off.

He pushed forward on the stick. The idiot was going to attempt an outside loop. We were pulling three negative Gs, which meant I now weighed 525 pounds, all of which was being held in by the narrow belt across my lap. My eyes bulged as the blood in my body raced to my head. I felt like toothpaste being squeezed out of a tube. I knew I'd gained at least two inches in height.

Losing speed as we climbed upside down, the airspeed dropped below the red line. It appeared the wings were not going to come off, but by God, he'd tried. We arrived at the top of the loop, back to straight and level flight—I thought!

Inside and outside snap rolls came in quick succession, followed by slow rolls, then inverted flight ending in a stall and an inverted falling leaf leading into an inverted spin. Keiffer watched me in his rear-view mirror hoping I'd get sick. I didn't. The truth was, I was so sure we were going to die I never had time to think about getting sick. I actually sat there laughing, which infuriated him further. Landing back at the navy yard, he taxied up to the flight line, signed the yellow sheet, and walked away without a word. I'd had my first flight in an airplane.

Lieutenant Keiffer showed up five minutes late the following morning, still anything but friendly, but without the obvious belligerence of the previous day. We took off without incident and flew to the practice area.

"Always make a 360-degree turn and look above and below before you start any maneuvers—no mid-air collisions."

I nodded as he started the turn.

"You've got it," he said as he held up both hands for me to see. I took the controls.

"Turn to the right, slight right rudder, and ease the stick to the right."

I tried. The plane responded immediately. I felt a surge of excitement flow through my body. I was flying.

"You're letting the nose drop," he shouted.

I pulled back on the stick. Again there was immediate response, and we were climbing. He grabbed the controls and took the plane back to straight and level flight.

"Try a left turn."

This time I'd get it perfect. I eased the stick over and applied left rudder, holding the nose on the horizon. I made the turn a little steeper and tighter. I was really flying. He cut the throttle. The engine noise ceased; we were without power. I hesitated; he didn't. He jammed the stick forward, sending the plane into a dive.

"The instant your engine quits, push the nose down to keep your airspeed up so you don't stall. What emergency field have you picked out?"

I searched the ground below us for a suitable landing spot.

"You should always have an emergency field in view, and you should always know the direction of the wind so you can land into it."

We continued dropping. We neared a field that I thought was suitable.

"Just one problem, you've got power lines and you're going to have to go through them." He added power, and we started to climb. This was going to be tougher than I thought.

During the first hour I learned to stall the airplane to get some idea of how it would feel when I made a landing. Armed with this information, we headed for the practice field at Camden. Our planes, being trainers, were painted a bright yellow to warn other pilots. These were of course known as Yellow Perils.

The field was swarming with them like bees around a hive. Working my way safely into the traffic pattern was no mean feat. Once in position, I started our glide to the field. Keiffer flew, with my hands on my controls following his movements of his controls. We bounced down in a reasonable landing on the grass field. I did it over and over for the next half hour, once making the entire landing without any help from the instructor.

Finishing the flight, we taxied to the flight line, where I got out and another cadet got in. I would have to take the bus back to the navy yard. In the meantime, I'd wait in the ready room, where all the student pilots stayed when they weren't flying. The room had an ample supply of magazines, but we were more interested in the newspaper and took turns reading it out loud. There were two trials going on at that moment, one in Los Angeles and one in the Bahamas. The L.A. trial was about sex, while the other was about sex and murder, and the newspaper carried the entire testimony of each trial.

Errol Flynn was on trial for rape; actually, statutory rape. He had had sex on his yacht with a sixteen year old. From her picture she could have been twenty-five. The Bahamian case involved a man who was accused of murdering his wealthy father-in-law. The testimony that impressed me the most in the Flynn case detailed the lovemaking the first night, then her refusal the second night, to which he responded, "I possessed you last night, why can't I possess you tonight?" And he came up with this without a script.

The other trial was even better. A young British beauty of royal birth testified that "British women took good manners for granted, American women took them to bed." My parents taught me manners, but I suspect they never had this in mind.

Deiter made some signals that we should go on with what we were doing, but to watch the small window in the ready-room door. Casually glancing over, I realized that Dr. Haberstam, the psychiatrist, had his head pressed against the window, observing us through those thick glasses as if we were rats in some sort of experiment. Perhaps we were.

"Did you have trouble with him?" I asked, nodding toward the door.

"Well, yes I guess, but he was no match for me."

We all waited as Deiter's eyes narrowed and he took center stage.

"When I went in to enlist, they sent me to his office. After a lot of stupid questions, he finally asked what I'd do if I saw a Japanese battleship? 'I'd bomb it,' I told him. 'And suppose a second battleship came along?' 'I'd bomb it.' 'And a third appears?' he persisted. 'I'd bomb it.' Then the crucial question, 'Where are you getting all these bombs?' 'The same place you're getting all those battleships.' I had him. No witch doctor's gonna outsmart old Deiter."

With the daily flights, I quickly got six and a half hours of instruction. We'd landed on the field after one such flight, but Keiffer didn't tell me to taxi to the flight line. Rather, he got out of the plane. "She's all yours."

I was dumbfounded. "I only have six and a half hours," I said.

"You graduated in engineering, you're supposed to be smarter than the rest of us."

My God, was my imagined brightness going to get me killed? I was about to add something, but he had already moved away from the plane, heading for a grassy area where he lay down. This was it. I taxied into position for takeoff, waited until two planes making approaches landed, then gave it the throttle.

Picking up speed, the plane swerved to the left, but I quickly added a little right rudder. Before I knew it, the tail was in the air. I eased back on the stick, and I was airborne. I was flying, alone! My God, was that front cockpit empty. The plane seemed to handle differently. Could Keiffer's weight make that much difference?

Swiveling my head, I tried to keep track of all of the other planes in the vicinity of the field. Climbing to five hundred feet, I leveled off and slid into the traffic pattern to land. So far so good. Easing back on the throttle, I started to glide toward the field, making a turn for final approach. Watch the airspeed; too fast and you'll overshoot the field, too slow and you'll spin in.

As I was approaching the landing spot I'd picked out, a plane on the ground taxied out, leaving me no room to land without risking a collision. I didn't want to abort the landing with my instructor watching, although there was one way: I could side-slip the airplane. Risky was hardly the word with my limited experience, but I was going to try. I dropped the left wing and added right rudder. The plane slid more than flew as I cleared the plane on the field and took it almost to the ground before I leveled off. Hitting the ground hard, I immediately rolled to a stop. Keiffer walked over.

"What the hell was that?" He waited, but I didn't answer.

"Okay, take her up for a half hour and see if you can find the field again."

I gave it the gun. I was off on my own without an instructor watching me. For the first time in my life I felt completely free—a feeling of exhilaration I didn't know was possible. I was free of the earth, and I was free in three dimensions. I looked down on the city of Philadelphia, which was now in miniature, like the model train set I had as a child. The Delaware River Bridge was in front of me, and I could almost see the Atlantic Ocean to the east. I thought of Antoine de Saint-Exupéry's description of flying along the coast of South America in his book *Wind, Sand, and Stars*, and the waterspouts that rose from the sea. He compared the love of flying with the love of a woman and the risk of death in quest of a greater value. I was beginning to have a glimpse of his meaning.

I was full of myself that night in the barracks. I'd soloed after record time in training, and I wanted everyone to know it. It was going well until Deiter stepped in.

"Did you do a loop?"

"A loop, hell no, are you crazy?"

"I thought you wanted to be a fighter pilot," he continued.

"I do," I answered resolutely.

"Well, yes I guess, you didn't show it."

"What do you mean?" I asked completely deflated.

"You had a chance to show what you're made of, and failed. Everyone does a loop after soloing, that is, if you have the stuff to be a fighter pilot."

I was devastated. I lay awake all night thinking what I should have done. The idea of doing a loop had never occurred to me. We'd had no aerobatic training, but I shouldn't have let that stop me. I had to do something to make up for this blatant flaw.

The following morning I took the bus to the field in Camden for my first hour-and-a-half solo flight. I climbed to three thousand feet and searched for something spectacular that I could do. The Delaware River Bridge lay before me. I could dive, fly below it, and come up in a loop around the bridge at the center where the suspension cables came down near the roadway. The problem was too many people would see me, and someone might take my number and report it—big trouble. I continued north and there it was, a blimp.

The navy had a lighter-than-air aircraft training base at Lakehurst, New Jersey. This was the same field where I watched my great-aunt take off on the first flight of the airship *Hindenburg* from America to Germany in 1936 and saw the same airship explode and burn in 1937.

There were a number of blimps in the area, each carrying six cadets and two instructors. I singled one out and turned toward it staying above it so that no one aboard could see me. Starting my dive, I picked up speed until the needle on the air-speed gauge was near the red line, then pulled up under the blimp. I climbed up one side of the bag and was upside down as I passed over the top. If I fell out of the loop, nine of us would die. The plane carried over the top, and I started down the other side. I'd made it. I hoped the gods of war would recognize this and forget my lack of aggressiveness the day before.

Deiter exploded. "You did *what*?"

"I looped a blimp," I answered as casually as I could.

"You maniac," he screamed, "nobody does anything like that. I was just pulling your leg last night."

I had everyone's attention as I took them through a step-by-step description of the feat. They all shook their heads in disbelief.

That night Duke came over before lights out. "Did you really do that?"

"You don't think I'd lie, do you?"

"I guess not, just don't do anything that crazy again. You'll get a chance to show everything you've got before this is over."

I slept soundly that night.

# SHOOTING CIRCLES, CHECK FLIGHT, AND FIRST LEAVE

No sooner had I settled into the routine at the navy yard than they moved us to a new field just outside of Philadelphia, and only twelve miles from my home in Ambler. The navy had taken over Pitcairn Field and turned it into Naval Air Station Willow Grove. I used to ride my bicycle out to this field to watch the experiments with autogiros. Our auxiliary field was Wings Field, where I used to sit in the cockpit of the wrecked airplane and dream of the day I'd learn to fly one, hopefully not to wreck one.

The accommodations were brand-new and excellent, with two to a room and our own bath. The field had one long runway, but we were restricted to taking off and landing on the grass, which was a little more forgiving. The officer in charge of cadets was Lieutenant Ducky Pond, the famous football coach from Yale. Once he found out I knew the area and had played football, he assigned me as his aide, which consisted of doing his banking in Ambler, using his Ford convertible for transportation. I loved driving through my home town in the snazzy car and dropping by home for lunch. My mother was delighted.

Although we covered every aspect of flying in our training, one thing stood out: preparing to make a carrier landing. At this point that preparation consisted of shooting circles. At the auxiliary field a circle was painted on the ground slightly larger in diameter than the wingspan of the plane, and I was required to make a full-stall landing, touching down in the circle using several different approaches.

During one approach I could use power as required, provided I landed in the circle tail wheel first. Once I mastered that procedure, I had to do the same using S turns into the circle, then glide in from five hundred feet altitude. On every flight, either with or without an instructor, trainees ended up making ten landings. When time came for the check ride with the head of training, I had to hit eight out of ten.

The day I dreaded finally arrived. I was going for the check ride. The chief instructor was a seasoned navy pilot with carrier experience, and he never smiled. My heart sank just looking at him. We took off and headed for Wings Field. Halfway there he cut the engine. I was expecting it and jammed the nose down so forcibly he would have shot out of the cockpit if it weren't for the seat belt. I already had an emergency field picked out and made a suitable approach into the wind. Nearing the ground, he gave it the gun and I started a steep climb out of the field. I was feeling pretty pleased with myself when he cut the throttle again. We were barely above stalling speed and in a nose-high attitude. Once again I jammed the stick forward and barely kept the plane in the air. He added power as we were damn near going in. Still shaken, I arrived at the field for the circle-landing test.

Checking the wind, I positioned myself for my first power approach to a circle. Easing back on the throttle, I started the downwind leg of my glide, using a little power to keep my speed up. Perhaps the second emergency the instructor had given me was still on my mind, but I ended up approaching too fast and overshot the circle. One down. I now had to hit eight out of nine.

I laid the next one in right in the center of the circle and felt a little more confident. My good luck held until the sixth one. I wasn't quite sure from my vantage point if I had the entire airplane in the circle or not. The instructor being in the front cockpit was slightly higher and could see, but he gave no indication one way or the other. I'd better be on the safe side and count it a miss. I had to hit all the rest.

Coming in for the last power-off landing, I realized I was a little low and a little slow. I still thought I could make it, although I would have to cross the road at the edge of the field at very low altitude. There was just one problem: a car was coming, and if I continued on my present course, I was going to hit him. I looked at the driver until I was sure I had his eye then held up my hand, indicating a stop. He stopped, and I flew past him and full-stalled in the center of the circle. The chief flight instructor turned in the cockpit and gave me one of the strangest looks I'd ever seen, then burst out laughing as he gave me a thumbs up, indicating I'd passed the check flight. I was so happy on the flight back to the base I didn't even care if he gave me another emergency.

Had he failed me on the check flight, I would have received some additional instructions, after which I would have had another check flight. Failing this, I would have gone before a board made up of the commanding officer of the base, the chief flight instructor, and Doctor Halberstam. The navy put a lot of stock in the opinion of the psychiatrist, and he would have had the final word as to whether I would flunk out or not. Washing out of flight school left two alternatives: request training as a line officer, or get out and be drafted the next day. Each check flight took on added significance. We never went to see a classmate that washed out; it was too embarrassing for both of us.

C Stage finally arrived, the fun stuff, nothing but aerobatics. The first thing to learn was how to recover from inverted spins. When you went into one, everything seemed in the wrong direction, including all of the forces acting on your body. Snapping out of one, you ended up in a regular spin, which now seemed almost normal. I spent each afternoon going through all of the maneuvers you can do in an airplane until I could do them with precision and confidence.

Recovering from the last maneuver close to the ground, I looked for a moving freight train. Finding one, I'd run my wheels along the top of the freight cars. Failing that, I flew over to the reservoir and after clearing the ice of skaters, ran my wheels on the ice as the hockey players watched. I was ready for the final stage, formation flying, after which I was ordered to Pensacola, but not until I completed five days of leave with my family.

My father's health was a real concern. He was aging rapidly, and once again I wondered about my decision not to take an assignment in Washington, but there was nothing I could do about it now. There were the usual parties, and it was at one of these that I learned of the combat death of one of my high school classmates. Bill had played tackle on the football team and always given his all. He was a big, handsome guy but very quiet. No one knew where he'd been killed, only that he was dead. I knew he was the first of many, perhaps including myself. His death made a lasting impression.

I had one beautiful Sunday dinner with my family on the last day of leave. My mother had saved her ration points, and the meal was superb. There was one slight hitch. Spec slipped into the dining room before we sat down for dinner and lifted a quarter pound of butter from the table and raced outside with it, the melting butter running from his jaws. He was in the dog house literally.

There was another side to rationing, and that was saving cooking fat or grease and turning it in at selected stores or butcher shops where it was collected to be used in the manufacture of explosives. Since most people shopped on Saturday and that was the busiest day, the local butcher put a sign in his window: "Ladies, please don't bring your fat cans in here on Saturday." No one had the heart to tell him.

EIGHT

# NAVAL AIR STATION PENSACOLA: TRAINING IN THE SNJ

The train going south from Philadelphia was first class. Before the war these trains carried tourists from the Northeast to Miami and were state of the art. The train we transferred to going west to Pensacola had never known the meaning of first class. It would have been ancient during the Civil War. The passenger cars had wicker sides, and the engine burned wood to generate steam. There was no ventilation, so the only alternative was to open the windows. This let the acrid smoke from the engine in, and aside from the smell, it covered our uniforms with soot. In desperation we stripped to the waist and let the smoke blow through. We wanted to complain to the conductor, but he was already locked in the only sleeping quarters on the train with an overaged blonde, never to be seen again. Arriving at Pensacola, we put our uniforms on over our blackened bodies and hoped they wouldn't hold an inspection on our arrival.

Naval Air Station Pensacola was a remembrance of things past joined at the hip with the latest in aviation. There were avenues of Victorian homes with wide lawns that served as homes for senior officers. The lawns swept down to a beautiful officers club and the bay. You could have been in the nineteenth century rather than January 1943. Airfields were only a short distance away, with swarms of planes circling above or parked in rows in front of the administration building. I loved the look of my new home. I also loved the feel of the warm sunshine, having just left the bitter cold of the North—my first taste of Florida.

My quarters, although older, were spacious, with a view of the bay. We were two to a room, and in short order I met my new roommate. I was surprised to find he had not come from Philadelphia but had gone through E Base in St. Louis. It did not take long to realize that Howell Cobb was different.

Tall, lean, and sardonic, Howell had a triangular face and dark, unruly hair. Above all else he was a gentleman, a Southern gentleman.

His great-grandfather had been vice president of the Confederacy. My God, I was living with history.

Howell had attended a small liberal arts college in Georgia, and I quickly realized he was the best-read man I'd ever met. He had read Saint Thomas Aquinas in Latin, and this was only the beginning. I was completely outclassed when it came to discussions of philosophy. Mother had been a member of two book clubs, and I read all of the bestselling novels during the 1930s, but an engineering education with only one elective a semester left little room for literature, must less philosophy. Partial differential equations were fascinating and seemed to show a flow of the physical forces in the universe. Quantum mechanics, on the other hand, was closer to philosophy than science, but I could certainly see I had my work cut out for me.

Deciding to start with the so-called Harvard Classics, jokingly referred to as the five-foot book of shelves, I checked the library at the base and started educating myself. Other than flying and working out each day, I had nothing but time on my hands. I frequently finished a book in a day.

The most exciting thing about Pensacola was I was getting an airplane that was almost a service-type fighter, the SNJ. Built by North American Aviation, it was used as a trainer by the U.S. Army and Navy as well as the British. It was the first plane I fell in love with, but first I had to learn to fly it.

Climbing in the rear seat, I stared at the instrument panel that contained at least twice as many instruments as the N3N, as well as a complete set for instrument flying. There were additional controls for the controllable-pitch propeller and the mixture. The instructor climbed in the front seat, and we were off.

Once at altitude, the instructor had me stall the airplane to get some feel for the plane at low speed. Better to make mistakes up here than near the ground on landing. Everything happened at higher speeds, and everything happened faster, with much less room for error. As beautifully as the plane flew, it was trouble on the ground, especially just before takeoff or just after landing. It had a strong tendency to ground loop, that is, spin around 360 degrees, usually with one wingtip touching the ground. It was something you didn't want noted in your flight jacket.

I was in the front seat for my second flight with the instructor in the rear. There was one notable difference in the front seat: there was a .30-caliber machine gun there, mounted above the instrument panel, jutting through the skin to fire through the propeller. This was the first indication in my training that I was preparing to shoot someone.

Once I was checked out in the airplane, I was assigned to a flight of eight. They included Howell, Duke, Pat Junkin, Jack McNeice, and two unexpected additions, two full lieutenants, Dixon and Macalis, both regular navy and both Annapolis graduates. The navy had a long-established policy of requiring any officer that wanted to go into aviation to serve seven years as a line officer before he could apply for flight training. Whatever the original reason for this, the effect was to assure that any Annapolis graduate assigned to a squadron would always be senior to any reserve officer and would therefore be captain or executive officer of the squadron.

We were dubious about having officers in the flight, but it turned out to be a godsend. There was no question we received preferential treatment in every respect, especially scheduling. It was always midmorning for our first flight, and we always got the first flight at night, but the best part was the officers themselves. They were gentlemen and treated us as equals, never pulling rank. They were experienced in the ways of the navy and smoothed over a lot of rough edges for us. On top of that, they were good pilots, and we were all equal in flight time.

Duke and I traded places as each other's wing man. I had absolute confidence in him, and he enjoyed the same with me. We seemed to know instinctively what the other was thinking and going to do. As a result, we would fly formation so close we were almost touching, including takeoffs and landings. One day it hit me. We were in a turn in a steep bank. I was tight under Duke's wing looking at his plane and Mobile Bay beyond. I looked at the machine gun and knew I was ready to take on a Jap. I was a military pilot.

We flew in two four-plane sections with an instructor trailing us. We practiced glide bombing, dropping a ten-pound practice bomb that contained a blank shotgun shell that went off on contact, sending a plume of smoke skyward to mark the hit. Although the odds were slim that I was ever going to drop a bomb on a Japanese ship, I worked like hell to become as accurate as I could.

Finally, we began training in the thing I'd been waiting for above anything else: gunnery. In each flight, one of the eight would tow a sleeve that would be the target. The ammunition in each of our planes was tipped with paint, each a different color. As the bullet passed through the sleeve—assuming you hit the sleeve—it would leave a circle of color around the hole, allowing your hits to be counted.

I was third in line for my first pass at the target. Flying on a parallel course fifteen hundred feet above the tow plane, I turned on my gunsight and made a diving turn toward the target, pulling out aiming for the sleeve. Carefully leading the target, I made sure I wasn't pulling any Gs as I moved into range and opened fire. The popping of the machine gun wasn't as loud as I expected as I pulled off to avoid hitting the sleeve. This became a routine I practiced day after day.

The competition between us was incredible. After all, this was what it was all about. I had to learn to lead the target, just as in dove hunting. Would that target ever be a Japanese Zero? The war still seemed so far away, and I was no part of it.

My gunnery scores were good. In fact, I set a new cadet record for hits on a towed target. That did it, I was sent to Barin Field for fighter training. I'd achieved my first goal: I was going to be a fighter pilot; that is, if I lived through Barin Field. It had the nickname Bloody Barin: a crash a day. I logged almost half of my time in the air circling the field as they cleared one crash after another off the runway.

Cadets at Pensacola had always enjoyed the privileges of the officers club until the sheer numbers of cadets overwhelmed the facility. I was in the last class that was allowed in. Jack McNeice introduced me to the civility and relaxation of a drink before dinner. He had graduated from Princeton and had been the member of an eating club. He had the largest vocabulary of anyone I'd ever known and planned to become a lawyer after the war. Nothing cemented a friendship and made for camaraderie more than a drink or two.

I especially got a kick out of the British naval pilots that were in training with us. They were an upbeat bunch and eager as hell to get back to England and their war with Germany. I was startled, however, by their casual acceptance of death, which gave new meaning to the expression "stiff upper lip." They had already been at war for four years, and perhaps they had seen so much that it was almost ordinary.

One afternoon four of them came in, jolly as ever, and started drinking to the other four in their flight. We thought they were just getting an early start, then word spread around the bar. Their flight of eight was practicing tactics when one section of four crossed beneath the other four a little too close, cutting the tails off the upper four planes. No one succeeded in bailing out, resulting in four deaths. The four continued drinking, toasting old Nigel and the other three as if they'd just come in from a game of cricket. None of us wanted to fly with them.

Finally, my day arrived, the one I'd been waiting for: my first dogfight, one-on-one with another pilot, the ultimate test. We were never allowed to do this with another cadet, only with an instructor, as the chances of a mid-air collision were tremendous.

The instructor I drew had graduated from Pensacola three months before me, and although he spent those months in advanced fighter training, he had little more experience than I. He was cocky, which was good. He laid out the program and the rules. We would engage in four fights. In two, I would start one thousand feet above him, and in the other two he'd have the thousand-foot advantage. In both cases we'd fly toward each other. If we ended in a dead head-on run, we were both to turn right, and pray.

Taking off together, we flew to our assigned altitudes, checked in on the radio, and headed toward each other. I had the altitude advantage on the first run. Heading toward him, I slowed my plane to near stalling speed. Then as I passed over him, I did a split S; that is, I rolled my plane on its back and let the nose drop until I was coming straight down on him. He passed under me, and I was on his tail before he even knew where I was. I sat there for a moment until he came on the radio.

"Where are you?" he asked.

"On your tail," I answered as casually as I could.

He was not pleased. I had defeated the instructor—big mistake!

The next morning the congratulations of my drinking buddies were still ringing in my ears from the night before as I strode up to the flight line, ready for my second victim. I hadn't reached the schedule board when I heard my name called out. I turned to face the head of fighter training, a marine captain. He had landed on Guadalcanal with the original marine fighter squadron and shot down thirteen Zeros in just three days. Unfortunately, during a scramble on the fourth day, he jumped in a plane hidden in the trees and started across the field to take off. Another plane came out of the trees from a different direction, and they collided in the center of the field.

The captain had recently reported for duty at Pensacola after months in the hospital. I was going up against one of the leading aces in the U.S. military. How good was he? Damn good! I did manage one draw, however.

This made me realize that no matter how good you were, there was always someone better. Dogfighting brought it all home. You were going out to kill someone or be killed. Despite this, I couldn't wait for my chance to prove myself.

I knew I was still a long way from combat, but I didn't realize how close I was to being shot at.

We were required to make a long, cross-country flight solo, north from Mobile Bay to Birmingham, west to a small town in Alabama, south to New Orleans, then back to base.

The weather was perfect, and the flight was beautiful, covering wooded countryside. Approaching a low mountain, I spotted a cleared area on the ridge of the hill. On closer inspection there was a log cabin with a large barn in the rear. It looked like a real piece of Americana, something out of Norman Rockwell. Slowing the plane, I banked into a turn as I nosed over to go down and take a closer look. As I approached the cabin at low speed and altitude, a man ran out of the building, rifle in hand. He took careful aim. Instinctively knowing what was coming, I jammed the throttle against the stop and took evasive action as I climbed out of there. He fired and missed. He either thought I was a revenuer or worse, a Yankee. The rest of the flight was uneventful.

A few more sessions of night flying and I would complete my training. The danger was that there were so many planes in the air, and it was easy to confuse the wing lights of a plane in the distance with a car driving down a deserted road, or even a star. My head was on a continuous swivel as I watched for other planes and watched the instruments at the same time. I felt a great sense of relief as I landed from my final night flight. Barring some unforeseen mishap, I was going to be commissioned an ensign in the Naval Air Corps.

Before that happened, I got a grim reminder of what this was really about. We were all required to take our turns as cadet officer of the day (OD), preparatory training for the time we'd be officer of the day, or officer of the deck if we were at sea. I was all decked out with an OD arm band to assume my duties when there was a crash. I rode the crash truck to the scene, a short distance from the field.

The cadet had been engaged in a dog fight with an instructor when he pulled the plane into a tight turn and went into a high-speed stall. This was sudden and violent. The cadet didn't wait long enough to allow the plane to pull out before he put the plane in a second high-speed stall close to the ground. He went straight in.

The nose of the plane was buried in the ground up to the windshield, and despite the fact that the cadet had secured his seat belt and shoulder harness, he was crushed beyond recognition. The corpsmen reached in and tied cords around the pilot's wrists and ankles.

"What are you doing?" I asked in all innocence.

"That's to keep him from sliding out of his flight suit," one of them answered as they picked him up by the flight suit and carried him to the ambulance. "The body is like jello, not a bone left; it'll slide right out," he added.

I quietly threw up. Sudden death was never far away.

We had just two weeks to go when our two officers came to us with a surprise. They'd wrangled weekend passes for the eight of us and were arranging a party for us at the Grand Hotel, on Mobile Bay. To make matters even better, Lieutenant Macalis had been stationed in New Orleans, and he'd invited eight girls he'd met there to come over for the weekend.

I'd had a slight introduction to Southern women at North Carolina, but that was just a taste. These girls from New Orleans had charm they hadn't used yet. It was difficult to comprehend what it would be like if they turned on all the burners. They were beautiful as well as very intelligent, but above everything else, they were sophisticated and beautifully dressed. What a combination; it shouldn't be allowed. We poor slobs from the North were simpering puppy dogs, and I have the feeling the girls weren't even trying. We all swore we'd make it back to New Orleans the first chance we got. None of us ever did.

We spent the nights drinking and dancing, and the days on the beach or playing tennis. Being from the North, I had no idea how strong the sun was this far south. I woke up back at the base on Monday morning and moved slightly. The pain was excruciating. I was burned to a crisp, as was everyone in the flight. The problem was, we couldn't say anything about it. The navy didn't recognize sunburn as a legitimate excuse to go to sick bay. We had to fly.

Gritting my teeth, I gingerly slipped into my shirt. I risked not wearing a tie and hoped no senior officer saw me; couldn't risk demerits now. Waiting at the flight line was the thing I dreaded most: a parachute. The crew chief tried to help me in the harness, which cut across my shoulders like a hot poker, and the flight was an hour and a half long. Three days of that and I was ready for anything the Japs could throw at me. I'd made it; I was commissioned on Thursday, May 18, 1943, seventeen months after the Japanese attack. What the hell was I doing? Why wasn't I fighting?

I received my wings from an admiral in a magnificent ceremony. I felt I was really part of the navy. While checking out of the base at Pensacola, I had to go by the Hardaway Officer. I had never heard of this command, but I knew there must be one. Things couldn't be this hard naturally; there had to be someone in charge. He'd done a great job.

I received orders to Naval Air Station Opa-Locka, Florida, for advanced fighter training.

NINE

# ADVANCED FIGHTER TRAINING IN THE BREWSTER BUFFALO

The navy had a prewar policy of building bases near resorts. Opa-Locka was no exception; it was just twenty miles west of Miami. The flying field was a beauty, with runways fanning out from the hangars in the center. Whatever the wind direction, you would take off and land away from the buildings. Green lawns stretched far beyond the runways, giving plenty of room in case of a short or long landing. There was a beautiful officers club with a marble dance floor that promised interesting evenings on those warm, tropical nights.

The training at Opa-Locka was pretty much a continuation of the fighter training at Pensacola, with one notable exception. The conclusion of this training would involve checking out in an operational fighter, the F2A Brewster Buffalo. Several years before the war, the navy held a competition for the next generation fighter. They chose the two most likely prospects and had each company build one for a fly-off. The companies were Grumman and Brewster. Grumman was already a supplier of aircraft to the navy, but Brewster was a newcomer, having built only one airplane, a dive-bomber.

The Brewster F2A, won the competition with a top speed five knots faster than the Grumman F4F. The navy ordered three hundred of them. The plane looked a lot like the racing planes of the 1930s: all engine, a barrel fuselage, stubby wings, a large canopy, and almost no tail. Carrier squadrons started to train with them, and the F2As took their place with the fleet.

There were a number of problems with the airplane. It was the first navy plane with hydraulically retractable landing gear. It was the custom of pilots to pull the gear up as soon as possible to show they were hot pilots. Such was not possible with the F2A. Retracting the gear was so complicated that pilots would take off and fly out of sight with the gear still down.

Retracting the gear required the pilot to throw a lever and pressurize part of the hydraulic system. Once pressurized, the control had to be returned to the neutral position and the next part of the system pressurized, and so on. This had to be done in the correct order or the system would lock, and the wheels could neither be pulled up or down. If this happened with the gear up, the system would have to be drained and the wheels lowered by using a pump. The handle was just to the right of the pilot's seat. If everything failed, there was a pair of wire cutters taped to the side of the cockpit. Using them, the pilot had to reach behind the instrument panel and cut two wires, being careful not to cut the aileron cables. The gear was now supposed to fall into place on its own.

Carrier pilots are the best pilots in the world, but they weren't up to the Brewster Buffalo. The moment the Buffalo arrived with the fleet, they started to lose airplanes. The canopy shielded the small rudder from the air stream, making it difficult to hold the plane on course, especially at the low speed required for carrier landings. Faced with the dilemma of having purchased airplanes that the most experienced pilots in the world couldn't handle, the navy did the logical thing: they made them training planes. After all, if you could fly the Brewster Buffalo, you could fly anything. The navy sent the remaining planes to Opa-Locka. By the time I got there, they had twenty-five flyable Buffalos. I walked along the flight line knowing I was going to have to fly one of them.

Most of our flying was done over the Everglades, and we prayed each day not to have an engine failure over that area, especially at night. To go down in the Everglades at night was a harrowing thought. Occasionally a pilot would go down, electing to bail out rather than to try to make a landing in the pitch black. The navy had a swamp buggy, but they wouldn't make an attempt to find you until sunup. The pilots would all return with stories of having spread their parachutes and sitting in the center with their knife out to fight off alligators or snakes. The instructors said it was great survival training, but one I'd just as soon skip.

And of course there were always field carrier landings. An LSO, or landing signal officer, would stand at one end of a runway, which was painted to simulate a carrier deck. Each pilot coming in would fly parallel to the runway, then turn 180 degrees to go downwind, then turn toward the end of the runway where the LSO would pick the pilot up and guide him to a landing using brightly colored paddles. The pilot made his final approach just slightly above stalling speed, and you hoped his judgment was perfect. If the approach was good, the LSO would give the pilot a "Cut." This meant taking off all power and letting the plane full-stall into a landing, with the tail wheel touching down first. In a real carrier landing, the tail hook would catch a wire and pull the plane to a stop. Everything was geared to making carrier landings.

One afternoon I finished flying early and stopped by the officers club to pick up a bottle of liquor. The bar was on the second floor, and while I waited I strolled out on the balcony, which overlooked the field. As I stood there, two other officers came out, the commanding officer of the base accompanied by an admiral. The admiral turned out to be the head of safety for the training command. I wanted to get out of there, but there was no way I could do it gracefully, so I stayed and listened to their conversation.

The commander was explaining to the admiral why this was the safest base in the navy. Just at that moment a Brewster Buffalo started its takeoff run on the far side of the field. The two men stopped talking as they watched the plane. The F2A gathered speed as it roared across the field. It kept coming but it didn't lift off, it just went on rolling as it increased speed. This wasn't going to be a Greasy Dan takeoff. In fact, there started to be some question if it was going to take off at all.

Coming to the end of the runway, it just went on rolling across the grass, finally into the woods, cutting down small trees and in turn having its wings sheared off by some larger trees. Finally, the fuselage came to a stop almost a mile away. Crash trucks screamed up to the gate below us, sirens on and lights flashing. The marine guards at the gate refused to let the crash equipment leave the base until everyone showed their IDs. I took one look at the face of the base commander and knew it was time for me to get out of there. No ensign should ever be near a senior officer that's that mad. I beat a hasty retreat. That night I took an extra drink before dinner. I was scheduled to fly the Brewster Buffalo the next day.

Nervously I walked down the flight line to the F2A. The one-thousand–horsepower engine looked tremendous. I had undergone a one-week training program on the airplane, including a blindfold check-out in the cockpit. I had to memorize the location of all of the instruments as well as the controls, emergency and otherwise, then get in the cockpit blindfolded and point out every item to the satisfaction of the instructor. He tried to tell me how it would fly, but with a single place fighter no one could take you up and check you out on your first flight. I was on my own.

I checked the date on the parachute to make sure it had been packed recently, since there was a good chance I might have to use it. A mechanic helped me in the cockpit. I went over everything very carefully and started the engine. It caught on the first shot. The noise was incredible despite the headset covering my ears. The instruments checked out, and I had no excuse, so I taxied out to the runway.

I was sitting in a real fighter plane waiting to take off. The F2A had already been in combat in World War II. The Dutch government had purchased a number of them before Pearl Harbor and had them shipped to Indonesia. They barely arrived before the Japanese attack, and some were still in crates on the docks, but a few were in service on airfields. The Dutch had coast watchers throughout the islands, giving them ample warning of Japanese attacks. The Dutch pilots could have been at altitude over the cities and airfields waiting for the Japanese bombers, but for some unknown reason they weren't. Instead, they sat on the end of the runway until the Japanese planes arrived, then took off and tried to climb straight at them, with disastrous results.

I couldn't put it off any longer. Running the engine up to full power, I checked the mags—everything satisfactory. I released the brakes. The plane surged down the runway, accelerating so rapidly it pressed me against the back of the seat, and at the same instant started to swerve off the runway. I corrected with both rudder and brake, but the rudder was of little use while I was in the three-point position. I had to get the tail up as quickly as possible, so I pushed forward on the stick. The tail came up, and I managed to keep the plane on the runway. The question in my mind was, would it take off or roar off into the trees like the plane a few weeks ago?

I eased back on the stick. I was in the air and picking up speed faster than in any plane I'd flown. Starting the operation to pull up the gear, I went through each step very carefully, and, miracle of miracles, the gear came up and locked.

I was already at twelve thousand feet; everything happened so fast. I throttled back and let the plane slow to try a power-off stall. Keeping the nose slightly up, I waited, but not for long. It happened suddenly. I was going straight down, in a spin, losing altitude at an alarming rate. No panic: I hit the opposite rudder and eased forward on the stick until the spin stopped, then gently pulled back on the stick. Everything was under control, but I knew I was going to make my first landing faster then I had planned. A stall and spin in this plane at low altitude would be fatal. I took the plane to maximum speed and felt it out. The exhilaration was incredible. Slow rolls, loops, Immelmanns, split Ss—I tried them all. I was ready, if only I could land it.

I started the procedure to lower the landing gear well away from the field. I didn't want to have to deal with that once I entered the traffic pattern. Good luck: the gear went down and locked the first try. I eased into the traffic pattern and picked up the active runway but didn't like what I saw. The active runway was the one used for field carrier landings, and there was a landing signal officer at the end of the runway. I would be required to make a carrier approach and follow his instructions. It was not what I had in mind for my first landing in a Brewster Buffalo, but if I didn't, I'd be on report.

The LSO picked me up on the crosswind leg. I was high and fast. As the old saying goes, "Stay ten knots above stalling speed, add five more if you're married, and two more for each child." I wasn't a husband or a father, but I was still high and fast. Reluctantly I pulled back on the throttle; I had no other choice. The plane slowed. I could think of only one thing. This is the plane that fleet pilots, the most experienced in the world, had trouble with in this maneuver. The plane slowed.

The LSO indicated a sharp turn to the left to line me up with the runway. I was rapidly getting into the most dreaded situation known to flying: low and slow. As I settled rapidly toward the runway, the LSO signaled, "Too slow." I hit the throttle and increased speed, barely keeping the nose up. He gave me a "Cut." I flared just in time to make a perfect, full-stall landing, tail wheel first. Dumb luck, but I'll take it any time.

Sitting at the bar that night I felt a new confidence. I was ready if the time ever came.

# TEN

# THE WORLD'S MOST UNUSUAL AIRCRAFT CARRIER

My advanced fighter training was complete, with just one more thing to do before I was ready to go to a squadron: land on a real aircraft carrier. I received orders to go to Naval Air Station Glenview to check out on a training carrier on the Great Lakes. No worry about enemy submarines there.

Eight of us traveled from Miami together. It was a real come-down going to Chicago on a train rather than a plane, but space on transport planes was on a priority basis, and this didn't qualify. There was a bright spot: the train was nothing but fun, just one big, moving cocktail party. Fortunately we didn't have to fly on the day of our arrival.

Once again we were faced with a line of SNJs, but with one notable difference: these were equipped with a tail hook that could be lowered by a control in the cockpit. I made my way to my plane, climbed in the cockpit, and hoped for the best. We were going out over Lake Michigan to search for the most unusual aircraft carrier in the world.

The moment World War II started it was obvious to the navy that they needed a safe place to train a large number of pilots in carrier landings and takeoffs. The few fleet carriers were required in the war zone, and we had nothing else. The navy decided to take over a ship that served as a pleasure boat for tourists around the Great Lakes, take off the superstructure, and replace it with a flight deck. The ship, named the *Wolverine*, was driven by paddle wheels.

Being the hot pilots we were, we flew to the rendezvous point in tight formation. It was a crystal-clear day, and we spotted the carrier with ease. I had only seen pictures of a carrier from this perspective in movies, but this was real, and I was going to land on it. We flew over the ship and continued in that direction until we were far enough ahead of it to break up and start individual approaches.

I remembered to drop my tail hook and checked to see that my wingman did the same.

The lead plane banked away to the left. I was third and waited until I had a five-hundred-foot interval from the man in front of me. I turned and started my downwind leg. Slowly losing altitude, I dropped my flaps and wheels and trimmed the plane for the slower speed. I could see the lead plane making an approach toward the stern of the carrier. He was high and fast. I started my crosswind leg as the first plane got a waveoff. The second plane was in the slot, approaching the fantail as the LSO directed his every move. Again, he was too high and too fast—another waveoff.

Turning toward the stern, I resolved not to come in high or fast. I let the plane slow as I made a sharp turn toward the carrier. The LSO picked me up. The paddles were straight out; I was in perfect position. The deck was getting closer. Leaning out the left side of the plane, I had the LSO locked in my sight. He made no movement with the paddles. I let the nose drop slightly as I neared the ship. I looked the LSO right in the eye. He gave me a "Cut." I chopped the throttle and hoped the plane sank; it did. I hit the deck tail first and caught a wire, which jerked me to a stop.

Before I could think about the fact that I'd just landed on an aircraft carrier, there were men running all over the deck. One signaled me to let the plane roll backward slightly while a crewman unhooked the arresting cable. Another gave the signal to pull up my tail hook, while another indicated full throttle to get my plane the hell out of there. I taxied forward to the center of the ship, where a signal officer motioned me to run the engine up to full power. I complied. After listening for a moment to be sure the engine sounded perfect, the officer gave me the signal to take off.

The first time making a takeoff run down a narrow rolling deck is an experience of its own. All of the training had been geared to making carrier landings, but no one ever mentioned taking off. The tail came up before I knew it, and in a moment I was off the bow, sinking toward the water. I eased back on the stick and was airborne.

Seven more landings and we were all qualified. Next up, thirty days' leave.

ELEVEN

# ACROSS THE CONTINENT BY TRAIN, BUS, FERRY, AND THUMB

I couldn't wait to get home and see my family and friends, but on arrival I realized my father was not the man I'd left only six months before. His heart was starting to give him problems, and he was aging rapidly. Nitroglycerin was the order of the day when he exerted himself. Dad never said anything, but I knew he was worrying about me, and I hadn't even made it into combat yet. On the other hand, my mother was her usual stoic self. If anything was bothering her, she didn't let it show.

I looked up several of my old girlfriends, but they were all engaged to someone that was gone in the service. I almost felt like a draft dodger being home with nothing to do. So much for the glamorous life and good pay.

The big scandal in town involved the pastor of the Brethren Church. His sermons had one message: if you were a true Christian, you could not kill anyone, and that included during wartime. He encouraged all of the young male members to declare for conscientious objector status. The town was immediately up in arms and literally ran the pastor out of town. I had thought long and hard about the same thing and concluded that a true Christian couldn't fight, which was more or less the Quaker view, but the Japanese attack took care of any thoughts I had of this kind. I'd worry about the morality later.

Life at home had changed. Every one was intent on their jobs, most of which were defense related, and they wanted to tell you at great length about every aspect of that job. Dad had gone with the War Production Board and was working long hours. The only other thing anyone discussed was the war itself. Many people had large maps hung on the walls and followed every campaign in minute detail. I was chaffing at the bit. Then the telephone call came. Duke had everything set up in New York. I was going to meet Helen, the cover girl, and she was going to bring a friend. The war could wait.

Duke was waiting on the platform at Pennsylvania Station as I got off the train. We were both in summer khaki uniforms, but these were no ordinary khaki uniforms. These were made of gabardine and custom tailored. Duke had somehow gotten rooms at the Plaza, and we had reservations that night for dinner at the Stork Club, the prewar home of so-called Cafe Society. We both agreed that the only attire that was up to this level of sophistication was our navy whites, the most beautiful and flattering uniform ever created. We had a drink at the Plaza before we ventured forth.

Duke looked particularly handsome in the uniform, with his dark, wavy hair and olive skin. More than a few heads turned as we were ushered to our table in the Stork Club. Maybe there was going to be a glamorous life, and in a few minutes we were going to be joined by two models.

It turned out there was just one, Helen. It seemed that something had happened and her friend couldn't make it. We both sat there staring at Helen, as was everyone else in the nightclub. I quickly realized that two naval officers were the minimum escort for Helen, and really beautiful women didn't travel with other beautiful women. She wanted all of the adoration for herself.

Duke was oblivious to everything except Helen. He was so in love it hurt. He was in another world. The orchestra started and Duke asked Helen to dance. I watched as he took her in his arms and disappeared from this world. He was literally in seventh heaven. After a set, it was my turn.

I took Helen in my arms and instantly realized that she felt even better than she looked, if that was possible. Her body melded against mine from head to toe. I didn't want to make a pass at my friend's girl, but she was almost irresistible. She placed her warm hand on my neck as she laid her cheek against mine. What the hell was she doing? Then I felt the tears rolling from her face to mine. I drew away and looked her in the face. She was crying profusely.

"I dance that badly?" I asked, trying to lighten the moment.

A slight smile flickered across her face. "Of course not. I haven't had anyone hold me like this for so long, I miss him and love him so much." She started to cry again.

"He's sitting right there at the table," I offered.

She looked at me with sympathy. "No, he's in England."

I was more confused than ever. "What do you mean?"

"The love of my life is a private in the supply corps; he's already been shipped overseas. It may be years before I see him again. I never thought they'd draft David."

"What about Duke?" I asked.

"He's lots of fun, but I've never been serious about him."

We dropped Helen off and walked back to the hotel.

"Isn't she sensational?" Duke asked.

"Absolutely," I answered.

"The first thing I'm going to do when we get back is marry her."

What could I say? Why did she have to tell me about David, whoever he was? Was it up to me to shatter Duke's fantasy? I didn't.

I was happy to board the train for the West Coast with orders to report in at the Naval Base, San Diego. However anxious they were for me, I couldn't get a high enough priority to fly and was lucky to get a berth on the train. Little did I know that this would be the train from hell.

The train was half-filled with soldiers accompanied by a contingent of MPs. The rest of the train was wall-to-wall people. I was lucky to have the berth. Most of the people were sleeping in their seats, and it was a five-day trip.

The third day the dining car ran out of food. They were down to serving cereal and milk, and the last day, cereal and water. When the train stopped at a station out in the desert, everyone jumped off the train and ran like hell for the restaurant in hopes of buying a sandwich. I lived on peanut butter and jelly sandwiches for a day and a half.

Arriving seven hours late in Los Angeles, I raced to make my connection to San Diego. The station was a zoo. The number of service men arriving and leaving was incredible. It seemed that every person in the country was on the move.

The only train to San Diego was scheduled to arrive at the station there only twenty minutes before I was required to report to the base. I had no idea how far away that might be. I held my breath and got on the train. I continued to hold my breath all the way to San Diego. There were no seats, and I was forced to stand the entire trip, wedged in between soldiers and marines. I could have slept standing up, as it would have been impossible to fall down.

The train was late arriving. Grabbing my bags, I ran out the front of the station and tried to get a cab. There were none to be had. I was going to be late, and this was serious. If I didn't make it by midnight I would go on report. There was also the chance that I would be shipped out immediately for the Pacific. In that case I'd miss my ship, which would be very serious. In addition, there was little prospect of getting a room for the night. There were seven hundred marines sleeping on the lawn in front of the city hall.

Standing at the curb, I'd about given up when I heard someone call my name. Bryan Caldwell, my roommate at Chapel Hill, pulled up in a car. "Jump in," he shouted. I did.

"When did you get in?"

"About thirty seconds ago and I've got to report in."

Bryan glanced at his watch. "You sure do, and we still have to catch a ferry." He let nothing stand in his way as he violated every rule in the motor vehicle code. Approaching the water, we could see the ferry boat. It was loaded, and the barrier was coming down. Bryan hit the horn and started tapping out SOS in Morse code. "I knew that code would come in handy sometime." The sailors on the gate recognized the message and held the gate. We drove on that ferry at full speed, sliding to a stop just short of the car in front of us. We looked at each other and couldn't help but laugh. I checked in just two minutes short of midnight. They assigned me a room. I wasn't going out to sea that night.

The following morning I got my first taste of life in Southern California, and I liked what I saw. It was early August, and the weather was balmy and clear. There was a large bowl of fresh fruit on each table, and I could look across the anchorage at an aircraft carrier tied up there. Bryan showed up to have breakfast with me. He had a beautiful navy nurse with him.

"I arrived three months ago and am assigned to a patrol plane squadron. I had to go in for a physical and met Nancy. It was love at first sight, fortunately for both of us. We've been married for eight days now." Bryan bubbled with pride as he related the story and introduced us.

"We're going to show you San Diego," Nancy added.

"You don't want me along," I offered, "like having your mother-in-law on your honeymoon." I couldn't dissuade them. "Before we go, I have to check in. I may not be here that long."

We walked over to the assignment desk and approached the duty officer. "Do you have an assignment for me?" I asked.

He went through some papers. "Come back Monday morning, nothing's going to happen until then."

Bryan laughed. "See, I told you."

Nancy was a delight as well as good looking. It wasn't hard to see why Bryan had made his move so quickly. And, they had a car. We were off and running in a Ford convertible, looking for the mystic La Jolla we'd all heard so much about.

Bryan knew it was north of the city, so we started up the road along the coast. We rode along the cliffs overlooking the Pacific. The stories I'd heard about Southern California were not exaggerated. We finally came to a sign that read "La Jolla." Since we were all from the East and knew no Spanish, we didn't realize the *J* in Jolla was pronounced as an *H*, so we kept on looking. Finally, we asked someone and felt like fools when he explained that we were already there. We found the Valencia Hotel and had a delightful lunch on the terrace overlooking the ocean. A few drinks, and life couldn't get any better.

I reported in early Monday morning, my future hanging in the balance. The duty officer looked up my name. "You're in luck," he said as he pulled out more papers. "You're going up the coast where a new air group will be forming." Assignment to a new air group was more than I could have hoped for.

"Where is the base?" I asked.

"I don't know exactly, somewhere near Santa Ana."

Now I was down to bus transportation. I checked in at the only hotel in Santa Ana, a sleepy little farm community. The next morning I asked the two men behind the desk where the naval air station was. They appeared confused but finally answered that they didn't know of a base nearby. I went to a map and found it. Unfortunately, there was no transportation that would take me anywhere near the base. I was stuck.

Naval officers were not permitted to hitchhike, but this was an emergency, so map in hand and bags in tow I got out on the highway. There were few cars on the road due to gasoline rationing and the fact that we were pretty far out in the country. Finally, I saw one coming and stuck out my thumb. He stopped and I got in. He not only knew where the base was, he offered to drop me at the gate. The gentleman was very pleasant and personable. After some conversation about the navy, flying, and the war, he asked, "Do you have any interest in the movies?"

"I sure do," I answered.

"If you'd like to visit a studio, namely 20th Century Fox, give me a call when you're free," he said as he handed me his card. He was director of special effects at the studio.

After he dropped me at the gate of Naval Air Station Los Alamitos, I walked to my first real assignment. I had been a naval officer for two months and had gone from flying fighter planes to taking trains with a berth to trains with standing room only, to a bus and finally hitchhiking. Things had to look up.

# TWELVE

# ENTER THE F6F HELLCAT

Wrong again. The base was beautiful, built in the middle of what had been an agricultural area thirty miles southeast of Los Angeles. There was only one runway, since the wind blew off the ocean 95 percent of the time. The bachelor officers' quarters, known by the acronym BOQ, were new and quite nice. There was just one problem: no airplanes. Well, that's not quite right; there was one Piper Cub sitting all alone on the flight line.

The base had been an elimination base and had just been reclassified as an operational base. The base personnel had been used to handling aviation cadets but would now host a fleet air group. I was the first to report in for the fighter squadron and had nothing to do but wait.

There was a problem. I had not been paid since I left Opa-Locka, and with the transportation to the West Coast, not to mention the trip to New York, I was almost out of money. I went to the paymaster's office and found that the paymaster had not reported in as yet.

There was another problem. In order to receive flight pay, you were required to fly a minimum of four hours a month. I was now in my second month without flying, and you could only carry flight pay over three months before you'd start losing it. And there it sat, the Piper Cub.

I talked the base commander into letting me fly it, intending to stay near the field. I didn't bother with a map. After all, I was a qualified pilot, soon to be finding my way back to an aircraft carrier.

The Piper was probably the easiest plane to fly that had ever been built. The takeoff was routine. Suddenly, the Pacific Ocean opened up before me, with Catalina Island thirty miles out to sea. I was mesmerized. I flew out to the coast and turned north along the shore. Something was wrong. I was flying north, but the compass read west. I had a problem with the compass, and if there was anything I didn't want to do it was get lost on my first flight.

I made a one-eighty and tried to reverse the course I'd taken to get there, but I couldn't rely on the compass, as it was obviously faulty. Fortunately, it was early enough that the haze hadn't set in. They called it haze then; now they call it smog. I spotted the field and stayed within sight of it as I built up a few hours of flying time.

Over the next few days, more pilots checked in, among them a senior lieutenant who had commanded an elimination base. If there was anything a man with a background like that couldn't stand, it was seeing someone, especially so recently an aviation cadet, doing nothing. We had a pool table, but if he found us using it, he'd immediately set out to find busy work for the lowly ensigns, such as filing AlNavs—official navy communications—which piled up every day. His name was Roger Boles, but we immediately dubbed him Smiley, because he never did.

The smart thing was to stay out of sight, but that was not so easy, as we were in effect on call all day. I hit on the perfect solution: I'd find a piano and brush up on my playing. I could tip off one of my buddies to find me if they called a muster, and I'd be on the base, which was required. I sure as hell didn't join the navy to file papers.

The BOQ had a piano, but I couldn't sit in full view of everyone. Then it hit me: the chapel must have a piano. The chapel turned out to be an auditorium used for religious services as required. I found it, but it was locked. In the best tradition of the navy, I'd go see the chaplain.

I entered the outer office and was greeted by an attractive young girl in a Red Cross uniform.

"We not only have a piano," she offered, "it's a brand new Steinway grand, the gift of a number of people in the area, but first you'll have to get permission from the chaplain. Just a minute, I'll see if he's free."

I waited while she went into the inner office, not knowing that I was about to meet the most interesting man I'd ever meet in my life.

The moment I laid eyes on Pardee Erdman, I knew there was something wrong—several things, in fact. He was tall and slim with white hair that waved slightly, set off by his dress blue uniform. The problem was his rank didn't go with his age. Civilians that were brought into the service once the war started were given rank commensurate with their station in civilian life. Since he was obviously over fifty, had he been the pastor of a prominent church he would have held the rank of at least a commander, perhaps a captain, but the chaplain had only two stripes on his sleeve. He was a full lieutenant.

This could mean only one thing: he came from an unknown church in a small town. Having grown up in a small town, I knew one thing about ministers: they were poor. He probably had a wife and four children and had to pinch every penny to make ends meet, but it didn't fit.

The uniform wasn't from the army-navy store or one of the many naval uniform companies that flooded Pensacola. If we'd been on the East Coast I would have said it came from the finest tailor in New York. I still hadn't learned about Beverly Hills. There was a gold cross above his stripes indicating he was a chaplain, but there was something else: Silver Wings over the left breast of the uniform—Army Air Corps wings. It didn't seem possible, but the chaplain had been a pilot, in World War I, no less.

Something about him seemed to fill the entire room without being in any way overbearing. His vivid blue eyes seemed to have lights behind them. I was in awe but at the same time felt that he had been a friend for a lifetime. His manner was so easy I immediately forgot he was a minister. He seemed more like someone you played golf with at the club.

"You're the first pilot I've met from the new air group," Pardee said enthusiastically, "I can't wait until you're all here and we have the commissioning. My wife and I want to give a cocktail party to introduce you to the base officers, and I'll ask Bob Hope to put his weekly show on from here. You'll get a kick out of him."

I had no answer; I was speechless. I finally got around to asking for permission to use the piano.

"Of course, anytime. If I'm not here, the keys are in the right hand desk drawer; help yourself."

Still overwhelmed by my meeting with the chaplain, I found my way to the auditorium and the magnificent new Steinway. The moment I hit a chord I knew I was going to have to practice hard to live up to this piano.

The men of the air group started to pour into the base, virtually all of them coming off leave. They had not been paid for several months, and there was no paymaster set up on the base to handle us. Then it happened. A shiny new paymaster reported right out of three-months' training at Harvard Business School, learning how to be a navy paymaster. We flocked to his office, where he requested we fill out slips for back pay. He'd total them and be set up to pay us the following morning.

The entire air group lined up in front of his office the next day. Right on time, the paymaster arrived in a navy station wagon complete with armed guard. He got out of the car carrying a small bag. Looking at the bag, we had but one thought: if that's our pay, it must be in very large bills. How's he going to break it down? Not to worry, this man had been to Harvard.

Setting himself up at the window, marine armed guard on either side, he slid the window open as the first man in line stepped up. The paymaster opened the bag of money and took it out, all sixteen dollars of it. The paymaster took one look at the money, closed the window, and disappeared. It turned out that he had totaled the payroll the night before and it came to sixteen thousand dollars, exactly. Nervously writing the first check he'd ever written on the United States government, he made it out for sixteen dollars. It took six weeks to rectify the mistake, leaving us all flat broke. Instead of taking Hollywood by storm, we were forced to stay on the base, eating our meals there and drinking at the bar on credit. Harvard would never be held in high esteem again.

Duke reported in, assigned to the same squadron, as well as a number of others I'd gone through training with. Missing, however, were Howell Cobb, who had gone into the marines, and Jack McNeice, who was assigned to another squadron. Every night in the bar was like a class reunion. Mixed in the group were a number of lieutenants junior grade and full lieutenants. Most of these men had been instructors for several years after getting their wings, and they were not backward about letting you know how experienced they were. They looked down on ensigns, and I was the youngest and lowest ranking in the squadron. This automatically made me the squadron mess treasurer, normally a thankless job, but as it turned out, the greatest thing that could have happened to me. I was in charge of everything the squadron did that did not involve the war.

We had barely assembled in the bar when Duke rushed up. "The skipper has just reported in."

"Have you seen him?" I asked.

"Yeah," Duke answered, "and you're not going to believe it."

"What?" I asked in apprehension.

"His age, I can't believe a man that age is going to lead us in combat. Imagine having it at that age," Duke said in awe.

"How old is he?" I ventured.

"Thirty-two."

The skipper, Hugh Winters, was an Annapolis graduate and regular navy. He was from the South and of an old naval family. He had an easy manner, but you knew instinctively that just beneath the surface was a no-nonsense commanding officer. You automatically respected him and knew despite his friendly demeanor you'd better damn well toe the line when it mattered. He was the perfect skipper for a fighter squadron.

We only thought the skipper was old until we got a look at our intelligence officer, Jack Wheeler. His hair was silver gray, and he seemed to have difficulty walking. He was fifty years old and a full lieutenant. Was the United States really that hard-pressed for manpower? It turned out Jack owned a seat on the Chicago Stock Exchange and was known as the Silver Fox of LaSalle Street.

The moment Jack turned eighteen he had volunteered for the Army Air Corps during World War I. He was accepted and went into preflight training, which at that time consisted of two weeks of marching. The day he was scheduled for his first flight in an airplane, the war was over. The base commander told anyone that wanted to get out to take two steps forward. Everyone did, and Jack was out. He'd gone through his entire life regretting the adventure he'd missed, and he wasn't going to let this one get away. He had enough connections to get ten medical waivers and had gone through school for intelligence officers. He was all ours.

The lonely Piper Cub still sat there on the flight line, the only plane on the base. Where were our airplanes? I was walking from the hangar area to the BOQ for lunch, thinking about our lack of planes, when I heard someone call my name. I looked over and saw the skipper and Jack heading in the same direction. I was flattered that they'd remembered my name, and hurried to catch up with them. We hadn't gone far when I saw the chaplain coming from the other direction.

"Have you met the chaplain?" I asked.

"No," the skipper answered.

"Let me introduce you," I said, waving to the chaplain to join us. He walked over immediately and knew who the skipper was, even though they hadn't been introduced. I introduced Jack, explaining that he was the squadron intelligence officer but had been a broker before the war. Jack had his eyes riveted on the Air Corps wings on the Pardee's uniform and wasn't paying much attention.

Pardee laughed. "Ah yes, brokers have always been my nemesis. I'm such a fool when I invest in the market." He then went on to describe an investment he'd made two years ago and how much money he'd lost by selling too soon. The stock had skyrocketed after he got rid of it.

We walked in the dining room and took a table for four. The skipper was doing most of the talking, as Jack had withdrawn and seemed deep in thought. Suddenly, he mumbled something under his breath. I was sure I'd misunderstood him.

"What did you say?" I asked.

"That son of a bitch," he said slightly louder. I was sure Jack was jealous of the Air Corps wings since he'd made the same attempt.

"You couldn't help it if the war was over before you got a crack at it," I offered.

"No, that's not it. It's the investment he described. People always do this as soon as they hear I was a broker. They tell me about some outlandish investment they've made. Do you know what this phony chaplain would have made from the investment he described? Three-quarters of a million dollars."

I found it hard to believe a minister would lie like that, but it did make me wonder about the wings. Without a word, Jack got up and left the table. I tried to catch up with the skipper's conversation and asked, "Have you heard anything about our airplanes?"

One glance at the skipper's face and I knew I'd made a mistake. He was livid. Gritting his teeth, he said, "There's a problem."

The chaplain spoke up. "Perhaps I can help."

The skipper laughed in spite of himself. "I know they tell sailors to take their problems to the chaplain, but I'm afraid this isn't one where your influence would be helpful."

"Why not give it a try?" Pardee answered, smiling.

The skipper leaned back in his chair, resigned. "Well, alright, everyone's going to hear about it anyway. When I received orders to form a new squadron, I was assured we were going to get the new Grumman F6F. I haven't seen one yet, but the reports say it's superior to the Japanese Zero in every conceivable way. Today I was told we're not getting the new plane, but rather the FM2, which is an F4F with a larger engine. As you know, the record of the F4F against the Zero is poor."

My heart sank as I heard the news.

"Perhaps something can be done," the Chaplain offered.

"I'm afraid not." The skipper began, "I've been on the phone all morning with the naval district, even got up to the admiral in command. I pushed as hard as I could, in fact, a little too hard. I have a feeling I came close to a court-martial. If I go back again, I could be in real trouble."

"Let's see if I understand all of the details," the chaplain replied as he went through the skipper's story.

"You've got it," the skipper replied.

"Excuse me for a moment," the chaplain said as he got up and left the table.

The skipper did not look pleased. "If he gets into this, there'll be hell to pay."

The skipper returned to his lunch, and I did the same. At this point, the less said the better. We were finishing our salad when we saw the chaplain walking toward us with a broad smile on his face. The skipper saw the grin and shuddered.

"Everything's taken care of," Pardee said as he sat down.

"What do you mean?" the skipper asked warily.

"The squadron is going to get F6Fs. They'll be arriving next week."

The color drained from the skipper's face. "There's no way the admiral could have reversed his decision, and there's no one else with that kind of authority."

Pardee smiled. "I didn't go through the naval district, I called Jim and explained everything to him. He reversed the decision, but no one will know we had anything to do with it. The order will come in a routine way from Washington. You'll be officially notified tomorrow."

"You called Jim who?" the skipper asked angrily.

"Jim Forrestal," the chaplain answered.

The skipper's mouth dropped open. "You phoned the secretary of the navy, and got him?"

The chaplain's smile broadened. "Jim and I were roommates at Princeton. We both volunteered when the U.S. got into World War I, he in the Naval Air Corps and I in the Army Air Corps. We both saw action and know how important it is to have the latest fighter plane."

In all the time I knew the skipper, this was the only time I knew him to be without an answer. It seemed he didn't know whether to laugh or cry. While we were still in a state of shock, Jack returned to the table with the same look of disbelief on his face.

Jack leaned over and whispered to me, "It's true. I had my old brokerage house check the transaction and it's true. He made three-quarters of a million dollars."

By this time, nothing that I could learn about the chaplain would ever surprise me. "You didn't think the chaplain would lie, did you?"

The following Monday the first F6F arrived along with the rest of the pilots fresh from leave. The plane was a monster, at twelve thousand pounds unloaded. There were six .50-caliber machine guns and lots of armor, both behind and in front of the pilot. All of this was powered by a 2,200-horsepower Pratt and Whitney engine. I couldn't wait to fly it.

The following Sunday, August 15, 1943, the three squadrons that made up Air Group 19—a Fighter Squadron (VF-19), a Dive-Bomber Squadron (VB-19), and a Torpedo Squadron (VT-19)—stood at attention in front of their respective planes as Air Group Commander Karl Jung read the directive commissioning the air group. The chaplain said a prayer. With his connections, there was no doubt in my mind that God was on our side.

THIRTEEN

# GETTING THE FEEL OF THE F6F

The men in the squadron came from interesting backgrounds. The skipper and the executive officer, F. E. "Toby" Cook, were both regular navy and graduates of Annapolis. The skipper had been in combat, having served on the carrier USS *Ranger* and had covered the landings on North Africa. The exec, however, had just graduated from flight training at the same time I did and had no combat experience, something that would haunt us later.

The rest of us were all in the Naval Reserve and had joined to learn to fly. The senior lieutenants no doubt expected to serve the required four years and then become airline pilots. The war put an end to that plan. Two of these pilots had combat experience. Bill Masoner had been a fighter pilot and had two Zeros to his credit. Redbird Burnett had been a dive-bomber pilot on Guadalcanal and had managed to switch to fighters.

Redbird, the only name we ever knew him by, had contracted malaria in the South Pacific. He suffered periodic attacks and treated them with his own home remedy. Feeling an attack coming on, he'd go in the bar and drink ten martinis, then go out and run ten miles. After a few days of this, he'd apparently sweat the germs out and be back to normal. Redbird looked like a pilot of the 1930s. You could imagine him with helmet, goggles, a white scarf, and boots. He had a thin, black mustache and the look of a matinee idol of that era. He was what we today would call a womanizer.

One pilot, Hal Silvert, was Jewish. His father had no doubt given Hal the olive skin, but his mother was Swedish, accounting for his blonde, wavy hair and blue eyes. He was capable of flying a fighter plane but couldn't drive a car. He'd grown up in New York City, where automobiles were a nuisance rather than a necessity, and he'd never learned. Another of the pilots, Joe Paskoski, was of Polish ancestry. Known as Pasko, he was extremely well built and kept himself in perfect shape. He would have been quite handsome if it weren't for a nose that knew no bounds. Just like Cyrano's, no one noticed or mentioned it.

Joe Kelley was our Irishman right out of central casting. Joe had a perfectly round face with a perpetual grin from ear to ear. He was a little pudgy and could always be found at the bar as soon as flight operations were finished each day. He never ran out of funny stories and regaled the bar every night.

Knobby Felt was another story. A tall, lean cowboy from Montana, he looked like anything but a pilot. He had suffered from polio as a child, and although he'd survived, he had a stiff neck and had to turn his shoulders to look to the left. He certainly didn't go through the same physical I did. One day I asked Knobby about the senator from his state who had a questionable reputation.

"Why, that son of a bitch is so slippery he can beat a fart through a keg of nails and come out without a scratch." Everything Knobby said came out like that.

It turned out that Smiley Boles was the most senior of the reserve officers, and therefore held the position of air officer, in charge of keeping everyone on their toes. Smiley appeared to have the weight of the world on his shoulders when he reported in; now, he did. His one pleasure was smoking a cigar every night—unfortunately, the cheapest cigars available. No one went near his room after dinner.

We assembled in the bar in the BOQ every evening before dinner. A group of us were drinking and telling stories when the air group commander's (Karl Jung's) wife, Hanke, walked in. Had one of us noticed her, we would have jumped up and offered her a seat, but she didn't give us a chance. Walking over to the nearest ensign, she drove her elbow into his side, knocking him off the stool. She looked down at him as she slid on the stool.

"I'm a commander's wife," she said with disdain.

I still had a great deal to learn about life in the navy.

The bar had one additional feature that was interesting: slot machines. Every officers club, both army and navy, had them. It was a great source of revenue for such things as athletic equipment or phonographs for the officers and enlisted men.

Additional planes arrived, and the time had come to check out in the F6F. I studied the manual until I knew all of the systems by heart, and read every bulletin that came out regarding flying the airplane. We took our first flights in order of seniority, which meant it would be a while before I got my chance.

I was reading a directive in the ready room when word came down that the next pilot scheduled to fly was sick and I was the only one available. Suiting up as quickly as possible, I made my way to the fighter plane on the line. A mechanic helped me up on the wing and into the cockpit, buckling the parachute to my harness. Another mechanic placed a blank shotgun shell in the starter as I primed the engine. Starting the engine was somewhat tricky until you got on to it. I was hoping to get it on the first try.

Hitting the switch to fire the shell, I jockeyed the throttle. There was a thunderous backfire as flames shot out of the exhaust pipe. A sailor with a fire extinguisher moved toward the plane, but the engine quickly caught and the flames disappeared as the engine started to purr with a mighty roar. I could feel the power through the throttle as well as my ears and every quaking fiber of my body. I gave a thumbs up to the plane captain and started to taxi for takeoff.

I never imagined a cockpit like this when I sat in the wreck on Wings Field. It was beyond anything I could have imagined, but now I had to fly it. Arriving at the end of the runway, I checked the mags: perfect, no excuse. I was going to take off.

Revving up the engine and my nerve at the same time, I opened the throttle. The noise was fantastic. The response was instantaneous. Correcting for the torque of the giant engine, I started straight down the runway. I glanced at the instruments and couldn't believe that I had only applied half the engine's power. I pushed the throttle against the stop; the surge of power and speed was incredible.

The tail came up immediately as I eased the stick forward. A slight pull back and I was in the air. Instantly I hit the switch and pulled the wheels up so that anyone watching would know I was a hot pilot. Crossing the end of the field, I was already at five hundred feet. This thing really sang the song of the birds. I was really flying, and I had six .50-caliber machine guns, unloaded at the moment, but I knew I was ready for those Japs. Revenge would be mine.

I put the plane through every maneuver I knew, and a few more. It was amazingly responsive for a plane its size. It flew like a small fighter. Approaching the field, I made a tight turn into final approach, I knew everyone would be watching. Rolling out of the turn, I stalled it at the beginning of the runway. Pulling the flaps up as I taxied to the flight line, I knew I was home. This is what I'd been training for; I was ready.

I was assigned my position in the squadron. The good news was that my division of four would be led by Bill Masoner. There was nothing like having a leader that had already been in combat and had two Jap planes to his credit. The bad news was that we were stuck in the second half of the squadron, which would be led by the executive officer, a man with no experience.

We were encouraged to familiarize ourselves with the area. Bill led us on a tour starting with the Long Beach and Los Angeles harbors. The activity of both merchant and naval ships was incredible. Los Angeles was up the coast, and the trick was to try to find Burbank Airport and the Lockheed Aircraft factory that bordered it. The area was entirely camouflaged with netting over it, which made the field and plant appear to be a golf course. I had seen nothing like this in the East, and it brought home the fact that the area might come under attack by the Japanese. The idea of an invasion was not too remote.

We flew on up the coast, as one of the pilots said he knew where the movie stars lived. Dropping to five feet above the sand, we flew past homes in the Colony on Malibu Beach. We saw some magnificent homes but no movie stars. The beach stretched on for sixty miles until we reached Montecito and Santa Barbara. One look as we rounded the point at the Biltmore Hotel and I knew I'd found the place I wanted to live—if I lived.

Now the real work began, melding the entire squadron into a fighting unit, acting as one. We did everything together, from takeoffs to landings. We never broke down to less than four of us, following the old adage, strength in numbers. We carried out aerobatic maneuvers until we could anticipate each other's moves. We discussed each flight after we landed and analyzed our mistakes.

Gunnery started immediately, as we fired on a towed target. We no longer used a sleeve but rather a banner that could be towed at higher speeds. By setting a weight on the tow bar, the banner could be made to fly vertical for high-side runs or horizontal for overhead runs. We each had to take our turns towing the sleeve. This involved going down the runway at full speed and jerking the plane into a maximum climb, to pull the sleeve off the ground cleanly without dragging it on the runway. After the flight, you were required to drop the sleeve at a designated spot so the hits could be counted. Firing six .50-caliber machine guns was a thrill. The recoil was so great it actually slowed the plane slightly.

Some days we'd fly sixteen planes led by the executive officer, and other times the entire squadron led by the skipper. The dive-bomber and torpedo squadrons were engaged in similar activities, and in a short time we were called on to fly the entire air group on a practice exercise. We were about to be judged by some top brass.

The marines were going to have a practice landing on San Clemente Island, about seventy-five miles off the coast from San Diego. Unknown to us, the Marine Corps had been pushing for their own aircraft carriers. They claimed navy pilots did not give them adequate ground support and only marine pilots could do it. This landing was going to be the test. Engineers built defensive positions all over the island, many of them well concealed. If we missed them the marines would have proven their point. Fortunately, word had leaked out.

The air group would fly to Naval Air Station North Island, where our planes would be armed with live ammunition and bombs for takeoff the following morning to cover the landing. That night at the Del Coronado Hotel our skipper gave us a briefing. "I have word that the marines have every type of weapon on the island, tanks, artillery, whatever. Some of these may be fake, wooden models, but I don't give a damn what it is, take out everything you see."

The next morning the entire air group took off from North Island and headed for our first real operation, armed to the teeth. Before the war, San Clemente had a few privately owned homes on it, the rest owned by the navy. At the start of the war, the navy took over the entire island and used it for practice landings as well as artillery practice.

Climbing steadily, we came into view of the island as we reached ten thousand feet. This was the first time the entire air group had flown together, and it was a magnificent sight. If only the target weren't the U.S. Marines—but what the hell.

My half of the fighter squadron was directed to cover the landing. We dove to fifty feet and circled over the marines climbing into the small boats. Once they were loaded and headed for the shore, we stayed over them, machine gunning the beach where they were going to land. The rest of the fighter squadron and the bombers were to circle, looking for targets of opportunity. They found quite a few.

Trenches lined the landing beaches, which we riddled with our guns. The dive-bombers found the luxury homes on the far side of the island. Opening their dive brakes, they headed straight down, dropping their 2,000-pound bombs on the homes, blasting them to sawdust.

Pulling up from the beaches, we followed the contour of the island, arriving at the hills that overlooked the area. That's when we spotted them: military vehicles, no doubt dummies, but they looked real. The marines had outdone themselves. If we'd missed the jeeps, half-tracks, and troop trucks, we'd have looked like idiots. Opening fire with our machine guns, we blasted them as we unloaded our 500-pound bombs directly on them. We got direct hits and wiped out the entire column, but we called in the torpedo bombers in case we'd missed anything. One more sweep of the island and we were relieved, and we headed back to our base.

What we did not know was that the column of military vehicles we'd destroyed was actually vehicles belonging to the marine brass that had come to observe the operation along with representatives from the Pentagon. They were all hunkered down in a ditch along the road. The only word we received from the navy was a "Well done." The marines never got their carrier.

Training started every day with a gunnery flight, the heart and soul of a fighter pilot. The range stretched from the tip of Catalina Island, and it was our preserve. No ships were allowed in the area. We could fire without fear of hitting anything on the water and most of us were getting good; a few, however, were not. Some of the squadron never got a single hit on the banner. The skipper came up with a solution.

All of the guns in our fighters were inspected regularly to be sure they were in perfect working order and aimed properly. The firing pattern called for fire from the two outboard guns to cross twelve hundred feet in front of the plane and the four inboard guns to cross at eight hundred feet. In order to check this, the tail of the plane was jacked up until the plane was level, then a periscope was inserted in the gun barrel and aimed at a spot in the distance. The skipper's idea was to place a banner one thousand feet in front of the plane so each pilot could see exactly how it looked at that range.

I was heading for lunch when I spotted Knobby. He waved and came over to join me. "How's your wife," I asked, "I didn't see her at the last party."

"Oh, the little heifer's down in San Diego, making the rent," he answered in his usual manner.

I was about to pursue his wise remark when I spotted the jacked-up airplane. "Let's check out the banner," I suggested. We headed for the plane. Climbing up, I got in the cockpit, turned on the gunsight, and looked at the banner target. It appeared about as I suspected. As I climbed out, Knobby got in. He looked through the gunsight. After a moment he looked again, then turned to me with a smile on his face.

"This is a gag, isn't it?" he asked.

"What do you mean?" I replied.

"You're putting me on, there's no banner out there," he persisted.

I looked at the bright orange banner in the distance and figured he was putting me on. "I've seen enough if you have," I answered, starting to climb down off the wing.

"I mean it," he continued, "there's no target out there—is there?"

I looked at him, dumbfounded.

Knobby jumped up and climbed out of the plane. "Wait here a minute, I'll be right back," he said as he took off toward the hangar. A few moments later he reappeared carrying his helmet and goggles. Climbing into the cockpit, he put on his goggles and looked through the gunsight. "I'll be damned," he shouted, "there it is."

"Let's see those goggles," I said as I reached for them. Knobby gave them up without a fight. I looked through them and almost fell off the wing. The prescription in the lenses was so strong I felt as if I was ten feet tall. "My God, Knobby, you're nearly blind, how the hell do you pass the physicals?"

"I have all the eye charts memorized, and I use the goggles when I fly," he answered without any concern.

"Knobby, you have to report this. You have to turn yourself in. You can't go into combat with this condition."

Knobby looked at me in a different way. "Bill, flying means more to me than anything else in the world. I fought through the polio and still passed the physical for the Naval Air Corps. I'm fine with the goggles, and no one is more eager to get the Japs than I am. I want to fight, and I'm not going to let this defeat me."

All the way through lunch my mind raced as I faced one gigantic problem: was it my obligation, no, my duty, to report this? I had some idea of how much Knobby wanted to do this, but he wasn't only risking his own life, he might be risking everyone else's. This was my first indication of what it took to be in command: the decisions you had to make, even if you didn't want to. I decided to go to Lieutenant Smiley Boles and tell him.

Walking to the operations office I felt terrible, like a school kid ratting on another student, a friend that you caught cheating. I gritted my teeth and went in. Fortunately, no one was there but Smiley. I stood for a moment, not knowing how to start. He looked up from under his perpetual frown.

"Well?"

"I have to report something," I started.

This got his attention. "What is it?" he asked.

"Knobby Felt . . . he's . . . he's damn near blind," I blurted out.

"Oh that," Smiley said, relaxing, "I know about that."

"You know?" I asked, incredulously.

"Sure, he does alright with those goggles, nothing to worry about."

I walked away, stunned.

A new wrinkle was added to our training: coordinated attacks on a sled towed behind a boat. We carried this out with all three squadrons until we had perfected the ability for all of us to arrive at the target at the same instant so that the antiaircraft gunners could not concentrate on one group.

We also started field carrier landings with our new planes, as we would soon have to qualify on a ship. One unwelcome addition was night field carrier landings. Butterflies appeared in the stomach at the mere mention of night field carrier landings. A short section of runway was designated near the edge of the field for this operation, as these would be touch-and-go landings for which a long runway was not required. There was one problem: high-tension lines ran just outside the field on that side. Rather than high, steel towers, these were twin wooden poles about half as high. They were scheduled to be moved when the field was built, but the navy never got around to it.

The evening before our first night flight, we all rendezvoused in the bar at six o'clock, as was our usual practice. There was always a suspicion that the navy made bars available and drinks cheap as a way of helping us relax after a hard day of flying. Whatever the reason, we fell into a pattern of drinking every night. It also seemed to help the men bond as a unit.

This particular night the bets started to flow along with the liquor. The group I'd gone through training with, Duke, Pat, and Hal, started betting how many waveoffs each of us would get before we got a signal to cut. Not to be outdone, I bet that I could get a cut on every approach, including the first one.

"No way," Duke interjected. "The LSO won't give anyone a cut on the first pass; he'll want you to make one just for practice."

"Want to put twenty dollars on that?" I responded.

"All right," Duke answered.

The others asked if they could get in on the "easy money."

"I'll cover all bets," I said with assurance.

There were no drinks the next night, just a light supper then into our flight gear. It was pitch black as we went to the flight line and got into our aircraft. Eight of us taxied out and took off, following each other around in a low traffic pattern, simulating the pattern around a carrier. I could barely see the tiny light on the turtleback of the plane in front of me. All of the field lights were off. True to Duke's prediction, the first plane got a waveoff, as did each succeeding plane. They were all coming in too high and too fast. As I observed each waveoff, I dropped my altitude five feet and slowed slightly. I started my final turn and picked up the landing signal officer and his lighted wands. He indicated I was slightly high, which I corrected immediately. The wands came down to horizontal, which meant I was in perfect position. I continued to slow slightly. He gave me a cut. Pulling back on the throttle, I felt for the ground and met it with a hell of a bump. I was a little high, but I'd gotten a cut, and the bet was looking better than ever. Gunning it, I took off into the total blackness.

I started my next approach, dropping another five feet from my previous altitude. Again slightly high, I adjusted to receive another cut. The bet was in the bag. I dropped another five feet in altitude on my downwind let. This one would be perfect, and it was until I hit the high-tension poles just forty two feet above the ground. I went right through two of them, cutting 230,000-volt lines. There was a blinding flash, followed by another one, then half of Southern California was blacked out. I was headed for the ground, hit, flipped over, and slid upside down until the plane came to a stop. By that time I was five feet under the ground, stunned.

I snapped out of it in a moment, only to find I was suffocating, my nose and mouth packed with dirt. My hands were free, and I quickly tunneled through the packed dirt up to my face, swallowed a mouth full of dirt and gasped for breath. I was still alive, but the question was, for how long? I could smell aviation fuel leaking from the tanks, and the exhaust pipes and cylinder heads were hot enough to ignite it. Obviously, I couldn't lift the airplane, so I was trapped upside down in the cockpit with nothing to do but wait for the fire. Planes in crashes of this sort catch on fire at least ninety-five percent of the time, so I had little to hope for. It's funny the things that come to mind in a situation like this. I remembered a class discussion I'd had with a teacher in high school as to whether a man in extreme pain would hold out until the last moment in hopes of rescue or would commit suicide. I had a knife. If the pain became unbearable, I had a feeling I was going to find out the answer.

I lay there for some minutes expecting the worst, but nothing happened. I could smell fuel, but it must have been missing the hot spots. Soon I heard the crash truck pull up and the sound of the rescue crew.

"How will we get the body out?" were the first unsettling words I heard.

"Jaws of life," came the answer. They started to dig a pit alongside the cockpit and cut away the opening. I hopped out.

My first concern was the plane and the damage. A medical corpsman rushed up. "Sir, get on the stretcher."

"I'm not hurt, I want to look at the plane," I answered.

"Sir, it says in navy regs that after a crash you have to lie down on the stretcher and be transported to a hospital."

Rather than get in more trouble, I lay down on the stretcher. Before they picked me up, another corpsman lit a cigarette and put it in my mouth. Grabbing it, I quickly snuffed it out in the ground. "There's enough gasoline around here to blow us to Los Angeles. Besides, I don't smoke." They loaded me in the ambulance.

Pulling up in front of the base hospital, I jumped out and entered the building, heading for the operating room. I pushed open the door and walked in. The two doctors, Alter and Simmons, were scrubbed and masked, ready to see if they could save the poor slob that was being brought in. The surgical nurses were ready. They took one look at me, covered with dirt.

"Bill, get the hell out of here, this is a sterile area, we're ready to operate if there's any possibility of saving this guy," Dr. Alter shouted.

"I'm the guy, I'm the corpse, see what you can do for me."

Their mouths fell open. "You son of a bitch, you scared the hell out of us," Dr. Simmons replied in relief. "Come over here and let's have a look at you."

I climbed up on the operating table as they checked me over.

"Little dirt in the eyes is the only thing I can find," Dr. Alter said after an examination. "I'll have it out in a second," he said as he took a camel's hair brush and went to work on the dirt.

"I think this calls for a celebration," Dr. Simmons said, going to a cabinet in the corner and returning with a bottle of medical brandy. Everyone climbed up on the operating table, and we proceeded to get smashed out of our minds. Since a crash was not covered in the original bet, they were called off. I learned one hell of a lesson from this: even I can make a mistake.

FOURTEEN

# CARRIER QUALIFICATIONS ON THE USS *ALTAMAHA*

One would have thought that the first and foremost purpose of the squadron was fighting. I quickly found that fighting was in second place. Having parties was number one. This point was driven home the first time there was a promotion in the squadron. We'd all gone to lunch and on returning to the ready room found an AlNav had come in from Washington promoting seven of our lieutenants junior grade to full lieutenants. There's a tradition in the navy that anytime an officer is promoted, he's expected to spend one month's increase in pay on a party for his fellow officers. Since the pay increase was over one hundred dollars a month, they had seven hundred for the party. The skipper gave them two hours to set it up. Flight operations were suspended at three o'clock in the afternoon, and the squadron rendezvoused at the bar.

Ramsey Hardin was one of the promoted officers, who also happened to be married and lived off the base with his wife, "Ginger." "Ram" was not a regular at the bar; in fact, no one had ever seen him there. It turned out that he and his wife were devout Southern Baptists, and neither drank at all. Despite this, Ramsey suddenly had a full quart of bourbon in his hand and was pouring it down as if it were water. Phone calls had already gone out to the various wives to come join the party, and within twenty minutes they descended. It was too late to slow the party down; it already had a full head of steam and the throttle was wide open.

Ginger arrived and surveyed the room. "Where's Ramsey? I'm getting him out of here."

It took a few minutes to find him. Ramsey was sitting under a table giving himself a shampoo with the whiskey. Ginger took one look and screamed, "Ramsey Hardin, you'll burn in eternal damnation." Turning on her heel, she left.

Somehow, Ramsey didn't seem to mind. He shouted to anyone that would listen, "God wouldn't damn me for just one night, would he?"

No one could answer this, so we went searching for the chaplain. We found him with a glass of Scotch in his hand and explained the problem.

Pardee climbed under the table with Ramsey and had an interdenominational conversation, Episcopalian to Southern Baptist. It was apparently successful, as they toasted each other at the conclusion.

The party went on until we ran out of booze. The wives, who had been more discreet about their drinking, took the married officers home, while the rest of us slept where we dropped. The following morning it was flight operations as usual, with hangovers that defied description. That's when we learned the beauty of pure oxygen, as we slipped into the cockpits of our planes and sucked on the oxygen hose in the hope that it would relieve our headache. It helped.

The word, which in naval usage means unconfirmed information, was that next week we would go to sea and qualify on a carrier off the coast of Southern California. We heard this same information repeated week after week. We finally became convinced that the navy had forgotten about us. It was nearing the end of the year, so we started to make plans for the holidays. The most important was New Year's Eve. A big party was in order. As squadron mess treasurer, I assessed everyone twenty dollars for a total of over one thousand dollars—a small fortune—to go for food and drink. This was going to be one hell of a party.

Naturally, the navy had other plans. The day before Christmas we received orders to go to San Diego and board a jeep carrier, the *Altamaha*, for qualifications. At the start of the war, carriers were in short supply. Since it took so long to build them, someone came up with the idea of taking cargo ships that were already under construction and putting a flight deck on them. These were smaller and slower than our *Essex*-class carriers. In fact, there had to be a fifteen-knot wind blowing for them to launch or land airplanes, but they were very useful and available in a short time.

We put out to sea on Christmas Day, one of the most beautiful days I'd ever seen. The sun was brilliant, and the sea calm with no wind. This was planned as a three-day cruise, but there was no wind, so we couldn't operate. We steamed up and down the Santa Barbara Channel in a dead calm for three days. Then, the forecast was for winds the next day. We'd still be back in time for the party.

"Winds" was putting it mildly; they were beyond gales, nearer hurricanes. We not only couldn't operate, we couldn't go topside. We bounced around in the channel as the ship endured the most pitch and roll it had ever recorded since it was launched. Acey-deucy and gin rummy were the order of the day as we hunched at tables in the ward room. The winds continued for three days, bringing us to the morning of New Year's Eve.

That morning, the winds abated slightly, and the staff decided flight operations might be possible. They wanted three volunteers to see if it could be done. The unwritten rule in the navy is, "Never volunteer for anything." Mulling it over in my mind, I thought this might be an exception. I volunteered, joined by Pat and Duke, probably the three most junior ensigns in the squadron. The senior lieutenants' disdain for us was brutal, as they told us in no uncertain terms that we weren't good enough to fly in this weather: they couldn't, so there wasn't a chance in the world that we could.

The carrier was too small to mount a catapult, so a free deck takeoff was the only option. Starting slightly more than half way back from the bow, I gave it full throttle and ran down the deck, hoping to be flying by the time I reached the bow. To go down in these seas was to be lost.

It was difficult keeping the plane going in a straight line due to the roll of the deck, but somehow I was in the air. The turbulence was violent as I climbed to three hundred feet. Flying a short distance ahead, I made my first turn. It was all I could do to keep the plane under control. Turning into the downwind leg, the plane picked up speed with the wind behind her. I prepared for final approach.

The landing signal officer picked me up. He looked as if he were doing calisthenics as he raised and lowered the signal flags: too high . . . too low . . . too high. The ship and I were all over the map. In addition, it was rolling badly.

We volunteers made three of the wildest approaches ever made on a carrier without a single landing. Then, the message I'd been waiting for came over my radio: "Impossible to land, return to base." The three of us stupid ensigns headed for the field over one hundred miles away, where a thousand dollars worth of food and drink was waiting, not to mention thirty dates. Maybe we weren't so stupid.

We took turns with the squadron carry-all, navy for station wagon, and picked up everyone's date. It was one of the memorable New Year's Eve parties of all time, ushering in 1944. Of course, we had to go into hiding when the rest of the squadron returned two days later. We also had to go out to the carrier later and complete our qualifications.

Word went around that we would be going out to the Pacific momentarily, but week after week dragged by, and nothing happened. Just as we'd given up hope, orders arrived: we were going out the next day. The place was in turmoil as I packed everything I owned in two large bags. The following morning I stored the bags in the fuselage of my airplane. We were ready: unfortunately, the weather wasn't. It started to rain. I'd seen rains, even hard rains, but I'd never seen anything like this. When it rains in Southern California, it really rains.

I dashed to my plane, climbed in, and closed the canopy to try to stay dry. The poor mechanics had to stand out in the driving rain as we started our engines. The skipper led the flight to the runway and started his takeoff run. At full power, all 2,200 horsepower, the plane could not accelerate to takeoff speed. There was too much water built up on the runway. Three-quarters of the way down the runway, he cut the throttle and gave up, taxiing back to the line. We all followed.

The skipper sent one plane out each hour to give it a try, but no one could get airborne. We gave up at nightfall and went back to the BOQ. The problem was, we'd already given up our rooms, and all of our uniforms and shaving equipment were stowed in the planes. This didn't appear to be much of a problem; after all, you can put up with anything for one night. The problem was, it continued to rain for two more days. We looked more and more like bums and no doubt smelled the same, not exactly fitting the image of naval officers.

The fourth day dawned bright and clear as we took off for Naval Air Station Alameda. I got my first look at San Francisco as we flew up the bay, and ended up flying under the Golden Gate Bridge, as the air traffic pattern stretched far beyond the field. Once on the ground, I taxied across the field to a dock where the aircraft carrier *Intrepid* was tied up.

Following the directions of sailors on the field, I maneuvered directly under a crane on the ship. Cutting the engine, I watched a hook come down. A mechanic opened a small door on the top of the plane and attached the hook to my plane. The crane lifted the plane, with me in it, to the flight deck of the carrier. I climbed out as crewmen pushed the plane out of the way as the next plane came up.

That night we saw San Francisco, every bar of it. We got down on our hands and knees to watch the cable running under the street for the cable cars, but in general stayed out of trouble. The following morning at eight o'clock we set sail. We were finally going into combat. Of course, fate had something else in mind for us.

FIFTEEN

# FROM FIGHTER PILOT TO SOCIAL DIRECTOR ON MAUI

Our first night at sea, the carrier we were scheduled to serve aboard was torpedoed off Kwajalein Atoll. The carrier did not sink, but was damaged enough to require repairs in the United States. The name of the carrier was never revealed to us as damage to ships was secret. The torpedo struck the stern and bent one of the four propeller shafts. The carrier was diverted to Bremerton, Washington, for repairs. The air group was sailing west aboard the *Intrepid* with no place to go.

We knew nothing of this, but senior officers in Pearl Harbor were busy at work trying to find someplace to put us. The island of Oahu was overflowing with servicemen, and there weren't a lot of other choices. Our future hung in the balance.

There's an old wives' tale in the navy that if a ship suffers an accident during launching, the ship is cursed. This seemed to apply to the *Intrepid.* It was launched at a shipyard on a river, and as it slid down the ways, the lines that were supposed to stop it failed. The ship went across the river and ran aground on the other side. From that point on, it seemed plagued with problems. It was known in the fleet as the "Evil I." The ship had not yet been in combat, so it was in mint condition. The crew was eager to make life as comfortable as possible for us, so we had a pleasant three-day cruise to the Hawaiian Islands. On arriving at Pearl Harbor, the carrier ran into one of the cranes on the dock.

Jack Wheeler, having lived through prohibition in Chicago, arranged for the air group to purchase two hundred cases of liquor, tax free, of course, to take along on our cruise. It was illegal for us to take this on the ship, so we had it crated and marked as "Top-Secret Radar Gear." We had our own officer's armed guard down in the hold patrolling the crates. One afternoon the captain of the ship came down while "Whiskey Bill" Cravens, a full lieutenant with the bombing squadron, was on patrol.

Bill snapped a salute, which the captain returned.

"Son, I'd like to take a look at the new radar. I haven't heard anything about it," he said. Bill didn't hesitate a second. "Sir, are you specifically cleared for BuAir 3771638?" The captain thought for a moment. "I don't recall that I am."

"Then, with all due respect sir, I can't let you examine this equipment."

The captain stared at Bill, who was in turn holding his breath. Finally, he said, "You're right, son. Carry on."

Bill took a deep breath. The liquor was safe.

The night before we docked at Pearl Harbor, the skipper sent word that he wanted to see me. I reported on the double. It's never good news when the skipper sends for the lowest-ranking ensign. I knocked on the door of his room.

"Come in."

I braced myself for the worst and entered.

"Bill, it hasn't been announced yet but we've just received word of our destination. They've been building a new airfield on Maui at Kahului. The runway is complete, and they have crews working around the clock to finish the quarters. We'll be moving in tomorrow. The islands are under martial law, so the civilians have not been able to have a real party since Pearl Harbor. I want a party the night after tomorrow to introduce the squadron to the people there. I want the greatest party the island has ever seen."

I stood there waiting, but nothing more came. "That's a great idea, sir, but I don't understand . . ."

"You're the squadron mess treasurer; you're in charge. I want you to take the first plane they unload from the ship and fly ahead to Maui. The rest of us probably won't come down until later in the day, by the time they get us all unloaded. There will be a jeep waiting at the field in my name. Take it, go into town, find the newspaper office, and ask to see the society editor. Explain what we want, and let nature take its course. Any questions?"

I was too stunned to think of anything. "No sir," I answered resolutely.

"Carry on," he said, and the meeting was over.

I walked down the passageway in a state of shock. What in the hell had I gotten myself into? What did I know about throwing a party for an entire island? And there was that vague mention of martial law, nothing to be trifled with. On the other hand, I had my orders.

The following morning the carrier entered Pearl Harbor. Evidence of the Japanese attack was still obvious, particularly the battleship *Arizona*, which was barely visible above the water. The moment the carrier tied up, I went ashore and waited for the first F6F to be unloaded. Once the Hellcat was fueled, I taxied out to the runway and took off. Suddenly, the island of Oahu lay before me, the harbor, airfield, beaches, and Diamond Head. The beauty was breathtaking.

I was more than a little apprehensive as I headed south. Although I had a map of the area, I was totally unfamiliar with the islands. What if I couldn't find Maui? My worries melted away as I climbed and saw the islands stretched out before me. I could see Molokai and Maui on beyond. There was no question, this was paradise.

Approaching Maui, I started a slow descent toward the narrow waist nestled between two extinct volcanoes. The water was a vivid blue, with hints of iridescent coral just below the surface. The land was lush and green and appeared soft enough to jump into. The navy had built an airfield consisting of one runway in this narrow valley, running to the beach at one end.

The runway was the longest I'd ever seen, extending almost ten thousand feet in length. There was just one slight hitch: it did not face into the prevailing wind. The story went that the navy sent meteorologists to determine the prevailing wind. They set up all of their technical equipment and took readings over a period of time. Once they determined the direction, they laid out the runway.

Locals watching asked why they were building the runway there.

"Planes take off and land into the wind," the navy men informed them.

"Wind doesn't blow in that direction," the locals replied, "only the last three months, no other time in history."

The navy men smiled. They'd run into local superstition before, but, of course, it was no match for science. With science as their guide, the navy built the runway thirty degrees out of the wind. Landings on this magnificent runway were hazardous, especially in high winds. Being totally unaware of this, I made a routine landing and taxied to the flight line where the skipper's jeep was waiting. I found the keys and took off.

Having spotted the small town from the air, I had little trouble finding Puunene. To say it was quiet would have been an overstatement; it was dead. I found the newspaper office in less than a minute and entered the building. Funny, everything was exactly the way the skipper said it would be, and he'd never been on the island.

I asked for the society editor and was introduced to Mrs. Potter, a delightful, middle-aged woman who turned out to be the wife of the owner of the paper. I started to tell her about the arrival of the air group, but she interrupted and said they'd already heard about our expected arrival, and all of the island's civilians were going crazy in anticipation of meeting us. Maybe this was going to be easier than I'd expected.

I explained that we wanted to give a party for all of the civilians the following night. A look of absolute amazement and pleasure covered her face. "This is incredible," she said as she picked up the phone. She repeated the information I'd just given her and finished by saying, "we'll be right over." Hanging up, she turned to me and said, "We're going over to meet Mrs. Cook. She's the social leader of Maui."

Driving through fields of cane on deserted country roads, we arrived at an undistinguished driveway that led through pineapple groves to a beautiful, low, rambling house. Mrs. Cook lived up to her position, formal but charming. She immediately put me at ease as she explained that due to the immediacy, she would phone everyone and issue an invitation personally.

She reached for the phone. "Lucette, would you please get me Harry at the country club?" She turned to me while she waited. "We don't have to bother with numbers out here. Our operators know everyone by name." Momentarily, she told the person on the other end of the line, "Harry, an Ensign Davis will be over shortly. Rent the club to him for tomorrow night. Thank you."

Turning again to me, she said, "Now, you'll be wanting entertainment. I've made a list of the hula troupes available. I've listed them in the order of their professionalism. Lucette leads the best one, and she'll be off her shift in fifteen minutes. However, I suggest you audition at least two, just to be sure."

When I stood in front of that commander in Philadelphia and was sworn into the navy, I never imagined in my wildest dreams that auditioning hula troupes would be my first assignment. It was going to get even better.

Mrs. Cook walked us to the car. "I can't tell you how excited everyone will be at the prospect of a real party. You know, we've been under martial law since the attack on Pearl Harbor, and civilians can't be out after six p.m. I'm sure you have something in mind regarding martial law."

Dropping Mrs. Potter off at the newspaper office, I took off for the country club. Harry met me at the door.

"How late will the party last?" he asked in all innocence.

Thinking of our parties in California, I answered, "All night."

He gave me an odd look as I gave him a check.

"May I use your phone?" I asked. Harry ushered me into his office. I picked it up. "Yes," a delightful voce on the other end answered.

"Lucette?" I asked.

There was a slight pause. "Forgive me, I don't recognize your voice."

"That's because you've never heard it before," I answered, "I'm Ensign Davis."

"Of course, you're renting the country club. How can I help you?"

"I'd like to audition your troupe," I answered as unemotionally as I could.

"I hoped you would," she replied with a lot of emotion. "I can be home and have the troupe together in less than half an hour." She gave me directions.

I, in turn, headed for the office of the provost marshal, the man in charge of martial law. After a short wait, I was ushered into his office. I snapped a salute. Major John Berry looked annoyed as he half-heartedly returned the salute. He was short and bald with thick horn-rimmed glasses. He quickly informed me that he had been a lawyer in civilian life and had volunteered out of patriotism. To me, he looked like Mister Milquetoast with a major's oak leaves.

"Our air group is arriving later today," I informed him, "and we're giving a party tomorrow afternoon to introduce them to the island. We'd consider it an honor if you would attend."

"I don't go to social functions. I don't have time, and I don't want to diminish my authority by becoming friendly with the local population," he answered curtly.

I was about to retreat when I had an inspiration. "We know nothing about martial law, so this might be a chance for you to explain the rules while you have everyone together," I offered.

For the first time, he stopped writing and looked at me. "That's a good idea—a chance for me to read the riot act to your men. What time will the party start?"

"Fifteen hundred hours," I answered.

"I'm too busy for that. I'll be there at four-thirty, sharp."

"Thank you, sir," I said as I got the hell out of there. At the same moment I made a decision that no pipsqueak army major was going to spoil the fun of sixty-four fighter pilots. I returned to the newspaper office.

"Are there any young eligible girls that will be at the party?" I asked the society editor. She laughed as she answered, "Most of the families sent their children to school in the States after the Japanese attack, but there are two that didn't, and they're on the guest list."

"I'd like to meet with them this afternoon," I said.

"I'll call them and have Maria go over to Gloria's house; it's the easiest to find," Mrs. Potter offered graciously.

A short time later, I met two of the loveliest girls it's been my good fortune to meet. They were not only attractive but bright and full of fun. They'd heard of our arrival and were more than anxious to meet the group. I assured them that I would introduce them to every single one, but first they had to do something for me.

With that out of the way, I headed for Lucette's home. I had never been any place in my life that was so peaceful. The roads were narrow but devoid of traffic, and the view in any direction was spectacular. Finally, I turned off the main road onto a dirt road. Trees arched over the road, turning it into a country lane. Nothing was further from my mind than the war.

I knocked on the door of a modest one-story house. A mongrel dog poked his head around the corner of the house, took one look, and went back to lie in the shade. He didn't even bark. Looking through the screen door, I could make out the figure of an old woman coming to answer my knock. She smiled as she opened the door. "You must be Ensign Davis. Come in, we've been expecting you."

I entered a small living room that was completely shaded by the overhanging trees outside. The room seemed almost cool as I flopped on the couch. A moment later, Lucette rushed in and introduced herself. She was as lovely in her way as Maria and Gloria, although I could tell nothing of her figure, as she was wearing the traditional muumuu, which hung long and loose.

"We're almost ready," she said as she quickly left the room. "Grandma will entertain you."

Grandma came back with some lemonade, which I relished. While we were talking, Lucette's younger sister came in and was introduced. I couldn't help smiling at her radiant young face. My eyes traveled down to her stomach; my eyes almost exploded. Grandma started to laugh. I was embarrassed that she'd noticed my stare.

"Oh, you noticed our Margie. Well, girls will be girls." She continued to laugh as if it were a big joke. Margie was unconcerned. "After all," grandma continued, "she is fourteen, its time she found out about things."

I couldn't believe what I was hearing. Here was a fourteen-year-old girl obviously pregnant, and no one was concerned. It's as if it was the most natural thing in the world—which it was, but . . . .

Grandma went to the phonograph and turned it on. The soft strains of Hawaiian music filled the room. I was trying to forget about Margie when five gorgeous bodies swayed into the room. Their brown skin seemed to glow like velvet and appeared as soft. The loose-fitting dress on Lucette had hidden treasures that were now almost fully revealed.

Suddenly the heat in the room was overwhelming. Perspiration rolled down my face, but I was too embarrassed to take my handkerchief out and mop my brow. They were superb, and they could dance, too. I knew I wasn't going to audition another troupe. In fact, I didn't want to audition anyone but Lucette for as long as I lived, which of course might not be long, but what a way to go.

Gazing at those supple bodies, I caught my first case of Hawaiian paralysis, that marvelous mood that allowed you to forget the present and ignore the future. I felt lifted out of the mundane world and taken to a tropical paradise filled with balmy breezes, soft music, and brown bodies. Nothing else existed outside the room; everything in the world was here.

Lucette's younger sister walked past and broke the spell. I glanced at that bulging stomach and then at the fragile, thin waists of the five dancers. It hit me like a ton of bricks. I was going to bring these girls to dance at the party, dressed in next to nothing. Waiting would be sixty-four men whose sap had risen and was now boiling out of their ears. I looked at grandma and thought of her causal manner regarding sex.

"Are any of the girls married or engaged?" I asked.

"No," she laughed, "all of our men have been drafted. They've been alone for a year now."

Her answer exceeded my worst fears. They were probably as hungry as the men. I had heard that the hula tells a story. I already knew the plot, and I didn't know a word of their language. They spoke the universal language. I wavered but I knew my duty. I was a naval officer and I had my orders. After all, Sherman had it right, "War is hell." I hired the troupe.

SIXTEEN

# RAMSEY HARDIN'S LONG TALE

Driving back to the base, I felt completely self-satisfied, as I had carried out the skipper's instructions to the letter. Entering the BOQ, I feared my bags might have been overlooked, but they were sitting by my bed in the room I was to share with Duke.

It had been a long day, and the humid heat of Maui had drenched my shirt. A shower was my only salvation. Quickly unpacking, I headed for the shower. The building was built like most military installations of the time: two wings of bedrooms either side of a central area that housed all of the plumbing, and a large room at the entrance that served as a living room.

I started down the hall with a towel over my shoulder. Lefty Burman appeared, coming from the shower. He was the first person I'd seen who'd flown down with the squadron. "Hi, how was the flight?" I asked him.

Lefty looked up to reveal a dull, sullen face. He stared right through me, said nothing, and continued down the hall right past me.

"What the hell's eating him?" I thought. Before I could answer my own question, another squadron member appeared with the same look on his face. I waited for him to speak, but he too walked right past me without a word. Suddenly, it hit me. We'd lost someone on the flight from Pearl Harbor. Instantly, I felt sick. I shivered in spite of the heat. Then I realized the squadron was not out conducting a search of the ocean; this could only mean the man wasn't lost at sea but must have been killed outright on takeoff or landing.

Knobby appeared in the hallway with the same dejected look. He was going to go right past me, but I stepped in front of him. He looked up, agitated.

"What happened?" I demanded to know in a voice already mad at the unknown loss.

Knobby stared at me with glassy eyes, insulted that I would press him for an answer he didn't want to give. Finally, reluctantly, his lips began to move.

"You haven't been in the shower yet . . . ." he let his voice drift off.

What in the hell could the shower have to do with it? My God, someone had been killed and he was complaining about the shower. His head dropped, and his shoulders sagged as he started down the hall with all of the signs of a defeated man.

"Ramsey," he said, almost in a whisper. "You haven't seen Ramsey."

I headed for the shower more confused than ever. I had never seen a group of men as up as the squadron. They were fun, confident hinging on arrogant, sure of themselves, and ready for anything. Now, suddenly, for no apparent reason, everyone walked around looking like a whipped puppy.

It was just the same in the shower room. No one was talking—no horse play, no witty remarks. It was like a funeral parlor with steam. All of the open showers were going full force, but no one was speaking. Suddenly, the silence was broken.

"Hey, Bill, how'd you make out, you flew on ahead didn't you?"

There was no mistaking that Southern accent. In the mist of gloom, Ramsey Hardin's voice cut through like a friendly beam from a lighthouse. No one else in the shower paid any attention. They were all locked in their secret despair.

"What's wrong with everyone; did something happen on the flight down?" I ventured.

"No, it was a great flight," Ramsey replied with his usual enthusiasm. "Isn't the base great, and brand new? What did you think of that runway? We could land across it?"

Smiley came out of the shower next to Ramsey with no signs of having been invigorated by the cold water. Ignoring his unfriendly attitude, I stepped into the shower and prepared to remove that layer of sweat I'd accumulated. The water hit my body and in a flash took away all of my worries about what might have happened. The hell with it, if it's important I'll find out soon enough.

I let the water beat on my head. It made so much noise, I couldn't hear what Ramsey was saying. I leaned out of the stream of water toward Lance.

"What?" I hollered.

"You notice anything funny about the guys?" he asked in all innocence.

I brushed the water out of my eyes and looked at Ramsey for the first time. I looked, looked again, checked once more, then put my head back under the shower. Instantly everything was clear.

Ramsey was married and had lived off the base during our stateside duty. This was the first time the entire squadron had lived together. This was the first time any of us had seen Ramsey naked. I took my head out of the water and looked again. There it was; it really needed a shower of its own.

What an inspiration his parents had when they named him Ramsey. How could they have known, or was it obvious from birth? The mental picture made me laugh out loud. There was baby Ramsey in the hospital nursery, just born, fourteen pounds twelve ounces. Not an oversized baby, just seven pounds six ounces of baby, the other seven pounds six ounces was cock. I'm surprised if the nurses in the hospital didn't dress Ramsey in two blue caps, one on his head and the other . . . . If they were both peeking out from under the covers, from a distance they might have looked like twins.

It almost hung to his knees, and he was standing in a cold shower. Knobby later described Ramsey as just like an old hound dog, all ribs and prick. Ramsey totally demoralized the squadron more than the Japanese ever could. Of all the attributes of a fighter pilot that have been mentioned, there was one that was automatically understood:

He was irresistible to women and, above all, the world's greatest swordsman. This even applied if the pilot was still a virgin and didn't know how to ask a girl out on a date. They all knew in their hearts that each one of them was the personification of Errol Flynn in *The Dawn Patrol*. Suddenly, in one moment the entire squadron was reduced to a bunch of babies, stripped in an instant of their masculinity—a squadron that proved Sigmund Freud was right. The sight of Ramsey had taken the fight out of a fighter squadron. The medical officer that gave Ramsey his physical should have rejected him as unfit. A few men like Ramsey in the service, and we might lose the war.

"Ramsey, I'm afraid you're the reason the squadron's going to pieces," I offered.

He looked dumb for a moment. "Aw, that couldn't be it." Then he thought for a moment. "Well, maybe it could be. The guys in my fraternity were kinda funny."

"What happened?" I asked hopefully.

"Well, I was just seventeen when I went to the university. I was from a small town and hadn't been around much. Anyway, I joined a fraternity, and as soon as I was accepted, I moved into the house. The first night I went in to take a shower, a couple of the guys looked at me and let out whoops and raced out of there. They came back in a minute with the entire fraternity. They just stood there and stared at me. Finally, the president of the fraternity said, 'Come on! I know what Lance's initiation is going to be.'

"They dragged me out of that shower, threw a towel around me, carried me to a car, and drove into Charlotte. They parked in front of this big old house in a questionable part of town, the rest of the fraternity all following in their cars. They hauled me out and carried me right into this house and stood me in the center of a big room, sort of like a living room. Sitting on sofas around the room were twenty lovely young girls. Funny thing, they were all dressed in just panties and bras. I knew it was hot, but was that any way to receive company?

"Without a word, the president whipped the towel off, and there I stood, naked as a jay bird. A gasp went up from all the girl's, 'cept it didn't seem like they were embarrassed about seeing a naked man. It was something else. Then, this nice looking older woman that looked like the other girls' mama walked over to me. You'd never in this world believe what she did next. Just as calm as could be, she reached down and took my privates in her hand, kinda like a judge at a Four-H fair judging a side of beef. Then the other girls came up, and they all handled me. It didn't seem like anything personal, they were just doing an examination.

"I was cold, scared, and embarrassed, but despite that it started to grow when those cute girls put their warm hands on it. The more it grew, the more they stared. A few of them started to hold their stomachs and others looked as if they were going to be sick. Finally, the president of the fraternity said, 'Which one of you girls is gonna take this on?' There was silence for a few minutes, then one of them said, 'How much?'

"The guys got their heads together and pooled their resources. 'Fifty bucks.'

"This was 1936, and that was a lot of money. Despite that, no one made a move. Then this one girl came over and really took a hold of it. She kept squeezing it and shaking her head.

"'Okay, I'll try with the understanding that I get paid whether I'm successful or not. Agreed?'

"The guys talked it over and agreed. With that, she took me to a room upstairs. We walked in, and she took off all her clothes.

"I'd never seen a naked woman before, and try as I might to look away, it was a small room, and all the walls and ceiling were covered with mirrors. She was all I could see. I got so damn hard I could barely stand it myself. With that, she pulled me down on the bed and did things to me I couldn't believe. She had more tricks than a Southern politician, but nothing worked. She didn't even come close to getting it in, but with all that messing around, I suddenly exploded. After that, we just lay there, exhausted. Finally, she said I had a problem, that maybe only one girl in ten thousand could handle me, maybe none.

"I went on through college and never messed around with women. Then I met Ginger, and we knew we were in love right off, but we're both Southern Baptists, so we never did anything but kiss each other. We became engaged, and I knew I had to tell her something, but we never talked about sex, and I didn't know how to bring it up. I couldn't just come out and say I've been to a whorehouse; you know, that was a whorehouse they took me to.

"Finally, it was the night before our wedding, and I figured I had no choice. I had to tell her. We were on the sofa, kissing each other, when suddenly I pushed her away and said, 'Ginger, there's something I have to tell you.' She knew right off from the sound of my voice that it was something important. She looked straight ahead, and I did the same.

"'Ginger, I have a physical problem: my sex organ.'

"I heard her gasp slightly. 'What kind of problem?'

"Never looking at her, I explained as delicately as I could. She was dead silent. Finally, I screwed up my courage and looked at her. She was just sitting there, smiling." When word of this got back to the other squadron wives, they felt it explained why Ginger's eyes bulged so.

SEVENTEEN

# THE GREATEST PARTY MAUI HAS EVER SEEN

Our first morning on Maui dawned bright and clear, the first of many similar days we were to experience. The temperature was perfect, and although there was some humidity, the trade winds seemed to blow it away. Six of us made our way down to the firing range to skeet shoot, which we were required to do every day. The navy was convinced skeet shooting would remind us of the need to lead a moving target. The loser bought breakfast.

We had one gunnery flight in the morning, again the loser buying lunch. On this first day, the squadron was secured at noon to get ready for the party. We broke out enough liquor to take care of the evening. This turned out to be a big hit with the locals, as we brought bonded liquor of the highest quality. The islands had been deprived of stateside liquor since the war started, as space on ships was at a premium. There was a local distillery, but the product was closer to paint thinner than booze.

The skipper dug up a bus to take everyone to the country club, but before they embarked, I gave them a lecture. "There will be two very attractive young girls at the party. Tonight they are off limits. Consider them on detached duty," I said in my most authoritarian voice. There was a mumble from the men.

"I'm not passing up anything for you," Pasko said with the disregard of a full lieutenant for an ensign, and still no doubt suffering from the Ramsey effect.

"If you do, you'll screw up the party," I answered in desperation.

The skipper saved the day as he spoke up. "I don't know what Bill has in mind, but he's the squadron mess treasurer, and he's in charge of the party. Better do what he says." We took off for the party.

We arrived slightly early, to give the fellows a chance to look the club over. There was a fine bar with a bartender at the ready. The club had a casual elegance that fit the surroundings. Mrs. Cook arrived and suggested a receiving line made up of the skipper, the executive officer, and herself to help with the introductions. It was barely in place when the first civilian guests arrived.

You could tell instantly that they were looking forward to this party. It was their first party in over two years, and it showed. The skipper was beaming. We were off to a good start. The civilians were as open and friendly as the pilots, and in a matter of minutes we were all old friends. Everyone headed for the bar, where the friendships were cemented. There was little reserve to begin with, and in a quarter of an hour the place was really swinging. I kept Gloria and Marie away from the crowd. We had work to do. I watched the entrance like a hawk.

At 0430 exactly, I was rewarded. Major Berry arrived flanked by two MPs, who remained by the jeep as the major entered. Finding the skipper and exec, I took them over and made the introductions. I explained that the major was the provost marshal and as such was in charge of the military police on the island. I said this loud enough for Gloria and Marie to overhear. They rushed up.

"Oh Major," Gloria said in a voice brimming with enthusiasm, "we've heard so much about you, we just couldn't wait to meet you."

"Our very lives are in your hands," Marie added.

"Why don't you get the major a drink?" I offered.

With one girl on each side, they led the major to the bar.

The girls laid it on him to such an extent it was almost embarrassing. They made him feel that he had saved the Hawaiian Islands single handedly, and he ate it up. I was almost ashamed of myself.

The party just seemed to grow and grow, and when I didn't think it could get any better, I raced over to the major, who was now being fed his seventh drink.

"Sir," I started, "I've made a terrible mistake."

He looked at me as a father might a child. "What's the matter, son?" he asked in a drunken slur.

Me as a twenty-one-year-old aviation cadet, December 1942.

N3N, my first airplane.

SNJ, fighter training.

Lieutenant Commander Hugh Winters, commanding officer of VF-19 (right) and Lieutenant Toby Cook, executive officer.

This is what happens when you try fly through telephone poles.

A party celebrating the promotion of seven officers from lieutenant (junior grade) to full lieutenant. I am seated on the floor in the center with a jacket on.

Me seated with Bill Copeland on the rim of the extinct volcano Haleakala, on Maui.

The skipper takes a shot at the hula.

The air group commander attacks the hula.

Me in an F6F over Maui.

Joe Kelley front left, with two drinks in his hands, suffered an unspeakable fate at the hands of his captors.

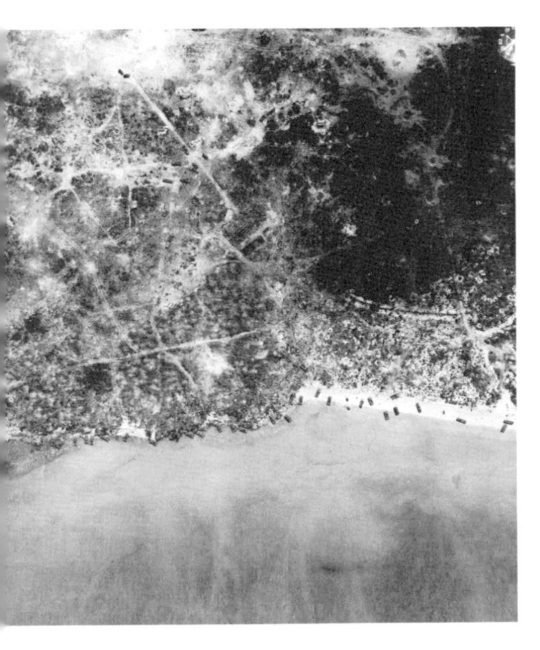

Landings on Palau, after bombardment by battleships and planes.

Admiral Marc Mitscher, commander of the Third Fleet, and Admiral Bull Halsey, in command of air operations, on the bridge of the *Lexington*.

Minutes before the takeoff for our first combat mission. I am seated in the second row, second from right.

Japanese carrier *Zuikaku* and cruiser *Oyodo* just before our attac[k] October 25, 1944.

The *Zuikaku*, showing my bomb hi[t] the white spot slightly after and to the right of the center of the deck. The bomb probably penetrated to four decks down. This photo was taken by Lieutenant Paul Beauchamp from 20,000 feet.

Me receiving the Navy Cross on the deck of the *Lexington* from Air Group Commander Winters.

The score: Air Group 19, 267; Japanese, 2.

Mogmog island in the Ulithi Atoll.

A photo of me taken December 20, 1944.

Me flying the world's only pulsejet-powered helicopter, designed by Corwin Denney and manufactured by Marquardt Aircraft Company.

"I haven't been keeping track of the time; it's six-thirty, and martial law is in force. What are we going to do?"

"Get me to a phone," the major ordered.

That's all I wanted to hear, as the girls and I almost carried the major to a phone. He made the call.

"This is Major Berry. I'm calling martial law off for the night. That's what I said. Martial law is cancelled for tonight. All of the MPs are relieved. That's an order!" Slamming the phone down, he turned to the girls. "Let the party begin."

It was fortunate that it all worked out so well, since we weren't serving food until nine and the hula troupe wasn't due to arrive until ten. As dinner finished, the lights dimmed and the Hawaiian music started. The room quieted instantly as the girls swayed onto the floor. They were dressed in bra tops and grass skirts, but no one had ever seen grass sway like that. It was as if they were from another planet, but in reality it was we who were from another planet—more like another galaxy.

A half hour into the dance, I suggested the skipper join the hula girls, which he did. He seemed to learn the hula instantly and was soon integrated into the troupe. With Hugh's obvious success, Karl Jung, the air group commander, demanded his turn. No one had rank enough to stop him. Karl was more at home on a football field, as he lurched rather than swayed and soon lost his balance despite the efforts of the girls to keep him on his feet. Suddenly, he was on his head, still dancing, then he crashed to the floor. We carefully carried Karl to a couch, where he slept if off.

At midnight the president of the country club took the microphone. "I want to welcome all of you to Maui and thank you for the greatest party the island has ever seen. It appears the entire board of directors of the country club is present, so I would like to call a special meeting of the board to discuss an urgent problem."

A murmur went through the audience. "Can't it wait until the next regular board meeting?" someone called out.

"No," the president replied, "we have to act on this right now. If you'll all form a circle on the dance floor, we can get this over in a hurry."

The members dutifully formed a circle as the president stepped into the center. "I declare this meeting in order with a quorum present. I would like to propose that every member of the squadron be made an honorary member of the country club, with full privileges for as long as they are stationed on Maui, and of course, free. I'd like to take a vote. All in favor? It's unanimous. You are all members."

A cheer went up as we helped the board members to their feet and shook their hands. With that, we all headed for the bar.

As the sun came up, we headed back to the base, in many cases carrying one or more of the squadron. We also had invitations to dinner with the various families on any day we were off duty. At seven o'clock a.m., the duty officer did a bed check then took the carryall and combed the island for the missing pilots. It was immediately evident the officer having the duty on Saturday night or any other party night had to be able to lift any of the other members of the squadron. There was no question we'd thrown a sensational party.

Three days later we found out how sensational a party it was. Admiral Nimitz's chief of staff, a captain, paid us a visit. It seems that the brass at Pearl Harbor didn't view calling off martial law favorably. The captain assembled us and gave us a tongue lashing that was reminiscent of Captain Bligh on the *Bounty*. He not only spared no words, he used some I'd never heard before, but I had a fair idea of what they meant. He made it quite clear he didn't want to hear anything about us in the future. The captain, still shaking with emotion, finally left and flew back to Pearl Harbor. Leaving the room, I ran into the skipper.

"I'm sorry I caused so much trouble," I offered.

"Forget it, Bill. As far as I'm concerned, you earned a 'well done.' That was a hell of a party. You're a fighter pilot. When you have a chance to take a shot like that, go for it, let the bureaucrats worry about it later."

As I started to walk away, he called after me. "Start thinking about the next party." I was stunned.

EIGHTEEN

# GUESTS OF THE MOLOKAI LEPER COLONY

We settled into one of the greatest routines in the history of warfare: skeet shooting, a gunnery flight, lunch at the club, golf or tennis, and an evening of drinking, bridge, or poker. This was all wonderful, but we were beginning to think our motto was that of John Paul Jones, when he said, "I have not yet begun to fight." It looked as if we were never going to. Major battles were being fought thousand of miles to the west of us, and we just sat there.

We were not in combat, but there was still plenty of danger. Steve Simoncik was making an overhead run on a banner target when he led the target too much and cut the tow line. The target broke loose just as he flew past, and the heavy weight at the front of the target hit his windshield, smashing it. Something went through and hit Steve in the head. The plane continued straight down, with the unconscious pilot hanging in the harness. We watched in horror as the plane continued toward the sea with no parachute in sight.

We circled the diving plane and prayed for him to bail out. It was not to be. It was over in one tremendous splash. One of the group dropped a dye marker and called the field. In short order, all of the squadron were out searching the sea for a yellow life jacket or life raft.

A rescue boat arrived as we continued the search in ever widening circles, but to no avail. Steve was gone. A day later we inaugurated the chapel at the new base with a memorial service. At the same time, we received word that Howell Cobb had been killed in a training accident at the El Toro Marine Base. He was the first of our cadet flight to be killed.

We had not gotten over the shock of their deaths when we received orders to attack Pearl Harbor. It seems that the brass in Pearl were worried that the forces on the island were becoming lax, as they knew the war had pushed the Japanese far to the west and there was little thought of them trying another sneak attack. The brass felt the

Japanese might make a suicide attempt and again find us asleep. They decided to use our air group to find out.

The air group was to take off from Maui, fly northeast 125 miles, then turn west and attack Pearl Harbor and the island of Oahu. We all had one question in mind: How will the gunners on the ground, not to mention any planes that get aloft, know this is a test and not try to shoot us down? We had the reassuring answer that the brass would alert the troops at the last moment that we were friendly and not to fire. If ever there was a chance for a gigantic screw up, this was it.

We took off at dawn and flew northeast, staying below one hundred feet. Once out of radar range, we dropped to twenty-five feet above the water and headed for Pearl Harbor. The air was bumpy, and I had to concentrate to stay in tight formation at so low an altitude. I couldn't help but feel something of what the Jap pilots must have felt as they carried out the same operation two years before.

Climbing slightly as we crossed the coastline of Oahu, we split up and headed for our various targets. We were not carrying live ammunition; everything was to be recorded on gun-camera film for analysis later.

We caught the fighters trying to get airborne out of Kaneohe. I sat on the tail of an F4U as it pulled its wheels up, and rolled the camera. He would have been dead meat. It had all the feel of real combat, and by some miracle the forces on Oahu had received word in time that no one shot back with real ammunition. From our standpoint, it was a real success.

Rendezvousing, we headed back to Maui at four thousand feet, our fighters closely escorting the bombers to protect them. Suddenly, one of the dive-bombers, piloted by Harry Bensen, started to drop behind the flight. "Engine trouble" was all that came over the radio from the pilot. The skipper took us in a large circle around the slowing plane. We were ten miles off the east coast of Molokai.

We watched as the plane went down toward the choppy sea. It was still early, plenty of time for a rescue. The SB2C turned into the wind and prepared for a water landing. The pilot leveled off just above the waves and pulled on the stick to effect a full-stall landing. At that moment, a large wave came up, and the plane crashed into it.

The bomber disappeared for a moment, then bobbed up. The rear gunner jumped out on the wing and inflated the life raft, but the pilot didn't get out. After a moment, the rear gunner lashed the life raft to the plane and slid into the cockpit, head first. The plane was sinking fast.

After what seemed like an eternity, the gunner pulled the pilot from the cockpit and floated him to the life raft. Harry Bensen appeared to be unconscious. The gunner slid him into the raft and waved to the flight as the bomber sank out of sight. The skipper assigned four planes to circle the raft until a rescue boat arrived as we turned and again headed for Maui. Looking back, I could see the bright yellow raft receding in the distance. It looked so lonely in that vast sea. Each of us watching envisioned ourselves in a one-man life raft alone in more hostile seas, with no rescue boat on the way. It was not a comforting thought. Although we could fly over a downed airman, we had no method of rescuing him.

Harry awakened about midnight that night to find himself in a hospital bed. Doing a quick assessment of his condition, he found he only suffered a headache from a blow on the head. He moved his body cautiously.

"Mister Bensen, are you awake?" the gunner, Tom Fry, whispered from the adjoining bed.

Harry started to answer in a normal voice but was immediately shushed by Tom. "Don't let them hear you."

"Why not?" Harry answered, this time in a whisper.

"We've got to get out of here."

"Where the hell are we?" Harry asked.

"In the hospital in the leper colony on Molokai; we're here for life. We'll never be allowed to leave." Tom answered in panic.

Slipping out of bed, Tom found his shoes and clothes. "How can we get off the island?" Harry shot back.

"I know where they pulled the life raft. We'll launch it and sail toward Maui. When they spot us in the morning, we'll tell them we were never picked up. What they don't know won't hurt them."

Creeping out of the hospital, the two found themselves on a spit of low-lying land bordered on the west by a sheer cliff nearly three thousand feet high. The only way off the leper colony was by sea to the east. They moved toward a low building.

"Behind here," Tom said.

Rounding the building, they found their life raft, somewhat deflated. A few minutes of blowing and it was filled enough to launch. Lifting the boat, they headed for the surf.

"Where the hell are you going?" the voice of a hospital orderly cut through the darkness.

"We're getting out of here; don't try to stop us," Harry answered in the most threatening voice he could muster.

"We pulled you out of the drink once. What the hell's the matter with you?"

"We're not spending the rest of our lives here," Tom shouted back, continuing toward the water.

"You guys have seen too many movies," the orderly shot back. "No one is restricted to the colony anymore; that went out over fifty years ago. You're being picked up in the morning."

"Don't believe them, sir, they're trying to trick us," Tom insisted.

Harry hesitated. "You mean, once you set foot here, you aren't required to stay for the rest of your life?"

"That's right," the orderly answered.

"How do I know you're not lying?"

"Well, I'm going home as soon as my shift is over," the orderly answered, "and I don't live in the colony."

Still apprehensive, the two men returned to the hospital, where they slept fitfully. They were relieved to be picked up the following morning and returned to Maui.

# NINETEEN

# LUAU TIME

By sheer luck I was having a drink with the manager of the country club on the veranda after a round of golf.

"Too bad you can't have a luau," the manager said.

"A what?" I replied.

"A luau, a combination of a native feast and a party."

"We'd never get away with a party like the last one," I replied.

"You could have it in the daytime—all day."

That evening the skipper walked past me on the way out of the mess hall.

"What are you thinking about for the next party?" he asked.

"A luau," I answered without hesitation.

"That's sensational, keep up the good work. Who will you get to actually put it on?"

"I was going to call one of the hula dancers; she should know." I walked away; I'd been looking for an excuse to call her anyway.

Picking up the phone in the BOQ, I called Lucette.

"Ensign Davis," came the reply without hesitation, "I was wondering when you'd call." Moving further into the dream, I asked, "Do you know anyone that can put on a luau?" "Only my mother," came the reply. "Why don't you come over after dinner, she'll be home."

Getting the jeep was a mere formality. All I had to do was tell the skipper I was working on a party, and I could have it any time, much to the displeasure of the executive officer, who was rarely allowed to borrow it. I knew the way to Lucette's house, even in the dark.

Dora was the epitome of a Hawaiian mother, big and friendly. She hadn't put on a luau since the war started, and she was determined to make this one the greatest she'd ever produced. "First," she said, "you'll have to get meat stamps. We'll need enough for an entire pig."

Meat stamps, I thought: that's civilian stuff. We don't have to bother with things like that, but of course, we did. The entire squadron had to go and sign up, and in two weeks we had enough points to get a pig. I hired Dora on the spot, and we picked a date.

"You'll have to pick up many things. I'll assign my daughter to act as your aide. She knows where everything is, and she has her own car when you can't get the jeep. Will that be alright with you?"

I tried to sound cool when I answered yes, but I'm sure I wasn't fooling Dora.

We set a date two week hence and worked out the schedule. I hadn't started to work with Lucette yet, but one afternoon I got a call from her.

"How do you feel about Japanese?" she asked.

I was stunned and didn't know how to answer. I'd already spent two years of my life training to kill them. "What do you mean?" I said lamely.

"You'll need flower leis for the luau. There's a Japanese village part-way up the side of the volcano. All of the men have been drafted, but the women are left there, and they have little in the way of work. They are magnificent with flowers, but I wanted to find out how you felt about using them."

"Weren't they all put in camps?" I asked.

"No, just on the mainland, they didn't bother the Japanese-Americans out here," she answered.

That's strange, I thought. I could understand why the authorities on the West Coast had rounded up people of Japanese decent. You couldn't risk having a force of over a hundred thousand, some of whom might be loyal to Japan, right in your midst, but why wouldn't you protect yourself out here nearer the war zone? It didn't make sense. "Perhaps we could visit their village together and you could make your decision," Lucette offered.

"Great idea," I said, getting off the hook. "I could pick you up at the gate tomorrow after lunch."

I couldn't wait.

Lucette picked me up right on time, and she was even more gorgeous than I'd remembered. She drove toward the volcano and started to climb. I marveled at the change in vegetation as we went up each thousand feet in altitude. It started tropical, but before long it looked like New England. Turning off the main road, which was minimal at best, we started over dirt roads that seemed to lead deeper and deeper off the main track. We left the paving behind and took to roads that had not seen a vehicle in a long time. One last turn and there it was, a village of almost dollhouse proportions. The entire town was only three blocks long.

Pulling up in front of a community building, Lucette parked and we got out. She led me into the building. It took a moment for my eyes to adjust. The hall was nearly filled with older Japanese women. Lucette started the introductions, and in a moment I was bowing to each woman in turn. It seemed that you should always be the last one to bow. I thought they'd never stop.

A nearby table was filled with a variety of leis, each more beautiful than the previous one, and since I ran a slot machine and had control of its abundant revenues, I ordered them all. Lucette made arrangements for us to return two days before the luau. We got a royal sendoff.

I sat back and thought as Lucette drove back down the mountain. These were the first Japanese I had ever met. I don't think I had ever seen one on the East Coast when I was growing up. This was the face of the enemy, yet they seemed to be the most gentle and polite people I'd ever seen. Their smiles were warm though shy. Could it be that the women were gentle and the men barbarians? The stories of the Bataan Death March and the atrocities on Guadalcanal were beyond belief. Could these be the same people?

The following week I spent more time with Lucette and her mother making preparations for the party than I spent flying. I duly collected the meat stamps and turned them over to Dora, but there were still a million things to do.

Two days before the party, Lucette called, suggesting we go up to the village to check out the flowers. "It would help if you could bring the jeep," she said.

I didn't ask why, but the skipper was very obliging. I picked Lucette up and was somewhat concerned driving a military vehicle with a civilian in it. I had no doubt that it was against regulations, but the traffic was light, so I took my chances.

Nearing the turnoff from the main road Lucette suggested, "I could drive from here on."

"Why?" I asked.

"It would be better," she replied.

I could tell she had something in mind, but I also knew this was an idiotic thing to do. "This better be good," I said as I stopped and we traded places. I sat on the right side as this beautiful young girl drove. I couldn't wait for the military police to show up.

Approaching the last turn into the village, Lucette turned to me. "Stand up," she said. I stared at her for a moment. "Stand up, quickly." I stood and held on to the top of the windshield just as we turned onto the main street.

They lined the street on both sides. Every woman in the village was standing there, dressed in the formal wear of ancient Japan, with their hair piled high, held by exotic combs. They were showering me with flower petals. A low murmur grew as we drove past. I realized they were saying, "Ensign Davis, Ensign Davis." I have no words to express my feelings. I thought I was the emperor.

The party started at eight o'clock Sunday morning. We dug a large pit and lined it with volcanic rock. A fire was set in the pit and allowed to burn for several hours. While this was going, on we played baseball, the squadron against the invited guests. We then extinguished the fire, placed the pig in the pit on the hot rocks, and covered it with dirt. By then it was time for cocktails.

By mid-afternoon, both the pig and the guests were done. Dora did a superb job of serving the meal, complete with our first taste of poi. With the number of drinks I had, anything would taste good. Midway through the meal, Lucette and the troupe made their appearance, and as usual they were sensational. After their performance, the girls became guests.

Lucette sat down beside me. "You *haoles* ["foreigner" in Hawaiian] know how to have a good time, but not like Hawaiians," she said.

"What do you mean?" I asked in all innocence.

"Some of my friends have invited me to a party Wednesday night, and I'd like to take you as my guest. You've been working too hard, and this will give you a chance to relax. It will be strictly native."

"Would it be alright if I brought some liquor?" I asked.

"You'll be the hero of the evening if you do."

Wednesday night, I stood in a freshly pressed uniform just outside the gate with a brown paper bag in my hand containing two quarts of bourbon. On top of everything else, I had the next day off so I was free as a bird. Lucette picked me up and headed for a part of the island I'd never seen. We pulled up in front of a small house partway up the far side of Haleakala. We could hear the music as we got out of the car.

The living room was dimly lit and one of the girls was dancing for the other guests. The music stopped as we entered.

"I want you all to meet Ensign Davis," Lucette said proudly.

The girls jumped up and placed leis around my neck and kissed me as the men shook hands. "We've all heard about you," they said in chorus.

"And look what he brought," she continued taking the bottles out of the bag. The cheers were ear shattering.

"This is strictly informal," they said to me, so I removed my cap, and my tie and shirt quickly followed. I picked up a spare ukulele and started to play along with them. We had a ukulele at home when I was a kid, and I could play about six chords, but you would have thought I was Segovia.

"I knew you were a Hawaiian," Lucette whispered.

Everyone could dance, both men and women, as they each took turns doing their favorites.

The family grandmother sat on the other side of me. "We're going to play our music, the real Hawaiian music, not the stuff we do for tourists. I'll translate the words for you." Suddenly the room was filled with music I'd never heard before.

The dance began with Lucette in the lead. To say it was sensuous would be to do a disservice to her and the musicians. It was subtly erotic. Grandma translated the words to the song, which under normal circumstances would have been considered pornographic, but somehow here it seemed natural.

The party went on for hours. "How will everyone get home?" I asked, "It's past midnight."

"They all live nearby; they can walk. The MPs never come back here anyway," Lucette answered.

"And you have your pass," I added.

"I won't need it; we've been invited to spend the night," Lucette added.

"Won't we be putting them out?"

"No, they have lots of room, but I want to give my mother a call so she won't worry about me."

Lucette went to the phone, which was just off the living room. I was near enough to hear the entire conversation.

"That's right, mother, we're staying overnight. No, we won't be a problem; we'll only need one room. I'm sleeping with Ensign Davis."

I sat there stunned. Did I hear what I thought I heard? This beautiful girl was calling her mother to say, in a voice loaded with enthusiasm, that she was sleeping with Ensign Davis. Who the hell is this Ensign Davis? The luckiest son of a bitch on Maui, the rest of the Hawaiian Islands, and all points east and west. So much for not trying to kiss a girl on the first date, or even the second if you wanted to pretend you were a real gentleman. This was real life at a level I'd never known. Thank God I didn't have to call *my* mother.

I was shown to our bedroom, and I undressed and stretched out on the bed. In a few moments she danced in, dressed in a borrowed negligee. She floated over to the bed and landed gently beside me. You will never understand the hula until you've been taught by a native, in the bedroom. There's more to the hula than meets the eye.

TWENTY

# TENNIS DUEL AT NAS KAHULUI

Since we were the first air group to report to the new base at Kahului, we arrived before the base officers. They started to trickle in, and the first one we had much contact with was the recognition officer, who was responsible for training us in aircraft and ship identification. His name was G. G. Glidden, and he was a great addition to the base. He was well built, although he had slightly sloping shoulders. He was no doubt restricted to non-combat duty because he wore thick glasses, which gave him the appearance of a college professor. We had an hour of recognition training every day, so we got to know G. G. in a hurry.

One day, coming in late from a gunnery hop, I missed the carryall going to the country club for golf. This would have to be a day for tennis. Arriving at the court, I expected to find a few of the regulars, but there was only one person there, G. G. I guess because of the glasses, I didn't take him seriously as a tennis player, but after a short wait and no one coming, I asked G. G. if he'd like to hit some.

"I'd love to," he answered enthusiastically.

We started warming up, hitting routine balls to each other. The court was clay, and his shots set up nicely. I found myself hitting the ball better than usual, and he in turn had no trouble keeping it in play. No other players showed up, so I finally asked him if he'd like to play a few sets.

"Love to," he answered.

The more I got into the game, the better I played. In fact, it was the best tennis I'd ever played in my life. I was quite elated until I realized that I was down love-four. I hadn't taken a game. In fact, as I thought about it, I realized I hadn't taken a point. G. G. had won sixteen straight points. That did it; I went all out. It didn't make any difference; he ran twenty-four points, beating me six-love. I didn't take a point.

"I realize I'm not much of a tennis player," I said as we stopped for some water, "but I've never lost every point before."

G. G. laughed. "I played a little in college, but I never considered trying to join the tour because of my eyes. I was just having a good day."

There's nothing like someone who can be gracious in victory.

A few weeks later, we received word that special services would have entertainment for us the following afternoon. The mail plane arrived as it did every day and, in addition to the mail, deposited Bobby Riggs and three other tennis pros. They were all in the navy, assigned to Pearl Harbor, and went to the various bases and put on an exhibition. G. G. and I were in the small stands to watch the show.

Bobby was a Wimbledon and Forest Hills champion, at the last tournaments held before the war started. Bobby played singles, then doubles, and then put on an exhibition that showed off his incredible skills. When he finished, he looked at his watch and announced,

"We have three-quarters of an hour before the mail plane goes back. Would anyone from the base like to play me a set?"

G. G. jumped up, "I'd love to."

G. G. went out on the court and started to warm up with Bobby. It was obvious from the look on Bobby's face that he didn't expect much. After a few minutes, they started to play. They each held serve to three all, Bobby no doubt thinking that he was carrying his opponent. G. G. told me afterwards that he could see the ball better than he ever had in his life, and he seemed to be able to put it exactly where he wanted it. He decided to try to break Bobby's serve.

Bobby served, and G. G. returned and came in behind it. Bobby looked up, surprised, then passed G. G. on the backhand side. G. G. threw his racquet behind him and placed the ball in the corner. Coming in behind the next return, Bobby hit the ball directly between G. G.'s legs. G. G. hit the ball between his legs for another placement. Riggs fell apart. Everything he tried failed. G. G. beat him six-three, running the last twelve points.

Bobby didn't come to the net to shake hands. Rather, he threw his racquet over the stands and rushed to his fellow pros for comfort. An unknown had walked out of the stands and beat the number-one tennis player in the world. I didn't feel so badly about my own loss. G. G. then told me he'd been captain of the tennis team at Harvard and had also been national squash champion. We became fast friends; he was one of the finest men I'd ever met.

Twenty-five years later I was a member of the Los Angeles Tennis Club. Bobby Riggs made regular trips to the club. On one of these, they gave him a locker next to mine, and we bantered as we both dressed. I took a chance.

"Bobby, do you remember a match on Maui about April of 1944?" That's as far as I got. His face turned dark as he looked at me.

"You were there?" he asked.

"Yes!" I answered.

"I hoped every son of a bitch that saw that match got killed in the war," he said without hesitation.

We never discussed it again.

# TWENTY-ONE

# THE MAUI SHIN BUN

One of the additional advantages of being squadron mess treasurer was that I got to meet a large number of the local civilians. As a result I started to receive a number of phone calls from young girls. The conversations all started the same way: "You probably don't remember me, but we met at the market when you were buying things for the luau. We're having a party tonight and we'd love to have you join us."

Since I considered myself spoken for, and Lucette was probably on the telephone line, I quickly found the two guys that had the next day off and lined them up for the party. This is what they call a win-win situation. I was actually running a dating service.

There was one problem, however, and that was our enlisted men. We had a small number attached to the squadron to supervise the maintenance of our aircraft and other ordnance. They also got a day off every two weeks, but they had no place to go. As officers, we could be out after six p.m., but enlisted personnel couldn't. In order for an enlisted man to get an overnight pass, he had to have a confirmed reservation at a hotel. The last hotel on Maui had closed in 1865, when the whaling trade came to a halt.

Suddenly, one morning two enlisted men rushed into the ready room, waving confirmed reservations for the Maui Shin Bun, a place none of us had ever heard of. The duty officer looked them over and issued the passes. From that day on, each of our men that had the day off came in with a confirmed reservation. We were all happy to see the men with a place to go and there was a noticeable improvement in morale.

A group of us were sitting in the lounge in the BOQ one evening, when Ben Buttenweiser, the administrative officer to the air group commander, rushed in.

"Does anyone know where the Maui Shin Bun is?" he asked breathlessly.

None of us knew for sure, but Pete Sprinkle thought he had some idea and gave Ben directions. "What's up?" Pete asked.

"The military police have found out the Maui Shin Bun is a Japanese whorehouse, and two of our enlisted men are there. It's about to be raided."

Ben took off in the carryall with tires squealing. He managed to find the house and get inside just in time for the raid. This is how a partner in one of Wall Street's most prestigious investment banking houses was caught under the bed in a Japanese whorehouse.

We were getting in deeper and deeper, between having martial law suspended the second night we were there, the country club party that brought a letter of reprimand, and now the whorehouse incident. The MPs had it in for us.

TWENTY-TWO

# PROMOTING THE ARTS, AND VISITING A FABULOUS ESTATE

Leaving the mess hall after dinner with a few of the squadron, I heard someone call my name.

"Wait up," Johnny Morrison said as he caught up with me.

"What's up?" I asked.

"Drop back a little. I don't want anyone else to hear this," he continued.

Slowing slightly, we fell behind the others.

"What have you got, something top secret?"

"Nothing that exciting. Three of the new enlisted men that have just reported to the base were professional musicians in civilian life. One of them played in a big band."

"That's great, but I don't see . . . ."

"I've invited them to play with us," John continued.

"We . . . I shouldn't say that, maybe you are but I'm not up to playing with men of that caliber," I answered.

"You're the only pianist on the base."

We both laughed.

"You're suggesting that the two of us jam with professionals," I said in disbelief. "One other thing: we're not permitted to fraternize with enlisted men, and besides, there's no place to do it."

"The officers club," John continued.

"The officers club, are you crazy?" I shouted. "Not a chance."

"We can meet down there at midnight on weeknights. The bar closes at ten-thirty and it's like a tomb after that. I've checked it out, and it's far enough away that no one will hear us." John's enthusiasm would not diminish. I had no choice but to go along.

The officers club was on the beach, not far from the end of the runway. John, carrying his tenor sax case, and I walked in the pitch dark along the only road. Arriving at the officers club, we went to the open dance floor with its small bandstand and took the tarp off the piano. I struck a chord, and with that three enlisted men appeared out of nowhere carrying their instruments, a bass, guitar, and snare drum. Introductions were made all around, and, of course, each of them answered "sir" with everything we said.

"Let's get one thing straight," I said finally, "down here we're all musicians, and you can forget the sirs and call us by our first names."

They quickly agreed, and we set up on the bandstand.

"Since I'm the ranking amateur," I said, "I'll pick the key. 'Body and Soul,' in C-sharp." The only sound was the waves breaking on the beach.

I gave the beat, "One, two, three, four." We were off.

I listened as I played. It was beyond my wildest expectation. It was really good. John had a soft tone that seemed to fit the situation, and the solid backing of the three professionals made us play up to them. We were really making music. Two hours later we gave up for the night, but agreed to try to get together two or three times a week. The professionals were very complimentary.

Subsequently, when I passed one of the musicians in uniform, he snapped a sharp salute, which I returned without any indication I knew him. However, if no one was around we gave each other a knowing wink.

A group of us were finishing breakfast when Pete Sprinkle got up and started to leave. "Where are you off to? We're not flying this morning," I asked.

"I'm going to class," Pete replied.

"What class? I haven't heard about a class."

"This isn't navy, it's an art class," Pete said as he tried to break away.

"An art class? You've got to be kidding," I responded.

"Actually, the problem is deciding which class I want to go to," Pete answered. "You know, A. Q. Jones is a world renowned architect in civilian life. He's trying to convince me to go into architecture after the war. And, of course, there's G. G. "

"What do you mean, G. G.?" I asked.

"Didn't you know? He's a well-known artist. Both of them are giving classes, and both of them are superb."

It seemed the base was turning into a summer art camp.

The next time I ran into G. G., I put it to him: "I understand you're something more than the best tennis player in the world."

He laughed. "I majored in art, and I make a living doing portraits of corporate presidents for the board room. I do about six of them in half the year, then I go to New Mexico for the rest of the year and do landscapes. That's my true love. Why don't you stop by the class Saturday?"

Now it was my turn to laugh. "I have no talent whatsoever in that area. Besides, I have to go to Pearl on Saturday on squadron business."

I caught G. G.'s interest. "If you have the time, there's a place in Honolulu that has art supplies that I can't get here on Maui."

That was as far as he had to go. "I'll make time. Give me the address and a list."

Friday evening, G. G. gave me both.

"Are you thinking of staying over night?" he asked.

"I'd like to, but there's only one hotel open. All of the rest have been taken over by the military for rest and rehabilitation."

"I have an aunt and uncle that live there," G. G. offered. "They have great guest quarters, and they'd love to see you if you'd care to give them a call."

I was dubious about calling someone I didn't know and inviting myself to stay overnight, but G. G. convinced me that they'd treat me as if I were their nephew. They'd been after him to come up, but there was no way he could do it.

Saturday, I found my way around Honolulu and got G. G.'s supplies as well as tennis balls at the submarine base. I went to the Muana Hotel and tried to get a room. They didn't even bother laughing at me; there were no rooms. I could just make it back to the field before martial law went into effect. I would have to be off the streets, as this was Oahu and the curfew was strictly enforced. I looked at the phone booth in the lobby and at the number G. G. had given me. I debated a moment, then went to the phone.

Uncle Monte was delightful and insisted that I come right over. He assured me that it would not be an inconvenience. I got directions and took the bus. The bus wound its way up Diamond Head and continued along a residential street. The surroundings didn't seem to fit the description I'd been given, so I got off at the next stop and went up to a house. A man answered and I asked where the Cook house was.

"Which Cook, there are several up here," he answered.

"C. Montague," I said.

He smiled. "Just go on up the street to the end, you can't miss it."

I went to the end of the road and approached a set of gates that resembled the gates at Buckingham Palace. The man had been right, you couldn't miss it. Starting up the long driveway, I was struck by the landscaping. It had to be on a par with the finest estates in England, but everything was tropical. As I was admiring it, Mister Cook approached from the house.

"Bill, welcome." His enthusiasm was infectious.

"Thank you, Mister Cook . . . "

"Call me Uncle Monte. Any friend of G. G.'s is one of the family."

How could I resist?

We went up to the main house, which was situated on twenty-five acres at the top of Diamond Head. This was the home of the Cooks, one of the big-five families that owned most of the Hawaiian Islands. Monte was the grandson of one of the missionaries that had come to the islands in the 1800s. As the saying in the islands went, they came to do good, and did very well.

The home was magnificent, the guest quarters occupying an entire wing. At dinner that night, there was a servant standing behind each guest. You had to merely glance at something on the table and it was instantly served to you. That evening we listened to classical music from the most complete record collection I'd ever seen. Aunt Lila was equally hospitable, as I felt I was in a home away from home.

The following morning Uncle Monte took me for a tour of the gardens, entirely planted in orchids. This was the largest orchid collection in the world. When Monte graduated from Yale in botany, he decided to make orchids his life's work. He had visited the most remote islands in the Pacific, collecting specimens. The navy contacted him regularly for information on many of these islands before they invaded them. He had been to Guadalcanal long before most Westerners had heard of it.

Twenty-five full time gardeners, all of Japanese descent, took care of the plants. As we came into sight along the winding paths, the gardeners would take off their hats and bow, and remain bowing until we were out of sight. It was another world and another time.

Aunt Lila and Uncle Monte invited me to come back any time I could, with two exceptions. The following weekend, Madame Chiang Kai-shek would be staying over the weekend on her way to Washington, and three weekends later General Douglas MacArthur would be staying there. Other than that, it was all mine. I was traveling with exalted company. I did manage to make it back three times.

TWENTY-THREE

# FLYING UNDER THE INFLUENCE

So far we hadn't lost one round to our nemesis, the military police, and we'd probably have been home free if the air group commander hadn't taken independent action. Karl Jung and three junior officers, Del Prater, Dan Hubler, and Joe Paskoski, were returning from a cocktail party in the jeep, with Karl driving. They'd tried to keep him from driving, as he was quite drunk, but he pulled rank. Despite this, they weren't too worried, as there were no other cars on the road.

As they careened along the deserted road, Karl spotted it, just sitting there, begging to be driven.

"I've always wanted to fly a train," Karl exclaimed as he slammed on the brakes.

The sugar cane planters had a railroad that ran around the island to bring the cane to the mill. At six p.m. the engineer had to bring the train to a stop, regardless of its location, and come back the following morning and continue the trip. No train could move at night during martial law. The military had some vague fear that the Japanese might use the train for a terrorist attack.

"You can't do it, sir," Danny shouted.

Karl ignored him.

"We'd better stop him," Joe suggested.

"He can get pretty mean when he's drunk," Del remembered.

They made one desperate try, first with words, then an attempt at physical restraint. Karl threw them both off with disdain. "I'm a full commander," he reminded them.

Lying on their backs, the three junior officers watched as Karl climbed up on the cab of the engine. The boiler still had steam up, and after a few moments of trying all the levers, Karl took off with the engine and fifteen railroad cars across the fields of Maui. Hanging his head out the side like a golden retriever, Karl seemed to be having more fun than he did flying a fighter plane.

Approaching the first road crossing, Karl dutifully blew the whistle, alerting anyone in the vicinity that the train was in motion. Immediately, the MPs were in motion—all of them. They stationed themselves at each road crossing and waited. It must have blown their minds when they saw the train approaching with a full commander in full naval uniform at the controls. Despite this, they attempted to jump on the moving train. Their first attempt failed, as they were thrown in the dirt alongside the tracks. It did not improve their disposition.

Racing to the next crossing, they made another attempt. Learning from the first failure, a big sergeant made a leap at the last car and hung on. Slowly, he worked his way up along the cars, then through the tender and into the cab. Karl saw him coming and was ready. When the MP tried to arrest Karl, he tried to throw the sergeant off the train. The battle teetered back and forth, as the sergeant hung on for dear life. Finally, youth, training and the fact the MP wasn't drunk paid off. He got the cuffs on Karl, and as they say, the shit really hit the fan. Karl, a full commander and Annapolis graduate, was going to be court-martialed.

For reasons unknown, the command at Pearl Harbor wasn't involved. This was local and was left in the hands of a naval captain, the senior officer on the island of Maui, Captain "Scratch Ass" Murphy. The captain had been stationed on Guadalcanal early in the war and had picked up a skin disease that was unknown to Western medicine. There was no treatment. The only symptoms were continual itching, especially of the ass. He couldn't sit, so he stood day and night and scratched his ass. It did not help his disposition. Karl's future was in his hands.

As a court martial would bring Karl's career to an end, something had to be done. The three squadron commanders met to decide what they could do. They determined that Hugh Winters, our fighter skipper and by far the smoothest of the three, would pay a call on Scratch Ass and see if he would consider any other course of action.

(I happened to mention the situation to Lucette, who suggested we go see a Chinese herbalist. I thought this over but decided to stay out of it.)

The captain was in a particularly mean mood when Hugh arrived. Hugh did everything he could to sooth his ruffled feathers and pointed out the pressures Karl was under. The captain was understanding and made a deal that if Karl didn't touch another drop of liquor while he was on Maui, he would drop the charges. Hugh agreed.

The problem was, Karl didn't. He depended on booze, and he wasn't about to give it up graciously. The three squadron commanders made a decision and locked Karl in his room in the senior officer's quarters. Two large enlisted men took him his meals. Otherwise, Karl was incommunicado. Ugly sounds blasted from that room as Karl fought a major battle with delirium tremens. Apparently, he wasn't beset by pink elephants, but rather imaginary MPs.

Training continued for the rest of the squadron day by day. Our gunnery scores increased as our golf scores decreased. The problem was, we weren't fighting the war. I felt like Ulysses in reverse. It took him ten years to get home from the war; it appeared it was going to take me ten years to get into the war.

Other than flying, parties were still a major part of our existence. One deterrent was that after the original party, we could never have another one that involved the entire squadron. The high command was still concerned about another attack on Pearl Harbor and required that half of every fighter squadron on the islands be held on alert over every weekend.

Never a group to take arbitrary orders at face value, we finagled with another squadron to spend a weekend with our entire squadron on alert so they could be off, and we, in turn, would have a complete weekend off when they returned the favor. We presented this to the air operations officer at Pearl and received his approval.

The following weekend the entire squadron was on alert, which meant no drinking, an almost supreme sacrifice. Two weekends later, we went about setting up another slam-banger with everyone participating—everyone except Karl.

The parties had gotten into somewhat of a routine. We all dressed in our freshly laundered uniforms and went to the officers club. There we had a small orchestra and a beautiful buffet. All of the proper civilians would attend with their wives, and the evening would start out very formally under the guise of an elegant cocktail party.

The male guests would soon settle in at the bar as the eager young officers asked their wives to dance, luxuriating in the smell of perfume and the feel of a warm body. Fortunately, we had all been told we were officers and gentlemen, so we made no passes.

Three hours later, the scene had all of the elegance of a barroom brawl in an old South Seas island movie. The problem was that there were women but no eligible ones. We resolved the frustration of so near and yet so far by drinking, or literally dousing the flames with booze.

The invited admirals were no exception. They began the evening resplendent in their regal uniforms, with a dignified bearing that made them unapproachable. Twenty drinks later and the shore patrol would have picked them up if they saw them in a public place.

The orchestra stopped playing at two o'clock in the morning, and the bar closed at the same time. The civilians took their wives and headed back to their quiet plantations, and we were left at the tables, finishing drinks we'd stockpiled for just such an occasion. By three, we crawled back to our quarters, drunker than a human should be allowed to get.

While we were drinking our minds into oblivion, military minds were hard at work. Once the air operations officer had given us permission to be off duty for the weekend, he promptly forgot. He scheduled us to supply eight fighters to cover a practice landing by an amphibious marine assault group on Kahoolawe island in preparation for the landing on Kwajalein. Of course, he never bothered to inform us, that is, not until three-thirty a.m. the morning of the operation. We were required to put eight planes, fully armed with machine gun ammunition and a 500-pound bomb, over the landing at five-thirty a.m.

Ramsey watched his squadron buddies crawl into the BOQ to flop on their beds in a state of total collapse. Now he stood over them, teletyped orders in hand. He had to get eight pilots ready to fly in less than two hours. He had already decided to lead the flight himself, as he was cold sober. That left seven, and there was no such thing as a designated pilot.

Entering the first room, he had to fight to get his breath from the alcoholic fumes emanating from the two bodies there. He shook the first man as hard as he could. Nothing. The man could have been dead. Shaking the second man, he got a moan, a favorable sign. Shaking harder, the man made a motion to push him away; here was a prospect. Soaking a towel in cold water, Ramsey applied it to the pilot's head. His work was rewarded with a stream of curse words.

"You're flying," Ramsey announced to the almost conscious man.

Repeating this from room to room, Ramsey found seven that moaned. Fortunately, most of them were still dressed. Ramsey's job was to keep them from going back to sleep as he arranged transportation to the flight line.

I was one that moaned when Ramsey shook me. I can remember Ramsey trying to hold me in an upright position as he tried to force my feet into shoes. My drunken toes curled and suddenly found themselves jammed into the shoes in that position. Since I was unable to walk anyway, Ramsey dragged me to the lounge as I made my feet move as if I were a ballet dancer on point. The crew chief drove up in the squadron van and helped carry the seven and dump them in. Ramsey was very considerate and tried to seat everyone so that his head was resting out the window, partly to get air, but mainly to be sure we didn't throw up all over each other.

The enlisted men were lined up on the flight line and snapped to attention as we drove up. This quickly turned to snickers as we fell out of the van as the doors were opened. Without an order, they ran forward and lifted us off the ground and carried us to the ready room. They attempted to dress us with the essentials—parachute harnesses, oxygen masks, and life jackets. Finally, we were ready to fly; unfortunately, we couldn't walk.

Two enlisted men picked me up and carried me out to my plane, where two additional men were waiting on the wing. They raised me to the waiting hands that in turn tried to slip me into the cockpit. Once I was in, they hopefully fastened the parachute harness to the parachute and the oxygen hose to the mask. They strapped the mask on my face and turned the valve to pure oxygen in hopes it would sober me up. I hadn't even noticed the five-hundred-pound bomb under the wing.

The crew chief gave me the sign to start the engine. At this point, years of training must have taken over. Although I was too drunk to walk, I reached down and tripped the switch firing the shotgun shell to start the engine, working the throttle until the engine caught. Two thousand horsepower were now surging at my finger tips as I started to doze off. An enlisted man jumped up on the wing and shook me, pointing to a plane taxiing down the line. I tried to follow it.

Finding the runway I carefully counted seven sets of lights making takeoff runs. Waiting a few seconds more, I gave it full throttle. With the size of this runway, I should be able to keep the plane straight enough to get it into the air.

The noise was phenomenal. I almost cut the throttle from the sheer din. I was gaining speed but continued to have the feeling that the whole thing was unreal, that I wasn't actually there.

I almost panicked—what was that? Something white just flashed beneath my wings. My God, there it was again. It took me a moment to realize that they were waves rolling toward the beach. I had come to the end of the runway, crossed a stretch of beach, and was now flying over water, just a few feet above the water, and I still had my wheels down. I pulled the plane and the wheels up simultaneously. The G force was doing a job on the alcohol in my stomach, but that would have to wait. I was losing air speed, and if I stalled at this low altitude it would be all over. Pushing forward on the stick brought reverse Gs and a healthy shot of booze to my mouth. I started to throw up, but I was wearing an oxygen mask. I choked everything back and tried to concentrate on flying.

Specks of light from the turtleback lights on the other planes appeared before me as I approached the rest of the flight. They were flying in a very wide formation, as everyone was afraid to get close to another plane. I pulled up a hundred feet from my section leader. We started climbing and headed for the rendezvous point over the fleet.

The minutes seemed like hours as we droned on. I glanced at my instruments, but they were almost meaningless. I prayed I wouldn't have a mechanical problem, as I was in no condition to make a decision of any consequence.

Suddenly, there it was: the rising sun. That great ball of fire shoved the blackness back from the horizon and swept across the ocean below us. It struck my bloodshot eyes and sent a flash of pain through my head. Ramsey was unaware of our plight and kept the flight turning toward the sun. Having taken off in the dark, I was wearing clear goggles and had no sunglasses. I tried to shield my eyes with my hand, but to no avail. Finally, Ramsey turned the flight toward Kahoolawe.

The island rose from the Pacific like all of the Hawaiian Islands, too beautiful to be believed. Perhaps God was having some fun. This spot was so far removed from any other place on Earth, he may have thought they'd never be discovered by man. Perhaps he was trying to see how beautiful he could make a place if he really put his mind to it. In any event, he succeeded.

Kahoolawe was no exception—from a distance. Up close it was different. It was a perfect example of what man could do to the most beautiful place on earth. The navy had commandeered the island as a target range and proceeded to pepper it with every form of explosive known to man, leaving one mass of craters and a jungle of unexploded shells, making it a literal hell in the middle of paradise. The marines were going to liberate a tiny portion of that beach that had been carefully cleared of unexploded ordnance.

The gray hulls of the ships became visible on the still-dark sea as we approached the island. Small boats were milling around the troop transports like a covey of quail around their mother. We'd made it, and on time. We circled overhead as the marines loaded into the landing craft. Our orders were to wait until the boats were half-way to the beach, then dive and unload our bombs on the beach in front of them. After a few minutes, they arrived at the half-way point, and Ramsey pushed over.

This sort of an exercise was normally an excuse for fighter pilots to dive on the beach, drop their bombs, then stay at ground level and shoot up everything in sight. This morning would be different. Ramsey flew true to form going into a steep dive, but the moment the rest of us pushed over, that lump in our stomachs started to rise, and we modified our dives.

Ramsey dove until he was out of sight. The rest of us dove only five hundred feet, let go one burst with our machine guns, dropped our bombs, and recovered into straight and level flight. Much to our relief, each bomb exploded safely on the beach, and we didn't hit Ramsey, who was down there someplace. As far as we were concerned, it was a perfect run.

Ramsey finally came up and joined us. "Where were you guys?" he asked. No one answered. After what seemed like an eternity we were relieved and headed back to the base, still in wide, safe formation.

Word had swept the base that a bunch of drunks had taken off on an operation and were now headed back to the field. Everyone was there, standing well back from the runway, anxious to watch the landings. They were not disappointed. We broke up over the field and started a cautious descent as we turned on the downwind leg. The palm trees seemed awfully close, but my altimeter indicated I was still at one hundred feet. It was one of those mornings when you didn't know whether to trust your instruments or your senses.

We kept a very large interval so we wouldn't pile into a crash, if there was one. Ramsey, of course, landed normally, much to the disgust of the crowd. Maybe there wasn't going to be any fun. The next plane dispelled that idea. Del was literally feeling for the ground. Coming over the end of the runway at seventy-five feet, he let the nose drop, then leveled off to see if the ground was there. It wasn't. He tried again, and again. The runway was long enough to allow several tries, but Del ran out of speed, and the plane dropped like a rock and hit with a loud bang. However, by some miracle, everything held together, and Del brought the plane to a safe stop.

I took a shot at it. Taking off my oxygen mask, I raised the seat to its highest position, so I could lean out the side of the plane to get as much fresh air as possible and a better look at the runway. I decided on a gradual descent: sort of let the plane fly into the runway. I had to be near the ground. I gave it another five feet, then eased back on the stick and throttle. The plane kept gliding, but I stuck with it. Finally, it stalled. I waited for the bounce, but it just kept dropping. Suddenly, it hit. I couldn't believe it when the plane rolled down the runway as if nothing unusual had happened. When they designed planes to make carrier landings, they built them tough.

I made it to the flight line, shut down the engine and collapsed. The plane captain jumped up on the wing.

"How do you feel, sir?"

I leaned out and threw up all over the outside of the airplane. "That should answer your question," I answered. We all made it back safely.

TWENTY-FOUR

# FAREWELL TO PARADISE

It took two days for the hangover to recede, then for the realization to set in of what we had done and how lucky we were to be alive. While in recovery, I received a telephone call from Lucette.

"How are you feeling by now, almost normal?"

"What do you mean?" I asked innocently.

"The drunken flight," she replied without hesitation.

"How did you know?"

"Everyone knows. It was all over the island by Sunday afternoon. This is a small island, you know."

Smaller than I'd realized.

"You've been working too hard," she continued. "You need some R&R, and I have just the thing."

"I'm all ears," I answered.

"I want to fix dinner for you."

"Great, at your mother's?"

"No, this will be a surprise. I'll pick you up at six."

At six p.m. I was standing outside the gate with the brown paper bag of booze in my hand. Lucette was right on time.

We headed toward Haleakala but took a different road at the base of the volcano and headed for the beach.

"Where are we going?" I asked finally.

"I told you this would be a surprise. We're here."

We turned into a hidden driveway and pulled up in front of a small beach cottage.

"This is my aunt's. She's been afraid to use it since the Japanese attack, so I look after it for her."

We entered a beautiful cottage with a deck overlooking a beach.

"Why don't you go take a swim while I start dinner?" she suggested.

Changing quickly, I came out on the deck and viewed the surf below. From my vantage point it did not appear too high, so I took off on the run down the path to the beach and dove in. It wasn't until I got out beyond the breakers and looked back toward the house that I realized just how high the surf was: higher than anything I'd ever been in before.

Swimming leisurely beyond the breakers, I enjoyed every second, knowing that shortly I was going to have to try to get back in to shore. The time had come. I measured the rhythm of the waves and made my sprint for shore, catching a gigantic wave just behind the crest. I looked down and realized I was twenty feet above the water below. I used all of my skill to stay behind the crest, but I went over and crashed down the face of the wave into the shallow water below. I tumbled until I had no idea of up or down. I was being battered by tons of water and almost buried in sand. I had to get my footing and get the hell out of there before the next wave came in and swept me back out. I felt my toes dig into the sand, and I ran up the beach just in time.

"Enjoy your swim?" Lucette asked as I came up on the deck. "I didn't know you were that good a body surfer."

"It was nothing," I lied.

"Dinner isn't quite ready. Why don't you try the hot tub? I fired it up for you."

I looked skeptically at the tub on the end of the deck but decided to give it a try. I climbed in and didn't think I'd be able to stand anything that hot, but in a few moments I adjusted and went into total relaxation. Lucette brought me a drink. I was in heaven, and the best part was yet to come.

We lay there all night under the stars on a large, padded, deck lounge, making love. The sounds of the trade winds mingled with the sound of the surf below. Could life really be like this, or was this just a trick the gods played on man? Here on this tiny island that had risen from the floor of the Pacific Ocean, life had evolved into a near perfect union of beauty and love. Too bad Western man discovered it. The undiscovered islands could have remained unknown as an example of what life on earth could be. Once discovered, all the white man could think of was how to make money from it, and all the Japanese could think to do was bomb it.

I was as far removed from the war as I could be. Little did I know that at that moment things were taking place further west in the Pacific that were going to destroy this idealistic existence. I felt Lucette's touch and immediately took her in my arms. She was so yielding and at the same time so passionate. We let the trade winds caress our naked bodies.

"I'm off nights now," she began. "We can come here every night."

I quickly agreed, although I knew deep in my heart that if the gods show you something as perfect as this, they're not going to let you live.

The following morning we had a high-altitude gunnery flight. We had just arrived at twenty-five thousand feet when we received a "Return to base immediately" message over the radio. We dove for the field. Upon landing, we were told to pack our bags and be prepared to fly to Pearl Harbor within the hour.

Throwing everything I owned into two bags, I ran to the phone and tried to reach Lucette, but to no avail. The word going around was that the fleet had fought a carrier engagement with the Japanese fleet, but our pilots had gone past their range trying to find them. Succeeding in finding the Japanese force about dusk, they carried out an attack and destroyed a number of ships, but many didn't have enough fuel to make it back to the carrier. The result was that our fleet was out there with no aerial protection. We were the closest air group, and we were on our way. We were going to get to fight after all. I tried Lucette one more time, but no luck. Soon I was taxiing out on the runway for takeoff.

Pulling my wheels up, I slipped out of the pattern and swung toward that small, beautiful beach with the crashing surf. I swooped down with my canopy back and spotted Lucette standing on the deck. I flew close and waved and hoped she understood.

Arriving at Pearl Harbor, I taxied near the awaiting aircraft carrier and was hoisted aboard. We set sail within the hour.

Our senior officers shared rooms with the ship's officers, but the junior officers were given cots on the forecastle deck. This wasn't exactly first-class accommodations, but at least it was cool. Somehow it didn't compare with the night before.

Bill Masoner was always prepared for any eventuality. Having been in the Pacific before, on Guadalcanal, he carried an inflatable mattress with him. We envied him the first night when we hit the hard cots and he had a soft mattress, but the second night out we had a hell of a storm. Water swept over the forecastle deck from the tropical downpour. We were all forced to cram toward the center of the deck for protection, but when Bill tried to move his cot, the wind caught his mattress and almost took him and the mattress over the side. Several of us grabbed him but could barely hold him.

"Let go of the mattress," I shouted.

"No way," came the answer over the roar of the storm.

Our grip started to slip.

"You're going to go."

Bill reluctantly let go of the mattress and watched as it spiraled toward the sea. Sometimes you can be just too damned experienced.

The throb of the ship's engines was different as we sailed at full speed to the west. Despite this, it was three days before we entered Eniwetok Atoll. The better part of the Third Fleet was anchored there, but our carrier was still at sea. We would rendezvous with it in two days. In the meantime, we got to explore Eniwetok. There really wasn't much to explore. The marines had taken it and then picked it over, taking anything that might be Japanese booty and any cat's-eyes that might be found in the coral reefs between the small islands. There was nothing to do but swim, lie in the sun, and read. The night before the rendezvous, the skipper called a meeting.

"Tomorrow we're going aboard the USS *Lexington* for an extended stay. This ship has a long and distinguished record, as did the air group that preceded us. They're going to be a tough act to follow. We want to make the best first impression possible, and since we're only going to land on her, that means interval: the time it takes for one plane to land, clear the arresting wire and taxi beyond the barrier so that the next plane can land. Their present fighter squadron had it down to thirteen seconds. I know we can't match that yet, but we want to get as close to it as possible. I want everyone sharp. We're not only going to be appraised by the ship's crew, but also Admiral Mitscher and his staff. This is the admiral's flag ship, and he's in charge of all air operations for the fleet. Give it your best. Admiral Mitscher is the thirty-third naval pilot and the father of carrier warfare. It'll be a tough audience."

Most of the squadron had been flying together for ten months, and we knew everyone's ability, but we had a number of replacement pilots join us in Maui, and we knew little of them. One was a Lieutenant Junior Grade J. F. Hutto. He was a fighter pilot but also had special training as a photo pilot, and his plane was specially equipped. The malocclusion alone should have been enough to keep him out of the Naval Air Corps, but there was more. It wasn't just that he was small, but he had a furtive look, which, combined with the teeth, made him look like a small rodent peering out of a hiding place. He looked scared to death. He turned out to be the comic relief that probably saved our sanity.

The following morning dawned bright and clear, with little wind. Once again I packed everything I owned into the fuselage of the plane and prepared for takeoff. There was one problem: We were at anchor. We were going to be catapulted off the deck, one at a time, while the ship was motionless in the water, with almost no wind over the deck.

I hadn't been aware that this could be done. I didn't know a catapult was that powerful.

We started engines and taxied up to one of the two catapults and waited our turn. I had never made a catapult shot, and I was more than a little nervous as I was directed to the starboard catapult. I let the engine idle until a mechanic hooked the sling up to my plane. The signal officer made a small circular motion with his hand, and I ran the engine up to full power. As he listened for a moment, I tightened the friction knob on the throttle and pressed my fist against it so that I wouldn't pull power off when I was hit with the G forces. I braced my right elbow in my stomach so that I wouldn't pull back on the stick, and waited. The launch officer dropped his hand

The force pinned me back against the seat. I had no control whatsoever over the airplane until it left the end of the deck. As instructed, I tried to make a right turn to clear the deck of my prop wash so they could launch the next plane. I was barely five knots above stalling speed and literally staggering into the air. It seemed nip and tuck for a moment until the wheels came up and I gained speed. I was going to make it.

The entire air group joined up, and we flew out a hundred miles to the carrier. We were in as tight a formation as possible to try to impress our new hosts. The fighters are always the first to land, so we broke off and dropped to three hundred feet over the carrier. The formation was perfect, and we felt damn good. We dropped our tail hooks and started to break up for our approach to the ship.

The skipper made the first approach and got a cut, followed by the rest of the squadron. So far, no one got a wave-off. I made a left turn to approach the stern of the ship. They were clearing the plane ahead of me as I picked up the landing signal officer. I was high and fast but quickly corrected until he had me in the groove. I wanted a cut so badly I could taste it. I kept approaching that tremendous ship, but my eyes were glued on the LSO. I got a cut. Catching the third wire, I was slammed to a stop. I released my brakes and let the plane roll back a little while they uncoupled the arresting cable, then pulled my hook up and opened the throttle to get out of there as quickly as possible. I taxied past the barrier as they were landing the next plane.

It was going better than we might have hoped. I could watch several of the planes as I climbed out of my parked plane and headed for the ready room. The last fighter was approaching. It was Hutto, and he was making the wildest approach anyone had ever seen. He kept coming, but the LSO gave him a waveoff out of self-preservation. The first bomber was the next to land.

We sat in the ready room, waiting. The skipper was standing in the front of the room, and he didn't look happy. Hutto continued to make passes, but no landing. The entire dive-bombing squadron landed, then the torpedo bombers, but no Hutto. He just kept flying around. Finally, out of desperation, the air officer got on the loudspeaker:

"If he doesn't land this time, shoot him down."

The LSO got the message and gave Hutto a cut. He was little high and a little fast, but he cut his engine and dropped it in on the deck. Drop was the right word; he blew all three tires. The skipper wasn't amused, and we'd missed the opportunity of making a hell of a first impression.

We were assigned rooms. I had two roommates, Duke de Luca and Pete Sprinkle. We'd been friends since the start of training and got along extremely well. The room was the second one aft of the forecastle deck, with two bunk beds on the inner wall and one bed above the sloping side of the ship. To make sure no one had the better bed all of the time, even though they were virtually equal, we rotated every two weeks. We each had a set of drawers and a desk, as well as a safe for our valuables. We kept our liquor in the safe and our valuables in our pockets.

It took a while to find your way around the ship. It was easy to get lost down a passageway you'd never been down before.

The one thing you had to learn and learn quickly was how to get to the ready room when general quarters sounded, wherever you might be on the ship. That was the battle station for fighter pilots in an emergency. When general quarters sounded over the ship's loudspeaker system, pilots racing down the passageways had the right of way over everyone else, including admirals.

The Japanese interpreter on the admiral's staff, Skip Hensen, roomed right across from us. He monitored Japanese transmissions almost all day and was always on call. Skip was extremely loose for a naval officer, but he could afford to be. No one else knew what he was doing, and no one else could replace him. His uniforms were usually wrinkled as if he'd slept in them, and he had a fierce black mustache. He also had a hell of a sense of humor as well as a formidable collection of Oriental pornography—all of this despite the fact, or perhaps because of the fact, that he had been raised by American missionaries in the Orient. Skip introduced me to a number of the staff officers.

As a group, they were somewhat different from the usual run of officers. Many of them had been brought into the navy because of special skills, like Skip with his Japanese. They were from many walks of life and covered a wide range of ages. One, Hal Weiner, had been an English professor at Harvard. He was widely read and had seen every play that had ever appeared on the stage in New York. He was delightful to talk to, and although we became good friends, I never knew exactly what he did—no doubt something in intelligence. As pilots, we were shielded from any secret information, in case we were shot down and tortured by the Japs. The less we knew the better.

We fell into an easy routine of drinks in Hal's room before dinner, then a social meal and bridge in the evening. Somehow this just didn't seem like war. That would all change very suddenly.

The fleet sailed from Eniwetok, and the word was that we were going to Guam to cover the landing there. The moment we were at sea, we maintained a combat air patrol (CAP) over the fleet. For the *Lexington*, this consisted of four fighters circling the carrier at ten thousand feet. These hops lasted four hours, at which time you were replaced with four more, and so on, as long as there was daylight. The flights were boring, as enemy planes never showed up so far from Japanese-held territory, but you had to be prepared just in case.

My first flight off the carrier was on a CAP. Once again, I experienced the thrill of the catapult, as four of us were sent to ten thousand feet to circle for four hours. Despite the fact that there was little chance of enemy planes, and the ship's radar would pick up anything within a hundred miles, there was an excitement, as this was classed as a combat flight.

The real excitement was my first look at the entire fleet under way. The Third Fleet, which was spread out over miles of ocean was made up of sixty-four ships, including sixteen aircraft carriers. Watching from almost two miles above the fleet, I could see the perfect formation of the ships and the precise parallel course they all followed.

When the order was given to change course to launch or recover aircraft, the entire fleet turned as one. The wakes from all of those ships were perfectly symmetrical with each other, like a perfect corps de ballet, but some of these ships weighed thirty-five thousand tons. I looked down on this power and wondered what kind of fools these Japanese were. They had made one of the greatest miscalculations of all time, and boy, were they going to pay a price. I couldn't wait to get to Guam so that I could contribute my share.

TWENTY-FIVE

# COVERING THE LANDINGS AT GUAM AND THE PALAU GROUP

The night before our arrival in the waters off Guam, the skipper gave us our first combat briefing. There was no pep talk; it was all rather matter of fact, in the sense that this is what we trained for and now we were going out and do it. He gave us no special instructions and no mention of feelings, such as fear. It was as if it didn't exist. There was not even a mention of, "I expect each man to do his duty." It sounded like another routine flight.

That night, Duke and I turned in before Pete came down to the room, as we were on the first flight and would be getting up at three o'clock for a predawn launch that would put us over the target at exactly sunrise.

We were both lying there awake in the darkness.

"How do you feel about tomorrow?" Duke asked.

I thought for a moment. "A little nervous," I admitted finally. "How about you?"

"I can't wait," Duke answered with a real edge in his voice, "I can't wait to get at them."

"I can't wait either, but I'm still a little nervous. No one knows how they'll react in combat."

"I know," Duke answered.

It was a long time before I went to sleep. Three a.m. came suddenly.

I felt entirely different as I jumped out of bed, like I'd finished one life and was about to start another. My hatred of the Japanese had not diminished; in fact, it was even greater. It wasn't that; it was something else, something intangible. I think it may have had to do with the fact that I was going into battle where everyone had live ammunition.

The ready room was also unusually silent as the pilots on the first strike got ready. I glanced around the room and noted a strained look on everyone's face. I suspect this is the moment of truth, when you face all of your worst fears and hidden doubts. Your thoughts meant nothing. It was simple: you were going, that's all there was to it.

Leaving the ready room, I was plunged into total darkness. It's really black at sea at night. My crew chief caught my arm and led me to my plane. I could make out the 500-pound bomb as well as the 1,000-pound drop tank. In addition, there was the unseen ton of .50-caliber ammunition in the wings for the machine guns. I was spotted far enough forward that the takeoff was going to be a catapult shot. My heart sank. I might never make it into combat.

My turn came on the starboard catapult. I set the trim tabs in the dark and hoped I'd set them right. The launch officer circled his hand, and I went to full throttle. He listened for a moment, then dropped his hand. I was pinned against the back of the seat and went off into the darkness, struggling to keep it in the air. I used everything I knew about flying to keep the plane between those two narrow boundaries, the water eighty feet below and a stall if I pulled up too sharply. Once the wheels came up and I started to accelerate, I felt more comfortable. I looked for the turtleback light of the plane ahead of me and joined up. Once at a safe altitude, we spread slightly, took our guns off safety, and fired a few rounds to be sure they were working properly. We slid back into tight formation.

Climbing steadily, we flew toward Guam, concentrating on the flying rather than what was coming. Guam rose unseen out of the dark sea, as we timed our approach to arrive over the target exactly at dawn. There was no point in giving the enemy additional time to get ready for us. As it turned out, they were ready. The moment we crossed the coastline, the antiaircraft fire started. It was accurate and plentiful. The air around us filled with black clouds from exploding shells. I couldn't hear them for the roar of my engine, but the noise must have been horrendous. In theory, I shouldn't have been able to see the tracers coming toward me, as the glow of the shell was on the rear of the projectile, but I could see them coming up very clearly.

They appeared to be climbing slowly toward me in an arc, like a soft lob in tennis, then suddenly they'd flash past me to explode behind my plane. The gunner hadn't led me enough. Now the shells were further in front, and I knew immediately it was going to be close. The four of us heading for our target took violent evasive action and avoided the next salvo.

Four of us had been assigned an eight-inch coastal defense gun that had been an American installation before the Japs took the island. We had examined photographs of the gun position but could not see it directly. We had to judge its position from its distance from two roads nearby. Bill signaled to break up and attack.

Duke and I increased the interval between us so that we could dive without fear of a midair collision. We started our dives, and immediately the antiaircraft fire increased. They were throwing everything they had at us. I glanced at Duke. One moment he was there, the next there was a tremendous explosion, then nothing. There weren't even any pieces visible. He had caught a shell, probably a 5-inch, and there was nothing left. I tore myself away and concentrated on the target and dropped my bomb. We all took evasive action after the dive and gave a sigh of relief when we were out of range. Then, we turned and went back over the target, hoping to see a parachute, but we knew it was hopeless. No one got out of an explosion like that.

I didn't remember the flight back to the carrier; all I could see was that explosion. It would remain riveted in my mind forever. Duke had made it through all of the trials and tribulations of growing up. He'd made it through college and two years of training as a pilot, only to be killed in the first twenty seconds of combat.

Dinner was tasteless, but I dawdled over it, not wanting to go back to the room and the job that awaited me. Pete was thoughtful enough to stay out of the room so as not to embarrass me if I broke down, or if we both broke down. I began going through Duke's things, starting with the easy stuff, the uniforms. I packed them as neatly as I could for shipment home. I left the letters until last.

I started with the letters from his family. I barely skimmed them, but I could tell from the tone that his parents were not happy with the fact that he'd volunteered for the Naval Air Corps. He was their only son. Perhaps this was even more important in an Italian family. Duke had started a letter the night before, expressing his thoughts about going into his first combat the following morning. He was eager: eager to show them what he was made of, that he'd made the only decision he could, given his feelings about the Japanese and his own country. He was where he wanted to be. He didn't finish the letter, but rather told them he'd finish it tomorrow after his first combat hop.

I reread the letter and decided that it wasn't going to help his family at all, and destroyed it. I only hope I did the right thing. I read the only letter he had from Helen Wellbank. It was hard to tell from the letter if she had feelings for Duke or was just carrying on a correspondence with him out of friendship. Unfortunately, I knew her real feelings, which didn't help. There were no indications of the feelings he had for her. Did he just need the imagined love of a stunning model to keep his spirits up? Should I write her and tell her what happened, or should I just let it die a natural death? No one would write Lucette if I got killed. Perhaps that was also just as well. I didn't write Helen. I sealed up all of Duke's things and sent them out for shipment home. Duke left home with such high hopes; now we didn't even have his body to ship home. It was dust on some hillside on Guam.

The reconnaissance photographs showed that we'd taken out the coastal defense gun.

We were now going to work every day bombing and strafing target areas behind the beaches. The second day, we lost a dive-bomber to antiaircraft fire, but both the pilot and gunner were picked up.

The third day a dive-bomber spun in on takeoff, and both of the crew members were lost.

Our routine had settled down to one strike a day and an additional combat air patrol over the fleet for another four hours. The takeoffs and landings were becoming routine, but of course they weren't. Every one took total concentration and expert flying. Sometimes it was hard to stay at that level, with the added hazard of combat that drained energy from you and left you less than sharp. I'm sure that most of the pilots, like me, relaxed when we left the combat area and were not at our best when making the landing. Losses around the carrier were mounting.

During our off-hours, battleships raked the beaches and fortifications with 16-inch-gun barrages. Life for those Japs on the island must have been a living hell. Even if you weren't in the line of fire, the noise of the continually exploding shells must have been nerve-racking.

After five days of softening up, D-day arrived. I drew the flight covering the landings, which meant a predawn takeoff and another flirtation with death. Once again, there was a three a.m. breakfast, but by now the chatter was back to normal, that is, for everyone except Hutto, who remained strangely silent.

Arriving near the island just before dawn, we circled off the shore while the battleships continued their barrages to at least keep the Japs' heads down.

The small landing boats loaded with the invasion troops were also circling near the larger transports. I felt for those men in the boats as they bobbed up and down on the rough sea. Most of them were probably seasick before they hit the beach, but they were going to have to fight regardless.

Precisely at sunup the boats started for the shore. Immediately, the battleships stopped their firing, and we were ordered to cover the boats. Diving down from five thousand feet to twenty-five feet, we flew over the heads of the invasion force and strafed the shoreline, hoping to hit some unseen targets. We continued in waves so that there were always fighters firing overhead as the men continued their endless trip to the beach. It must have been a morale booster if nothing else.

The instant we saw any flashes from Japanese guns, we turned toward them and strafed and bombed them. The action was continuous. The marines finally hit the beach, and we were right above them in full strength. We stayed until we ran out of ammunition, when another group took over as we headed back to the carrier to refuel and rearm. Then, we returned immediately for another three hours of ground support. By nightfall the troops had a strong foothold on the beach.

Going to general quarters that evening, we learned that since there was no air opposition, light carriers were going to take over the ground support and we were going to hit Palau, an island group to the west, as it might serve as a staging point for Japanese reinforcements for Guam. With that, our flight surgeons entered the ready room carrying small medical bags. The bags were filled with the elixir of forgetfulness, 140-proof medical brandy. Each pilot received one seven-ounce bottle. The best we could do for a chaser was a paper cup of warm water. This, coupled with the stifling conditions due to the fact that all ventilation was cut off during general quarters, gave mileage to that booze that was unbelievable. Within twenty minutes we had forgotten the fighting and the fact that the air group had lost six planes and ten pilots and crewmen in our first action. We had up a head of steam, and all of the stories were about close calls and miraculous survival.

The following morning I woke up with a hangover, but there was something else. It was as if our fighting had taken place at least six weeks ago. It seemed to be more of a dim memory than something that had happened only two days ago. I looked on the brandy as liquid grief counseling. I hadn't forgotten about Duke, but somehow the pain was lessened. Perhaps this was the only way we could survive, but somehow I didn't like it. It seemed as if we were cheating emotionally, as if I hadn't suffered enough for Duke's loss.

I was bothered for a long time that a close friend could be killed and it was almost as if nothing of significance had happened. I felt guilty and shallow, then it dawned on me: We were all so close to death everyday that you merely looked on the loss of a friend as something that happened to him today; you'd be along tomorrow. Somehow, this explained everything to me, and I stopped worrying about it.

Daily CAPs kept us sharp on the five-day trip to Palau. Toby Cook hounded the skipper to let him lead the fighter sweep scheduled for the following morning. As second in command, he felt that he was always left out of the good flights, and as a result his half of the squadron never got any gravy. Since I flew in Toby's half of the squadron, I had to agree.

The skipper gave in and let Toby lead the flight. We were sure there were Japanese planes on the island, and this was going to be our chance to get some. Spirits were high as we prepared for a predawn launch. There was a good chance that the Japs wouldn't know we were in the vicinity. Since we were coming in from the east and the Japs would be looking into the sun as it rose, we had a good chance for complete surprise and an initial run without antiaircraft fire. Wishful thinking.

We flew in low over the water in the dark, arriving at the island precisely as the sun came up, revealing up to fifty Japanese planes parked along the runway. There was no sign of activity; we had caught them completely by surprise. I turned my gunsight on and prepared to line up on a plane.

Instead of carrying out the attack, Toby started a climbing turn. We had no alternative but to follow him. We went to one thousand feet and by that time were at the far end of the field. At this point, Toby dove on the field, putting the sun in our eyes. We also had awakened the Japanese, who had quickly manned the antiaircraft guns and met us with a withering barrage.

Ignoring the fire, I lined up on a plane, set it on fire, and picked up another one. Every one else did the same, and after three runs we had every plane on the field on fire or badly damaged. Pulling up slightly from my last run, I spotted a Japanese seaplane base on an inlet at the far side of the island. We wiped it out in short order. Despite the heavy fire, no one was lost.

Debriefing after each flight had now become routine. Jack Wheeler was seated at a small table at the front of the ready room, and each pilot reported to him immediately as he entered the room. Most of the debriefings were carried out in a minute or two. Jack was interested in what you saw, especially the number of aircraft and the number destroyed. Ships were of great importance, and if you had seen a major ship such as a cruiser or battleship, that report would take precedence over anything else.

Once the pilots gave their reports, they took off their flight gear and relaxed in one of the chairs. Hutto was always the last to land, so everyone had finished their debriefing by the time he came in. He came into the ready room with a look of pure terror on his face, as if he'd just survived a near crash, which he had. It quickly became apparent that Hutto had been on a different flight from the rest of us. One other thing was unique: if Hutto had been on a four-hour flight, it took him four hours to tell Jack about it.

Once Jack got on to this, he pushed the microphone over so Hutto was talking into it and the rest of us could lounge in the chairs and hear what it was like to be a real carrier pilot. It was enough to scare anyone.

Hutto started with the orders by the skipper, or at least his interpretation of them: "While I sat in my plane on the deck waiting for the command to start engines, I thought about everything the skipper told me. I'm a fighter pilot first. Taking photographs, while important, is secondary. While I'm thinking that, they give the order, and I fire the shotgun shell, but the engine doesn't start. What if I don't make the flight? But the mechanic puts another shell in and I get it this time.

"I almost spun in on takeoff, but I pulled it out just inches above the water and joined up."

He'd then go on and tell how his instruments read on the flight to the island, how close he flew in formation—it just went on and on. Finally, he arrived at the island.

"I thought we were about to dive on the runway, when I realized that I'd forgotten to arm my guns. I hit the switches and opened the camera ports and turned on the intervalometer and we started our dive. I made my run and continued some distance out from the island before I made my turn. Then I saw it."

He just let the words hang there.

"Saw what?" Jack asked in exasperation.

Hutto's eyes went wide. "The battleship," he threw out triumphantly.

"A battleship?" Jack almost shrieked. "Are you sure?"

"I flew straight for it," Hutto replied.

Jack had already picked up the phone to call the admiral's staff. The rest of us stopped taking off our flight gear. We'd be going on another hop as soon as they could arm the planes, and this would be the entire air group. A coordinated attack on a battleship is something you only dream about.

Holding the phone to his ear, waiting for an answer, Jack questioned Hutto further. "Can you identify the battleship?" Then, as an afterthought, "Why didn't you make a contact report immediately?"

"Cause when I got closer I realized it wasn't a battleship," Hutto answered.

Jack hung up the phone and turned his full attention to Hutto. "What did you see?"

"It was a heavy cruiser, or at least a light cruiser, but one of the ones the Japs built that cheated on the five-five-three treaty—almost as big as a heavy cruiser."

"And?" Jack continued disgustedly.

"It was a destroyer."

"Did you get a picture of it?"

"Well, no. I flew straight for it, but as I got close, it submerged."

Jack blew up. "That was the rescue submarine, one of ours. They thought you were making an attack on it, and they had to submerge to protect themselves. You absolute idiot."

The next morning the entire deck was spotted with half the air group as we prepared for a strike on Angaur Island in the Palau group. Hal flew the fourth plane to take off. He came to the end of the deck and seemed to be struggling. He fought it but to no avail; the plane stalled and went into the ocean upside down. We all held our breaths as the trailing destroyer raced to the spot. We in turn were moving at twenty-five knots and were quickly out of sight. The launch continued. It seemed like a bad-luck omen to lose a plane even before we got into combat.

Once again, it was a pre-dawn launch, and we were over the target at sunrise. The antiaircraft fire over the small town was light, but there. We dove on the dock facilities and pretty much wiped them out, scoring hits with everything from five-hundred- to two-thousand-pound bombs. Rendezvousing out of range of the guns, we all gave a sigh of relief that no one had been shot down.

The fighter planes landed first as usual. I climbed out of my plane and headed for the catwalk along the side of the flight deck. I noticed the TBF torpedo-bomber making an approach at the stern. Something just didn't look quite right; perhaps he'd been hit.

The LSO gave him a cut, and the plane made a slight dive for the deck. Realizing that he was picking up too much speed, the pilot pulled back on the stick. The plane rose slightly and floated down the deck and over the triple barriers. It now hovered for a moment over the mass of planes parked with their wings folded, but only for a moment. It dropped squarely on top of the planes. Crash crews raced to the spot, as the potential for a disaster was incredible. All of those planes had partially filled gas tanks, and any leak from one of them could start an inferno that might be impossible to put out.

The pilot and crew were quickly pulled out of the TBF, then the men started pushing the damaged planes over the side, ten altogether. I stood there amazed as one plane after another crashed into the ocean, but it was done so quickly that no fire ignited. I went to the ready room, where I learned Hal had been rescued after crashing on takeoff that morning. All in all, it was not too bad a day.

That night, the fleet headed northeast, and in two days we arrived at Saipan, dropping anchor in the strait between Saipan and Tinian. American forces had already secured Tinian, but there were still enemy holdouts on the southern tip of Saipan. We watched a movie that night while the army fired 155mm shells from Tinian over our heads to destroy those holdouts on Saipan. The following morning we refueled and again set sail toward the northeast. We were going to Iwo Jima.

TWENTY-SIX

# AIRSTRIKES ON IWO JIMA AND HAHA JIMA

There had been a carrier raid on Iwo Jima about a month before, so the prospects of encountering large numbers of Japanese planes were dim. Instead, there would be ever-increasing antiaircraft fire. The Japanese had learned from bitter experience that as they lost aircraft, it was much quicker and cheaper to build antiaircraft guns and train crews rather than build airplanes and train pilots. Despite this, we kept a combat air patrol up at all times, and I drew one of these flights every day.

The night before our arrival at Iwo Jima the skipper briefed us:

"We are always looking for enemy aircraft, but as you know, the island has been hit before, so we don't expect too much. The other purpose of this strike is to get current pictures of the island with all of its fortifications. This is your show, Hutto." Hutto almost fainted.

Leaving the ready room after the briefing, several of us took a look at the next day's schedule and made a note of the fact that Hutto was on the second hop. We then went to Bill Masoner's room, which was somewhat larger than the rest. Hutto followed us for the first time.

The conversation was casual and touched on everything except the following day's strike. After about fifteen minutes, Hutto spoke up: "Hey fellows, which strike do you think will be the worst tomorrow?"

Without hesitation someone replied, "Why, the second one."

It was as if someone had struck Hutto with a club. He sat there in a daze. The rest of us went on with our conversation.

"Why?" Hutto asked finally.

"Why what?" came the answer.

"Why will the second hop be the worst?"

"That's easy. We'll probably catch them by surprise. We'll machine gun them in their sacks. We'll kill most of them, but there'll be a few left alive, and they'll want revenge. When the second strike arrives, they'll be ready, and they'll fight like maniacs."

Hutto was unable to speak.

We were wrong; the first strike was the worst we'd seen to date. When we arrived over the target at dawn, the Japanese were ready. The airfield was bounded on one side by a high mountain, no doubt an extinct volcano. It had a name, Mount Suribachi. There were several planes on the field, and we started a dive on them. I lined up on a twin-engine bomber and set it on fire. I pulled up to turn and make another run.

I had barely started my dive when tracer bullets flashed past me, coming from above. There must be Japanese fighters up there firing on us. They must have been up there waiting for us. I took evasive action, but the firing became more intense. Pulling up as I turned, I looked for the enemy planes but could not find any. I looked toward the mountain, which ranged high above us. The antiaircraft gunners were there, firing down on us. The entire mountain seemed to be alive with guns.

Redbird Burnett and his wingman burst into flames as they both took hits. I watched hopefully but saw no sign of a parachute. We went on and hit every target we could see and got out of there. Every plane was riddled with holes.

The second strike was more of the same but with less disastrous results. Everyone made it back, and as usual Hutto was the last to land. We all sat there, awaiting his debriefing. We were not disappointed.

After a lengthy description of the flight to the island, Hutto described opening the camera ports and turning on the camera's intervalometer. Lining up on the island, he started his dive toward the beach, starting to take pictures when he got down to fifty feet.

"The skipper told me they wanted pictures of any underwater barriers the Japs may have built off the beaches, so I came in low and got my pictures. Then suddenly I'm over the beach at twenty-five feet, and I see Japs in the trenches right below me."

"Did you shoot at them?" Jack Wheeler asked.

"Hell no, they weren't shooting at me."

We'd just about settled down when the skipper came in. "I've just taken a look through Redbird's stuff, and we've got a problem." He didn't wait for a comment but went right on. "It seems that Redbird is . . . was engaged to three different women."

We all sat there, not exactly surprised, but surprised just the same.

"Since his closest friend and he were killed at the same time, someone else is going to have to write some letters."

I thought for a moment. "Why not have three different guys write, one to each of the fiancées?"

The skipper thought for a moment. "That's a great idea, and you're one of the writers. I'll have the letters in my room after dinner."

I had violated the first rule for being in the service, never volunteer for anything.

Picking up one of the packs of letters, I headed for the ready room and our record player. I slipped a recording of Tchaikovsky's Sixth Symphony, the *Pathétique*, on the turntable and read the letters from Eleanor as I listened to the first three movements. I wished as I read them that I'd received letters like these from a woman. I didn't start writing until the fourth movement started. The despair in that movement is monumental, and it fit the mood perfectly. Of all the men in the squadron, Redbird had seemed the most immortal. I thought of his final moments and the effect it was going to have on this woman, who obviously loved him. Once again, I saw my parents receiving such a letter; there was never a way of shaking those thoughts. At least there was one bright spot: Redbird wouldn't have to come home and face the three women he'd promised to marry.

The following morning I took off as part of a strike on Chichi Jima, which, along with Iwo Jima, was part of the the Bonin Islands. The clouds and fog were bad, and we couldn't get in, so we went to our alternative target, Haha Jima. They had no doubt been warned, and they were ready for us.

The weather broke just as we arrived, revealing a small island with a wonderful harbor almost surrounded by land, with a small entrance at one end of the bay. There were docks suitable for large ships, and there were several tied up. Although intelligence had not told us, it appeared that this was the main port of the Bonin group. Without hesitation, we dove on the docks and ships.

Instantly, the air was black with exploding antiaircraft shells, by far the heaviest we'd ever seen. The gunners knew where we were headed and laid out a barrage over the docks. We had no choice but to fly through it. Two dive-bombers ahead of me were suddenly blown out of the air. I tried to concentrate on a cargo ship as I armed my bomb. I was being rocked by the concussion of the exploding shells nearby.

I pressed the bomb release button and pulled out, taking evasive action as I pulled away. Elvin "Lin" Lindsay, with his wingman, Joe Kelley, pulled out near me. A series of shells burst near them, sending them into violent maneuvers. Joe's plane yawed badly as it burst into flames. The plane was out of control, and he was awfully low. Moments later, Joe was out on the wing, trying to stick with the plane, hoping it would gain some altitude. He couldn't wait any longer; he slid off the wing and pulled his ripcord almost immediately. The parachute streamed out as his survival pack was ripped away by the hurricane-strength wind. He was screaming toward the water. The parachute billowed just soon enough to slow his fall before he hit the water. I held my breath, but moments later Joe bobbed up, apparently alright, but he had no life raft.

Lin regained control of his plane, but it was obvious even from a distance that it was badly damaged. He flew over Joe, and Joe waved. Lin flew away from the antiaircraft fire and slid his seat pack out from under him. He rolled the canopy back and flew back toward Joe. Dropping to less then ten feet, Lin held the seat pack out the side of the plane and flew right at Joe, dropping his speed to near stalling. At the right moment he dropped the survival pack and almost hit Joe on the head with it.

Joe quickly swam to the pack and inflated the one-man life raft. He had enough strength to pull himself in. He was safe for the moment. The Japanese had other ideas. They immediately put two small boats out to capture Joe. Ignoring the antiaircraft fire, we took turns strafing the boats, sinking both of them. The problem was Joe, sitting in the middle of the harbor. We could keep the Japs away, but there was no way we could get him out. It was too late in the afternoon to get a float plane in from a cruiser or battleship to try a landing in the bay.

Lin could not accept the fact that he was going to leave his wingman there. He headed for the rescue submarine about fifteen miles out to sea. Spotting the sub, Lin came in slow and made a water landing as close to the sub as he dared. Jumping out of the plane before it sank, he swam to the sub and was hoisted aboard. He was taken immediately to the captain.

Lin wasted no time on formalities. "Sir, we have a pilot down in the bay, I want you to take the sub in and rescue him."

"Inside the harbor?" the captain asked.

"That's right, right in the middle."

"I can't take the sub in there. I have no charts for that bay. Besides, they'd have a submarine net at the entrance, and the harbor is no doubt mined. We'd never make it. We'd lose your man and the entire sub."

Lin did not take "no" gracefully, but held his anger. "You have an inflatable boat with an outboard, don't you?" Lin asked, already knowing the answer.

"Yes," the captain replied.

"I'll take it in and get him," Lin said without hesitation.

"You couldn't do it alone, besides . . . ."

One of the seamen that pulled Lin aboard stepped up. "I'll volunteer to go in with the lieutenant, sir," the seaman offered.

"Let's go, we're wasting time," Lin insisted.

"I admire your courage and dedication, but I can't let you do it. There's no way you can make it in that harbor and out again," the captain said finally.

"Our fighters can keep the Japs away until I get out," Lin said as a last resort.

"Your shipmate is in the harbor. He'll be picked up by the Japanese and be a prisoner of war. Not a delightful prospect, but better than having both of you dead. If I thought you had a chance in the world, I'd agree, but the answer is no. You'll see him again at the end of the war."

None of us over the harbor knew of Lin's actions until later. We were still busy trying to keep the Japanese at bay, but we all knew we were running low on fuel, and the sun was going down. Forced to head back to the fleet, I watched the yellow life raft in the harbor as it got smaller and smaller. Finally, it disappeared from view.

The following morning we were over the harbor at the crack of dawn escorting a float plane, but there was no sign of Joe. He was a prisoner of the Japanese.

TWENTY-SEVEN

# "THE GREATEST INTELLIGENCE PHOTOGRAPHS EVER TAKEN"

One more day of strikes on Haha Jima and we pulled out and headed back to Eniwetok for rest and refueling. Once again, we received the drink of forgetfulness during general quarters, and after a few hours we forgot the horror of battle.

We were close enough to enemy territory that we still kept a CAP up, and in addition kept at least four pilots in condition eleven. This meant four pilots fully dressed in flight gear were ready to race to the flight deck and take off in one of the armed planes spotted on deck in case of an attack by a large number of Japanese planes.

Sitting there for four hours would have been a real bore, but the navy was more innovative than that. They had work for us. We censored enlisted men's mail. Every morning a large mail sack was deposited in the ready room, and the condition-eleven pilots went to work on it. It was required that all mail that left the ship be censored, as you could not reveal the name of the ship, the air group, where we were, losses, and so forth. The funny thing was, all you had to do was go to the ship's post office and buy a mail order for a dollar and send it home. It not only had the name of the ship but a picture of the *Lexington* as well.

Reading the deepest, private thoughts of four thousand men was a revelation. Of course, the thoughts dwelt on only one subject: sex. The letters broke down into two categories. The first covered all the things the writer was going to do to his wife or girlfriend as soon as he got home. The other covered all the things he didn't want no other son of a bitch doing to his wife or girlfriend while he was away.

The acts were beyond description or understanding. Most of them seemed physically impossible. No one could contort themselves into those positions. They also were going to put it in places most people would never have thought of. I wondered how the men made it through the day with such thoughts. Some of these men were maintaining our airplanes. If I'd had these sets of instructions sooner, Lucette would have thought that the volcano we were sleeping on had erupted again.

Hal Weiner was equally impressed with what he was learning about the English language—things he hadn't even picked up in graduate school. He had already decided on new lectures he was going to give once he returned to Harvard, for example, how to construct a sentence around one word; "Fuck the fucking fuckers."

After sailing for several days, we were once again in Eniwetok. We quickly adjusted to our relaxed schedule of reading, a little basketball, and swimming. I had seen a diving mask in a store in Long Beach and purchased one before we left the states. Several others of the squadron also had masks, including the skipper, so we decided to do some spear fishing. The cooks aboard the carrier assured us that they would prepare any fish we caught. Our squadron ordnance chief built us spear guns using the recoil springs from the .50-caliber machine guns. They sharpened the spears until we could sink one through a plank, three-quarters of an inch thick. We were ready.

Taking the boat in to the recreation island after lunch, we changed into swimming trunks and ventured out into the clear water. As you moved out from the island, the water was shallow, running from twenty to sixty feet in depth. Then suddenly, the bottom dropped out, as the depth in an old, submerged volcano went to two thousand feet. I peered into that depth, which was pitch black, and shuddered.

I was surprised to find few fish in the shallow water as the six of us fanned out swimming ten feet below the surface. Five of us were more or less in a line, but the skipper swam off nearer the dropoff to the deep water. We'd spot a small fish but had no luck getting close enough to take a shot. Feeling rather frustrated, I looked toward the deeper water. That's when I saw it.

At first it appeared as a large shadow moving slowly out of the depths. Then it got clearer. I motioned to the man next to me, and he signaled along the line. The shadow kept moving and becoming clearer. It was a shark—a very big tiger shark, perhaps sixteen feet long and it was moving our way.

The skipper was closest and beyond our signaling, but fortunately he saw it. The five of us started to backpedal toward the beach, all the time facing the oncoming shark with our spear guns pointed toward him—all but the skipper. The moment the skipper saw the shark he headed toward it. We couldn't believe our eyes. The skipper was far enough away from us that we wouldn't be of any help if he got in trouble.

The shark continued in our direction, and the skipper toward the giant fish. He swam right up to within a few feet of the shark, pointed his spear gun at its side, and fired. The spear hit squarely in the side of the shark, and bounced off. We all held our breaths. The shark didn't even turn; it didn't notice the spear and continued to swim lazily along, heading back toward deeper water. We relaxed and waved the skipper in to the beach.

Climbing out of the water, the skipper came up, breathless. "Did you see the one I almost got?"

"We saw it, and we want to talk with you. We'll follow you anywhere in combat, but the next time you attack a shark, you're going to be on your own."

I took advantage of the free time in port and practiced for the two emergencies I might face on any flight, either bailing out or making a water landing. I'd find a plane spotted on the flight deck or on the hangar deck and climb in the cockpit in full gear. I'd strap myself in, then assume I was going to bail out as quickly as possible. This meant disconnecting the wire to the earphones and releasing the tube to the oxygen mask, then the seat belt and shoulder harness.

A water landing required the same action with the radio and oxygen equipment, but here the seat belt and shoulder harness were pulled up as tight as possible, with the parachute harness loose. I'd jump on the wing, pull the survival pack and life raft out, and prepare to ditch. I took a lot of ribbing from my fellow pilots, but if the time came, I was ready.

We stayed in Eniwetok for over two weeks while the marines prepared for the landings on Peleliu, in the Palau group, and the fleet prepared to cover them. Once again, the entire fleet left anchorage and headed west. We had been there before, and the one thing you could count on was the fact that they would have brought in more antiaircraft guns. Combat air patrols were again the order of the day.

Since we hadn't been in combat for almost three weeks, the brass decided to stage a practice mission using the entire air group. We were going to carry out a coordinated attack on a target towed by a destroyer, with live ammunition and bombs, the full works.

The initial eight fighters had to be catapulted, as the deck was loaded with aircraft. Johnny Morrison's was the fourth plane to be catapulted. He seemed to struggle from the moment he left the deck. The plane was staggering and never recovered. He flew for a few moments and got his wheels up, but the plane never got out of the near stall. Suddenly it spun in. Johnny didn't get out.

I sat there in my plane on the deck watching and hoping, but to no avail. I thought of those nights at two a.m. on that tiny bandstand at the officers club on Maui, when we made music with that small group and the wonderful sax solos he improvised. I could almost hear them running through my mind. I wished I had a recording of them. It was all I had in the way of a memory of John.

A few days later we arrived at Palau. My division of four planes was assigned to act as a CAP over the main airfield in case any Japanese planes showed up from the Philippines. The antiaircraft fire was relatively light, and there was no activity at all until an American fleet of three cruisers showed up and contacted us by radio, asking if we would act as spotters for them. We agreed, of course, although we hadn't really been trained in directing naval gunfire.

The cruisers had orders to destroy all of the facilities on or near the airport. There were a number of buildings along the runway as well as a tower and warehouses just off the air field. We each became responsible for one cruiser, and of course, the competition was on. It was possible to identify the shells from each ship, as the explosions had a color marker in them. Each ship fired one barrage to get the range, then it was up to us.

I identified the color of my cruiser's rounds and instructed the gunners to raise the range thirty yards and over fifty yards. I watched as the cruiser fired its next salvo and waited for the shells to reach the target. The explosion was devastating as two buildings disappeared. I felt a surge of raw power flow through me as I realized the power I had under my control. The next hour was pure fun as the ships took out everything on this end of the island. I could only imagine firing those nine 12-inch guns at an enemy ship. The cruisers were very appreciative of our efforts and thanked us profusely. I had a feeling we'd done well.

The following day it was back to Peleliu, to soften it up for the invasion. Once again, we wiped out the only airfield and then went to work on the docks. There were a number of small supply ships, which we sank. Then we set the oil tanks near the dock on fire. The antiaircraft fire was heavy, and Whiskey Bill Cravens was shot down but managed to glide far enough out from the harbor to be picked up by the submarine. Boy, did we love having that rescue sub off every island we hit.

We ran into so little Japanese opposition that the brass decided it was time to make the first strike against the Philippines since General MacArthur left in 1942. Intelligence expected us to run into large numbers of enemy planes.

We flew toward the island in the dark after a predawn launch. The southernmost island, Mindanao, was nothing like the small islands we'd been hitting. This was quite large, almost three hundred by three hundred miles at its widest. The island had high mountains completely covered with forests and perhaps a number of newly constructed airfields.

The flight headed for Cagayan Harbor, which was filled with sampans. We dove on them, and I got one in my sight. One blast with my six .50-caliber machine guns and the ship burst into flames.

Bruce "Lucky" Williams lived up to his name. He chose a sampan in the center of the group. He went into his run and was down to two hundred feet when the ship exploded. It was the ammunition ship, and it blew sky high, literally. Lucky suddenly found himself at three thousand feet with the wings of his airplane bent upward. He had been blasted straight up twenty-eight hundred feet.

We continued across the island, looking for airfields. We were now well over the mountains when the skipper spotted a cleared area in the middle of the forest. It appeared to be long enough to be a runway, but it was hard to tell from our altitude. The skipper's voice came over the radio:

"Fearless Four, go down and take a look at that clearing." I was Fearless Four, and I went into my dive.

I kept expecting a sudden burst of antiaircraft fire, but it didn't come. If they were laying a trap for me, I was diving right into it. I wasn't really worried, however, as somewhere in the back of my mind I knew this wasn't an air strip. I continued down and confirmed my guess. This was a village. A dirt road ran through the clearing bounded on both sides by thatched huts built on stilts, perhaps twelve feet high, no doubt because of the crawling things in the jungle.

The huts were far enough apart that I could fly down the road between them. I slowed the plane and opened my canopy as I flew toward the building at the end of the road. It was completely out of place in the middle of this jungle. European gothic in design and painted gold, it was the Catholic church.

I pulled up, made a turn, and flew back down the street, staying below the level of the decks in front of the huts. All of the children of the village were now out on their decks cheering as I flew by only a few feet from them. I was overwhelmed by the smell of the forest. Being at sea, I had forgotten how land smelled. I took one last, large breath, waved to the children, and rejoined the flight.

The following morning we went further north and hit the Del Monte area, striking first at the airfield there. Having hit Mindanao the day before, there was little hope for surprise, and they were ready for us. We dove on the field and encountered a blistering barrage of antiaircraft fire.

Ruff Ruffcorn took a direct hit as he flew down the field. He was only twenty-five feet above the ground, but although the plane was engulfed in flames, he managed to pull the nose up and was gaining altitude. The fire reached the cockpit and forced Ruff out onto the wing, where he hung on, hoping to get high enough to jump. I watched as he tried to stay with the plane, but at two hundred feet he had to give up and jumped. The parachute had barely begun to stream out when he hit the runway and bounced up almost a hundred feet. At the same moment his plane exploded.

I lined up on the barracks and riddled them with machine gun fire, setting them on fire. Pulling out, I spotted a Japanese dive-bomber flying ninety degrees to my course. Despite the distance, I led him and opened fire. In a few moments, smoke was pouring from his engine. Before I could get closer, another of our squadron pulled in directly behind him and exploded the plane. It was on his gun-camera film and not mine, so he got credit for the plane. We not only had to fight the Japs to shoot them down, we had to compete with our own squadron mates to get them.

Leaving the field in ruins, we circled the countryside but couldn't find another target. Landing back on the carrier, we found that seven of our planes had sustained hits from the antiaircraft guns. In addition, Dan Hubler had a bullet come in through the side of the cockpit, taking the end of one finger off where he was holding the throttle. He was back in combat within a day.

The overwhelming resistance from the Japanese that we expected did not materialize, so the fleet moved north during the night, and a strike was scheduled to hit Cebu island the following day. There would be a fighter sweep, but I was assigned to cover the photo plane. We flew in as a group, then once over the island, Hutto broke away and I dropped in behind and slightly above him as he started his series of runs.

There was a great deal of activity with ships in the waterways around Cebu. The sky was clear and the visibility great. Hutto held a straight course as he began his first run. A Zero fighter plane appeared out of nowhere. Until that moment, I had only seen pictures of Zeros. I knew every detail, but seeing one in person was different. It's like seeing pictures of Ava Gardner for years, memorizing every curve and subtle structure of her face and body, then suddenly coming face to face with her in person. First of all, she's full size, not an eight-by-ten glossy, but most of all, the mental harmony your brain gave to her body is nothing like the real thing. I was dumbstruck for a moment as I stared at the plane.

Quickly getting over my surprise, I led the target and fired a burst from my machine guns. I led the target too much, sending tracers screaming past the nose of the plane. The Jap pilot immediately made a sharp turn to the left, putting me right on his tail. I closed until there was no chance of missing, and fired. It took only a short burst to blow the plane up. I was aware of someone screaming over the radio. I listened for a moment, but it had stopped. Then I realized that that screaming had been me. As I had fired my guns at the Zero, I had automatically screamed at the top of my lungs. That scream came from somewhere deep in my brain, from the primordial lizard part of my brain. Mankind has no doubt been screaming during combat since the beginning of time.

Hutto completed his photo runs without event, but the rest of the squadron had a field day. They caught the Japanese taking off to intercept us and shot down seventeen planes in the air and destroyed another thirty-five on the ground. The dive-bombers sank several large cargo ships, with the loss of one plane and crew.

The following day I went for the daily double, with two strikes on Cebu and Negros. Although there were a number of Japanese fighters in the air, none came near our flight. Since our first responsibility was to protect our bombers, we did not leave the group to chase fighters, much as we would have loved to.

Pulling out from a run on the airfield where I burned several planes on the ground, I approached a small island in the bay that was completely covered with an oil refinery. The cracking towers, tanks, and pipes covered acres of land, and I knew the possibility of doing any real damage was slight, but I decided to waste some ammunition on the facility. Even a few ruptured pipes would be something.

I flew low at about twenty feet and lined up on a complex at the heart of the refinery. I opened fire and could see my tracers ripping into the equipment. Our ammunition consisted of an alternating mix of general-purpose, tracer, and armor-piercing rounds, so things were flying in all directions. Suddenly, a fire erupted, sending a sheet of flame skyward and forcing me to make a tight right turn and pull up to avoid flying through it. As I climbed, I could see the entire refinery going up in flames. Explosions erupted all over the island as the refinery went up in a gigantic fireball.

Back on the carrier, I couldn't wait to tell Jack Wheeler about my good fortune during the debriefing. I barely got it out when Smiley Boles came over. He'd been listening to my story and appeared mad as hell.

"You blew up that refinery?" he asked in anything but a pleasant tone.

"Yeah, the whole damn thing," I answered proudly.

"God damn it, that wasn't on the target list," he continued.

"It was a Jap refinery, what the hell was I supposed to do with it?" I asked angrily.

"That refinery was the property of Texaco Oil Company, and I hoped it would survive the war. I own stock in Texaco," he said in disgust.

Sometimes you can't win for losing.

The following day we went back to clean up anything left over. Finding planes on the runway, I dove through the usual antiaircraft fire and set two twin-engine bombers on fire. A number of us were hit, and one plane went down. The pilot had just joined the squadron as a replacement pilot, and no one knew him. I didn't even know his name. What a sad fate to be a new man in the group, whom no one had time to get to know, and then be lost on one of your first flights. Who would write the letter home?

Once again, the fleet headed north, going to Luzon. This was the main island of the Philippines, with the capital city of Manila. The Japs had to have overwhelming power here, or they must be resigned to defeat. So far, we hadn't seen any evidence of the latter.

The night before our arrival off Luzon, we had our briefing for the following day. We were going to hit Nicholas Field, the main American air field before the Japanese conquered the islands. Intelligence was most anxious to get pictures of the field, to see how much the Japanese had expanded the facilities. Once again, it fell to Hutto to get the pictures. Since we might meet strong resistance, the skipper stressed that Hutto was to act as a fighter first and foremost, but if conditions permitted, he should get the pictures. The admiral was counting on it. The mention of the admiral created new furrows on Hutto's brow. That night, in our casual meeting in the bunkroom, Hutto didn't utter a word. He was scared speechless.

The predawn strike took off and headed for the docks on Manila Bay. We took off slightly later and flew toward Nichols Field. The flight consisted of torpedo bombers at twelve thousand feet, dive-bombers above them at fifteen thousand feet, and fighters spread above, below, and around the bombers. I flew in Bill Masoner's division, which was slightly ahead of the main body. As we approached the field, we could see Japanese fighters in the air at a distance. We were going to have a welcoming committee.

Approaching the edge of the field, our division dove, looking for the flashes of antiaircraft guns. We spotted some and took aim as we dove until we were in range, then opened fire. The more havoc we could create, the better chance our bombers would have. The rest of the flight fell in behind us, and the Japanese behind them. The Japs had stayed well out of range until then, but they no doubt had hopes of picking off a bomber or two as they pulled out. All hell was breaking loose everywhere.

Pulling out low over the antiaircraft guns, we headed for the rendezvous point so that we'd be in position if the Japs pressed their attack. There was a wild melee of planes at low altitude and high speed, trying to close ranks for maximum protection. Our fighters that followed the dive-bombers down got the gravy: they shot down six planes without the loss of a single one of our planes.

Flying in formation again, we headed back to the ship. The remaining Japanese fighters were still trailing us but staying just far enough away that we didn't break formation and go after them. It made my mouth water to see them so close and yet so far. If the skipper had released eight of us, we could have gone after them and cleaned house, but our first responsibility was to protect the bombers, and that's what we did. Apparently, word went around to other carrier groups that we were shepherding the bombers home, as we found ourselves escorting bombers from other air groups on their return flights.

Relaxing in our chairs in the ready room after debriefing, we waited for Hutto to land to hear what really happened. Finally, he came in, a limp rag. Jack Wheeler had only one question for Hutto when he sat down: "Did you get the pictures?"

Hutto slid further down in his chair but did not answer.

Jack asked again in a firm voice, "Did you get the pictures?"

Hutto finally answered, "No."

"What," Jack exploded, "nothing? What happened?"

Hutto perked up slightly. "You know, the skipper told me I was a fighter pilot first. That's what happened."

"What the hell does that mean?"

"Well, we got in there and . . . .you know, that's a really big field."

"The pictures," Jack said, trying to get him back on track.

"We got in there, and there were Jap fighters around us, and I remembered what the skipper . . . ."

"The pictures."

"Well, I was just about to go through my check-off list when the bombers dove with Jap fighters after them, so I pushed over too. I pulled out just over the runway, and I see tracers going past me. I've got a Zero on my tail, so I take evasive action all over the place. By the time somebody shoots the Zero off my tail, the bombers are rendezvousing, so I go along, remembering that I'm a fighter first of all."

"So, you never got a picture?" Jack asked in disgust.

"That's right."

"The admiral isn't going to be pleased. They'll probably have to schedule another strike." The phone rang, and Jack grabbed it. He listened for a moment. "Yes sir, right away," Jack hung up. Turning to Hutto, Jack said, "The admiral wants to see you on the double."

Hutto turned dead white. His knees almost gave way as he started to walk out of the ready room. He stopped at the door and looked around for help.

"On the double," Jack shouted.

The door closed behind Hutto.

Wending his way through a labyrinth of passageways, Hutto arrived at the ladder that took him up to the admiral's intelligence room. A guard stood at the door. "Lieutenant, j.g., Hutto, to see the admiral."

The marine corporal snapped a salute. "He's expecting you."

Hutto stepped inside. The staff stopped whatever they were doing and turned and stared at Hutto, whispering to each other.

Admiral Mitscher stepped away from the table where they were working. "So you're the photographic pilot?"

"Yes, sir," Hutto answered in a wavering voice.

The admiral, who was as short at Hutto, surveyed him up and down. Mitscher was the father of naval aviation and had fought the battles for carriers when battleships were king. Hutto was in awe of the man who faced him.

"In all my years in the navy, I've never seen anything like this," the admiral started. "How the hell did you do it?"

"Well, sir, the skipper said I was to be a . . . ."

"These shots right inside the hangar," the admiral continued, ignoring Hutto's remarks, "we're all waiting to find out how you did it."

All of the staff turned their full attention to Hutto.

"Inside the hangar?" Hutto ventured.

"That's right, you haven't seen them developed. Here, let me have some of them," the admiral retorted as an aide handed some wet photographs to him. The admiral studied them for a moment, and handed them to Hutto. He literally couldn't believe his eyes. He was staring at large photographs of every installation on Nichols Field. There was a photograph taken in the open doors of every hangar in which all of the equipment inside could be identified. Hutto just stared, speechless.

Finally he started, "Well, sir, I really didn't . . . ."

"I love modesty," the Admiral interrupted. "I'm recommending you for the Distinguished Flying Cross. These are the greatest intelligence photographs ever taken. Congratulations, son." The admiral held his hand out and shook Hutto's. "Well done."

Hutto left the Admiral's quarters in a daze. Finding his way down to the ready room, he walked in, still in a daze.

Jack took one look at Hutto. "My God, he must have really eaten you out. What did he say?"

"He's giving me the DFC."

Jack and the rest of us reacted in disbelief. "Why would he give you that? I figured he'd court-martial you."

Hutto couldn't believe it either. "The only thing I can figure is that I opened the camera ports and turned on the intervalometer just as the Zeros showed up, and I didn't remember I'd done it. When I was flying low down the runway, trying to shake the Zero on my tail, I did some quick turns, and every time I lifted a wing the camera snapped a picture. I just happened to be lined up with the open doors at the end of each hangar. I didn't know I'd taken them."

Jack just shook his head.

TWENTY-EIGHT

# R&R AT ULITHI ATOLL

I had fallen into a routine, the routine of war. It was not exactly the life I would have led going to the RCA plant in Camden every day, but somewhat the same. I got up every morning at around three, had breakfast, then got in a plane, and after the usual hair-raising catapult shot in the dark, commuted to work, usually about a two-hour flight. Rather than read a paper on the train, I was busy testing my guns and checking on the oxygen. Other than that, it was flying formation, just like driving on the freeways. Once at work, over some Japanese installation, things changed. Normally, work took only about fifteen minutes, and, of course, death was a constant companion, as far away as the next exploding shell from the ever-present antiaircraft guns. The Japanese never seemed to run out of ammunition.

Blowing up everything we could find of value, we beat a hasty retreat and headed for home. At the end of the commute, there was always the thrill of the carrier landing, just to keep you on your toes.

The afternoon brought another flight, and later, a four-hour CAP over the fleet. All told, I was flying twelve hours a day, capped off with a few drinks with friends, dinner served on white linen tablecloths by stewards, and then either bridge or classical music. Tchaikovsky's Second and Fourth Symphonies seemed to be the favorites among the group. When I listen to either of those pieces of music today with my eyes closed, I can still feel the motion of the ship. Then, it was get up the next morning for a repeat of the previous day. In three days of intensive strikes, we hadn't lost a single plane or pilot. How long could our good luck last?

The ship's radar picked up enemy planes, but they did not make a determined attack on the fleet. As a result, the CAPs were becoming boring. It was almost more fun censoring enlisted men's mail. We devised all sorts of diversions to keep ourselves amused while on CAP. I now took a paperback book along, as well as a piece of fruit and some lemonade in a canteen. Once at altitude, I'd spread out from my wingman and put the plane in a slight turn and read.

Taking a break from my reading, I glanced over at Pete Sprinkle's plane. I couldn't quite see what he was doing, but something didn't look right. I slid my plane over until I was in tight formation with him. Pete had sheet music propped up against the gunsight and was practicing his piccolo—not exactly the image we all have of the bloodthirsty fighter pilot.

That night, there were the usual card games, bridge and poker. Ramsey was not a card player, but some of the pilots shamed him into a poker game with high stakes. Everyone watched as Ramsey picked up his cards. His facial expression always gave away the quality of his hands. When they were good, he'd laugh and shout. They were good most of the time, and Ramsey cleaned out the experts. The saying went, "Ramsey doesn't have a poker face, just poker hands." They wouldn't let him in the game again.

The executive officer of the ship came in the wardroom for a cup of coffee. He surveyed the scene and said, "I'm not running a ship of war, I'm running a gambling ship."

The following day we pulled out and headed for the new fleet anchorage at Ulithi Atoll, about five hundred miles east of the Philippines. With no flights scheduled, Pete and I were relaxing over a game of chess in the morning when our steward, Elwood Gant, came in to clean the room and make the beds.

"Oh, I'm sorry, sir, I didn't know you were in. I'll be back later," he said.

"No, don't let us bother you, come ahead." We went on playing chess as Elwood cleaned the room. A few days later, I was in the room writing a letter when Elwood came in. Again, he started to leave, but I told him to go ahead with his work.

"Sir," he said after working in silence for a while.

"Yes," I answered.

"Can I offer a suggestion?"

I was surprised. "About what?"

"Your chess game. Have you ever studied von Neumann's theorem on finite dual games, in which he proves there is always a saddlepoint in the payoff matrix of such games?"

I sat there stunned. "No, I can't say I have."

"I have a copy in my footlocker which I'd be happy to lend you. It'll help your game."

"I gather you play chess," I offered.

"Yes, I won the chess championship in college," he said proudly.

"How far did you go in college?" I asked.

"I graduated with a BA."

"What in the hell are you doing here as a mess steward?"

Elwood stood for a moment with a slight smile on his face. "I wanted to be a fighter pilot like you," he answered finally.

"Why didn't you apply?" I asked in all innocence.

The smile turned to a broad grin. "How many black pilots have you met in the navy?" Suddenly, I realized how utterly ridiculous my question was. I'd never seen any.

"Did you try?" I asked.

"I tried. You could hear the laughter ring throughout the recruiting office. I walked out and was drafted two weeks later. I was in the navy and on my way to stewards' school."

I thought for a moment, not knowing what to say. "How bad is it?"

Elwood hesitated for a long time. "I can't criticize my commanding officer to another officer, I'll be in hack."

"It won't go any further," I said finally.

"Our general quarters station is passing ammunition. Our commanding officer is the marine captain who heads the contingent of marine MPs on the ship. He drills us continually when we're finished with our duties as stewards. He's from the South, and he can't stand to see a nigger sit down. He's killing us. If this ship had oars, you know who'd be pulling them."

"That bad?" I said.

"Worse."

"I'll see what I can do," I offered.

"You'd be making a big mistake," he said.

I made an appointment with our skipper. "Sir," I began, "I want to bring something to your attention regarding the marine captain and the stewards on board."

The skipper stared at me for a moment. "Bill, we never had this conversation, and never bring it up again."

"Yes sir," I answered and got out of there.

I tried to explain to Elwood the next time I saw him alone, but he wouldn't let me.

"I really appreciate your trying, but I knew you were headed for trouble. You're lucky you got off as lightly as you did."

I appreciated his letting me off the hook so easily.

Pulling in to Ulithi Atoll at dusk, we couldn't make out much of our surroundings except that it appeared to be another typical atoll, the remains of an ancient volcano. The entire navy support fleet of several hundred ships had moved forward to this anchorage. It was rest and rehabilitation time, and we were ready for it. All of the pilots slept in the next morning.

I was lying in the sack at about eight in the morning, deciding whether to get up and make breakfast or sleep in and wait for lunch. The decision was made for me when a thunderous explosion shook the ship all the way down to the keel. I hit the steel deck running to the ready room in my underwear to join the rest of the squadron, similarly dressed. General quarters was booming out through the loud speakers. Everyone shouted the same thing: "Are we under attack?" We ventured out on the catwalk along the side of the flight deck. The answer was obvious.

The first ship in line nearest the entrance to the atoll, an oil tanker, was burning fiercely. Destroyers were slipping past the anchored ships, dropping depth charges everywhere throughout the lagoon. Word reached us quickly.

The entrance to the lagoon was protected by an antisubmarine net, as well as a destroyer circling the approach to the atoll. That destroyer was being relieved at eight a.m., and as the replacement destroyer sailed out of the entrance with the sub net pulled back, one or more Japanese two-man subs slipped in. Since the entrance wasn't very deep, the sub couldn't submerge to a safe depth, and the destroyer rammed it.

Hearing the crash, one of the subs already in the anchorage lined up on the nearest ship and fired one of its two torpedoes. The torpedo made a direct hit amidships on the tanker and set it on fire. With that, all hell broke lose as every destroyer with steam up combed the lagoon to make sure any additional subs were destroyed. They continued until noon.

These small subs had been towed by a large sub to Ulithi and waited just off shore until the relief took place in the morning. The plan was to get all six subs in the lagoon, line up on six aircraft carriers, and fire their total of twelve torpedoes simultaneously. Had they been successful, they would have crippled six aircraft carriers and might have even sunk some. It was a bold plan and might have succeeded, except for the accidental ramming by the destroyer. We realized the war was always with us.

The following day, when they were sure all of the subs had been dispatched, we were free to go to the officers' recreation island, Mogmog. Unlike Eniwetok, Ulithi had not been fought over, so it was in its native state. It was beautiful, like the tropical paradises portrayed in prewar South Seas movies. There was even a native village in the palm forest in the center of the small island. The buildings were quite substantial, with sides open to about five feet high, and high-pitched thatched roofs held up by heavy, polished timbers. The open sides allowed the trade winds to blow through the living quarters, and the overhang was extensive enough to keep out all but a very heavy rain.

The navy had put a fine bar in the main building of the village, and everything we needed was there, except the natives. We quickly found out that they had been moved to the largest island at the far end of the lagoon, and it was off limits to all navy personnel. We sat there on the beach, drink in hand, and stared at the far island; all of us, that is, except two torpedo-plane pilots, Ted and Dave. They just sat there and plotted. The following day they put their plan in motion.

Finishing breakfast, they picked up food they could pack, including fruit, and went back to their rooms and changed into bathing suits, which they covered with a minimum of uniform. They found an extra TBF survival kit and removed the three-man life raft. Walking to the ladder, they convinced the officer of the day that they were going fishing, and were permitted to go down to the water where the captain's gig was tied up.

Inflating the boat, they put up the small sail and left the carrier. Negotiating between the large ships, they finally reached the limit of the fleet and continued sailing for the forbidden island at the far end of the lagoon. The weather was perfect and the sailing went smoothly. Another five miles and they'd find out what the mystery was all about.

The PT boats came out of nowhere and cut across the bow of the life raft sending it rocking wildly.

The voice boomed over the loud speaker, "Turn around, this is a restricted area, leave immediately."

"What do you think they'd do if we just go on?" Dave asked.

"I don't think they'd do a damn thing," Ted replied confidently. "Let's ignore them." They proceeded on course.

The lead PT boat came closer. "If you don't reverse course, we have orders to shoot you. These orders are from Admiral Halsey personally."

Ted and Dave looked at each other. "Maybe we'd better turn around. The bar opens on Mogmog right after lunch." Turning the life raft around, they headed back toward the ship, but now they were trying to sail into the wind, and they couldn't tack in the small inflatable boat. They had to paddle the rest of the day and barely arrived back at the carrier in time for dinner.

Years later I happened to see a copy of *National Geographic* that featured an article on Ulithi, complete with pictures. The women of the island were absolutely gorgeous and went around bare breasted. I took one look and knew why no one was allowed to visit the natives.

We were looking forward to a week of recreation, but suddenly the fleet was a beehive of activity. With little fanfare, we weighed anchor and put out to sea along with the entire fleet. This had been unplanned, but the barometer was dropping precipitously, and apparently it was safer to be out at sea in a bad storm than inside the atoll, where the highest land might be only five feet above sea level. America had no reliable weather stations along the coast of China, and of course not in Japan, so these storms could come almost out of nowhere, and they could be devastating.

The first day out gave little indication of anything unusual. I ran into the Glen Seagrave, the aerologist on the forecastle deck, the first evening.

"How's it look?" I asked.

"We can't really tell yet, but I don't think it's going to be too bad. It looks as if it'll pass to the west of us."

I had been talking to Glen a number of times, but we'd never introduced ourselves.

"By the way," I started, "my name is . . . ."

He held up his hand. "Don't introduce yourself." Immediately he looked embarrassed. "I don't want to seem unfriendly, but I got to know a couple of pilots in the previous air group, and it tore me to pieces when I'd see their names on the list of pilots lost the previous day. I enjoy talking to you, but I don't want to know your name."

The fact that someone didn't want to know who I was in case I was lost didn't do much for my confidence.

The following day the wind picked up enough that we didn't even put a combat air patrol up. That night we had our first taste of a typhoon. Starting at sundown the winds increased every hour. By midnight they were over one hundred miles an hour. The winds whipped the ocean up until it resembled mountains.

The only place we could look out on this was a porthole in the side of the bridge. We'd take turns going up and surveying the ocean from a point that was normally eighty-five feet above the waterline. At times it appeared that we were in a valley with towering peaks rising well above us on every side. If anyone ventured out on the flight deck, he would be instantly blown overboard. We started to make bets as to whether the carrier would survive or not.

By the second night, the ship was climbing the side of these mountains. As she neared the top of the wave, the bow of the ship would climb out into space and would continue until the center of gravity passed the point of balance, whereupon the bow would dive and the screws would come out of the water at the stern. The carrier would then dive down the side of the wave and bury the bow in the next one. As the carrier burrowed into the wave, the flight deck would go under water as much as twenty feet. The carrier would start to shake from side to side as she tried to pull herself up from the tons of water pressing her down. I held my breath as the carrier struggled with each wave.

There was a trick to learning to sleep under these conditions. You had to go with the flow. As the ship went over the top of a wave, there would be slight negative G, which allowed you to inhale effortlessly. As the ship pulled out at the bottom of the wave, there were positive G forces, which pressed the breath out of you. The storm was giving you artificial respiration.

Shaving was also tricky. When I learned to shave, we had nothing but straight razors in the house, so I learned with one of them. I never thought of buying a safety razor, as my father thought they were for wimps. Since we had to shave every day, I got out the straight razor and prepared to time the waves with each stroke of the razor. Ned "Spick" Bennett and Pete Sprinkle didn't have the stomach for this and had to leave the room while I shaved.

Increasing all day, the winds reached 150 miles an hour by nightfall. I thought back over my strength-of-materials classes from college and wondered if anything almost nine hundred feet long could continue to withstand nature's fury indefinitely. Would high-tensile steel and man's genius for construction meet its match that night?

At two o'clock a.m. we found out. The bow of the carrier dove into the next wave and a frightening, rending sound of metal on metal screamed through the hull of the ship. Not hesitating a second, I jumped out of my bunk and raced for the ready room in my underwear. In a few moments the entire squadron was there. We all slipped into life jackets, although the chances of survival in those seas were nil. We were all convinced the ship was breaking up. Word finally came over the loudspeaker system:

"We are not sinking. The ship is built with expansion joints above the water line so that the ship can flex in extreme conditions. We bent so far the joint went up against the stop, sending a shock through the hull."

We listened but decided to stay in the ready room the rest of the night playing cards. When I took that oath in Philadelphia, I had thought of many events that might occur in my career, but sitting in my underwear wearing a life jacket in the ready room of a carrier, playing cards, was not one of them.

The following morning the storm had started to subside, and we received word that we were on our way to strike Okinawa. We were also advised that we would be using Admiral Matthew C. Perry's ninety-year-old charts, as these were the most recent ones the navy had. No one could say we weren't up to date.

The storm blew itself out during the night as we prepared for a predawn launch. Heading straight for the main harbor at Naha, we caught a fair amount of shipping anchored there. My division dove on a light cruiser and inflicted a lot of damage, but our five-hundred-pound bombs were not armor piercing, so we didn't sink it. Our dive-bombers got a series of hits on a heavy cruiser with two-thousand-pound armor-piercing bombs, and it went down. After shooting up everything visible in the harbor, eight of us were assigned to circle the island and look for targets of oportunity.

The pickings were slim as we rounded the island. There was no air opposition and little activity elsewhere. I spotted something a distance away in the water. We headed for it. A lone Japanese destroyer was sailing from Okinawa to Taiwan, then called Formosa. We in turn were out of bombs. We couldn't let this juicy target go unmolested, and all each of us had were our six .50-caliber Browning machine guns. We dove on the destroyer and let go with long bursts aimed at the waterline.

All eight of us completed two runs, hoping to set off an explosion, but no luck. Preparing for a third run, I noticed something different. The ship seemed to be riding lower in the water, although it was still making good speed. As we watched, the ship continued to ride lower. "Let's hold up a minute," I said over my radio. We circled.

I made a quick calculation in my head. I estimated that there might be as many as two thousand half-inch holes drilled through the light skin of the destroyer, many of them below the waterline. The ship was sinking from perforation. As we watched, the ship sank from view. We'd sunk a destroyer with machine gun fire. It makes you realize how absurd movies are today, with their machine gun fights where no one gets hurt.

Landing back on the carrier, I watched as they threw one of our planes over the side. It was so shot up it wasn't worth saving. The pilot was uninjured. I was making my way off the flight deck when a dive-bomber taxied by. The pilot opened his bomb bay doors so that the plane could be rearmed. I stared in horror as the two-thousand-pound bomb he had been carrying dropped out. It seemed to fall in slow motion. If that bomb was armed, it was all over. Several of the deck crew also saw it dropping and raced toward the plane. It hit the deck and didn't explode. The deck hands immediately started to roll the bomb toward the side and pushed it over. We all held our breaths. It didn't go off as it hit the water.

The pilot had opened his bomb bay doors when he dove on the cruiser. He pushed the release and pulled out, blacking out for a short time. He of course assumed he'd dropped the bomb and didn't realize he still had it aboard. We were all lucky.

While we were off on the strike, orders were received on the carrier that would have profound effects on the squadron. Karl Jung, the air group commander, had been promoted to captain and was to take over as air officer on another carrier. Hugh Winters, our fighter skipper, was promoted to full commander and made air group commander, while the thing we all feared the most was inevitable. Toby Cook, our executive officer, was made a lieutenant commander and was the new fighter skipper. The poorest pilot in the squadron was now our leader, and there wasn't a thing in the world we could do about it. Several of us junior officers discussed going to Hugh and telling him, but we were all afraid to open our mouths. They were both Annapolis graduates, and if anyone would stick together, they would. In addition, I'd had my experience bringing things to the skipper's attention regarding the black steward. I wasn't going to volunteer.

The new command structure came close to costing Hugh his life.

TWENTY-NINE

# FIGHTER SWEEP OVER FORMOSA

There was one advantage to the new setup, and it was evident immediately. We were heading for Formosa, and there was going to be a fighter sweep. Since Toby was now skipper, he was going to lead it, and that included my division. We held a briefing the night before our arrival off Formosa. Intelligence expected heavy air opposition.

Ending the briefing, Toby introduced several replacement pilots that had just arrived. They were all ensigns, right out of flight training, and they'd never been in combat. This scared us all to death, as each of us was totally dependent on his wingman and had no idea how a new man might fly. In addition, we were now the senior squadron in the fleet, and we would be leading the show.

Following Toby's briefing, we received a briefing from one of the staff intelligence officers. This was a first, and we waited in expectation as to what he might tell us. We had been striking tropical islands, but this was going to be entirely different. We weren't too happy with the message the officer brought us:

Formosa is located 120 miles off the coast of China and has risen from a fault in the earth's crust running north to south. The eastern side of the fault is tilting up, giving rise to a range of mountains as high as thirteen thousand feet on that side, running the length of the island. The western side is a wide plain covered with rice paddies, but the land is firm enough to support fighter planes taking off and landing without concrete runways, making any field a potential fighter base.

The island was originally settled by aborigines migrating from Indonesia. Chinese followed from the mainland, forcing the aborigines into the mountains. The Japanese invaded and took control of the island in 1895. The aborigines were headhunters and had a special taste for Japanese, carrying out murderous raids on their farms on the plains. To protect themselves, the Japanese built an electrified fence the length of the island to keep the headhunters in the mountains.

The intelligence officer told us with a straight face that the aborigines would know we were fighting the Japanese and would be friendly to us if we fell in their hands. He suggested that if we went down, to try to make it to the mountains. There were also seven types of poisonous reptiles and snakes on the island and seven poisonous fish in the waters around the island—a true Garden of Eden.

Electricity was in the air at breakfast. We knew there would be Japanese planes waiting for us. Sixteen of us suited up in the ready room for the fighter sweep. Unexpectedly, Hugh Winters, the air group commander, accompanied by Joe Paskoski, came in and started to put on their flight gear. Toby's face fell.

"I'm leading this flight," Toby said angrily. "You're not in the squadron anymore."

"I just assigned myself to accompany you," Hugh answered with a smile.

"I don't want you," Toby said as firmly as he dared.

"You've got me," Hugh answered with a real edge in his voice.

Toby made no effort to hide his anger. He was fuming and was about to get into it when the order came over the loud speaker, "Fighters, man your planes." We all raced out the door. They'd have to settle it later.

Arriving at the southern tip of Formosa at sunup, we proceeded up the western side of the island. Toby led the top cover, flying at twenty thousand feet, with Del Prater flying his wing. The rest of us were spaced every few thousand feet, with Hugh and Joe flying low cover at twelve thousand feet. Straining our eyes, we searched every square inch of the sky looking for enemy planes, but so far nothing. Despite the tension, I could not help but admire the beauty of the island below me. The terraced rice paddies gave an architectural slope to the base of the mountains.

Weaving lazily across the sky, I looked up at the top cover, then down at the air group commander, easily recognizable, as his was the only two-plane section. I looked again; there was something wrong. The air group commander's plane was on fire. He and Joe were weaving frantically toward each other, trying to shoot the Zeros off each other's tails.

"Bogies, twelve thousand feet, the skipper's in trouble."

Toby went into a tight turn and surveyed the situation, but did nothing.

Del shrieked over the radio, "Toby, let's go!"

Still, Toby circled. Del pulled up next to Toby and tapped his hand on his head, indicating that he was taking the lead. With that, Del dove and the entire squadron followed, all except Toby. Arriving at twelve thousand feet, we found what we'd been looking for, maybe more than we'd been looking for: fifty Zeros. We were eighteen, with one already on fire.

Diving into the maelstrom, I found myself heading straight for a Zero, head on. This is not what they taught you in fighter training. You had a great shot at him, but he had an equal shot at you. Tactics and marksmanship had nothing to do with it. This was two knights in armor riding at full speed at each other, nothing subtle.

The Zero had two Vickers 7.7mm light machine guns firing through the propeller, backed up by two Oerlikon 20mm cannons in the wings. The fact that they fired through the propellers meant that they had a relatively slow rate of fire. On the other hand, the cannons fired exploding shells and would do horrendous damage to my plane. Flying straight at each other, there was no way you could miss. I dropped my seat as low as I could to take advantage of the armor plate in front of me and headed straight for him.

At five hundred yards he opened up with his machine guns. The flashes looked like someone flicking a small flashlight on and off. I could also see the tracers streaming toward me, all aimed directly at the pit of my stomach. They fell below me; he'd started firing too far away. He was out of range.

Moving closer, he started firing his 20mm cannons. These looked like large flashlights flashing on and off. I showed my contempt by not firing my guns. I was going to wait until I was on top of him. Finally, after what seemed like an eternity, I raised the nose of the plane slightly and opened up with all six guns. Immediately I could see large pieces flying off the Zero. He kept coming for a few more moments, then slid under my left wing and blew up. I heard myself screaming once again.

I watched the doomed Zero for a moment, then looked around. There were trails of flames from damaged planes all over the sky. It looked like an exotic fireworks display. Tracers flashed by me. Another Zero was making a head-on run on me. Again, I waited, as his guns blazed away, until I knew I was in range before firing. The moment I fired, pieces flew, and again a Zero burst into flames and blew up as we passed each other.

I glanced over at my wingman, Spick, only to see a Zero on his tail. "Spick, break left," I shouted over the radio. He turned immediately, and I turned right into the Zero. It was a full-deflection shot, and I nailed him first burst. I had shot down three planes in less than a minute.

Joining up with Spick, we looked for more of the enemy, but it turned out that all those trails of flame I'd seen were Japanese planes. We couldn't find any more. We had shot down over thirty confirmed, six more probable, and a few damaged. It there had been more, they'd turned tail and fled. Toby finally came down, and the entire flight joined up. We were short one plane. Robert "Doc" Tripp must have chased a Zero away from the fight and been jumped by a number of them with no one to help him.

Continuing up the coast, we reached Taipei and the large airfield there. Toby led us to the main runway, where there were a number of enemy planes on the field. He started a dive, and we all followed. We were coming in at a steep angle, and it was hard to line up on more than one plane. What was Toby thinking? I fired a short burst and had to pull out.

Del's voice came over my headset.

"Pull out! Toby, pull out! You're too low, you're going in. Toby!"

There was a tremendous explosion on the field. Toby had flown straight into the ground. The antiaircraft fire was so light, it was hard to believe he'd been hit, and his plane never wavered. We went in again and shot up all of the planes on the field, but despite the number of fires we set, none stood out in my mind like the F6F on the end of the runway.

We circled the rest of the island, but found no enemy. Despite our victory over the Japanese planes, the flight back to the fleet was a sad one. Once in the ready room, I was torn between jubilation over the big dog fight and sadness over the loss of Doc and Toby.

Toby had been our skipper for only one flight.

R.A. "Ish" Farnsworth came in to be debriefed on his first combat flight. It seems we worried about him unnecessarily. He also found himself in position to make a head-on run on a Jap. He never even hesitated.

"I saw this son of a bitch out there," Ish explained, "and I turned right into him. He did the same. Did that idiot think he could play chicken with me?"

"You heard of kamikazes?" Jack interjected.

"Shit, they can't scare me. I flew right at him, and I wasn't gonna give way," Ish answered.

"How close did you get before you opened fire?" Doug asked.

"I didn't," Ish replied.

"Well, what the hell did you do?"

"Flew right into him, I told you I wasn't gonna give way," Ish answered almost in contempt.

Doug was getting frustrated. "What happened?"

A crew chief poked his head in the ready room. "Excuse me, sir, but who was flying number twenty-seven?"

"I was," Ish answered.

"Sir, you've got five square feet of Zero wing wedged in your wing. Do you want me to save it?"

All of our mouths dropped open.

"You mean you actually hit him?" Doug asked incredulously.

"I told you I didn't give way to anyone playing chicken, just ask my younger brother. At the last moment that kamikaze Jap lost his nerve and pushed his nose down and rolled on his side. I took his wing clean off."

We didn't worry about Ish anymore.

Hugh came in and we were all relieved to see he'd made it back.

"I thought you were on fire," I said.

"I was; my battery caught fire from a Zero's first burst, but it went out," he answered with a smile. Then he turned very serious.

"I want to say a few words about Toby," he began. "You all know that he was not happy with my going on the fighter sweep. Perhaps he thought my being there somehow reduced his authority. Nothing could be further from the truth. I don't want anyone to think that he didn't come down to Joe and me because of any personal animosity. He was a naval officer through and through and would always do the right thing, even at the risk of his own life, as we all do. There is no doubt he was hit on that dive on the air field. He died a hero's death, and I'm recommending him for the Silver Star. I also want to inform you that Lieutenant Smiley Boles is senior and is now your commanding officer for the rest of our tour." Without another word, the skipper left.

I turned to Del. "You were right there next to Toby, could you see him?"

"Yeah, I could see him."

"What do you think? Why didn't he dive when we saw the Zeros?"

"I wish I knew. He saw me signal that I was taking the lead, but he did nothing."

"What about the dive on the air field?"

Del thought for a long time then said, "I didn't see any antiaircraft fire." That's as far as it went.

I lay awake through a good part of the night thinking over the day's events. What happened to Toby? Did he freeze being skipper in the biggest battle we'd had? Could he possibly have committed suicide over his failure to react? Whatever the truth, we'd never find out.

# SPLASHING JAPANESE PLANES, AND HUTTO'S FIRST KILL

The following day there were numerous strikes against various targets on Formosa. I was scheduled for the third strike, which was to consist of six dive-bombers escorted by twelve fighters. The Japanese had built a large hydroelectric plant high in the mountains of eastern Formosa. The dive-bombers were instructed to take it out.

The air group commander, Hugh Winters, came over to Bill Masoner and me at lunch.

"I'd like to see you in my room after you finish," he said.

"Yes, sir," we answered, wondering what in the hell we'd done.

Once we were in his room, Hugh asked us to sit down. "I've been going over the combat reports, and I see where everyone in the squadron has shot down at least one Jap plane except Hutto."

Bill and I stared at the skipper, then at each other. "I don't understand," Bill said finally.

"Bill, you're the luckiest fellow in the squadron when it comes to finding enemy planes. I want to put Hutto in your four-plane section tomorrow, and, *if* there are no Jap fighters around after the bombers hit the power plant, you're relieved to take your four planes on a search of the island and see if you can find him a plane."

"Do you think he'll go for that?" Bill Masoner asked.

"We aren't going to tell him. You know the rule, the first one to spot a plane gets first shot. Just make sure he sees it first."

The flight into Formosa was uneventful. The weather was clear, and it gave me a chance to study the eastern coastline of the island. There were sheer cliffs that appeared to rise out of the ocean to a height of over ten thousand feet. Numerous waterfalls tumbled over these cliffs to the sea below.

We continued into the mountains and easily found the power plant. The dive-bombers went into their dives and every plane scored a hit. The place was demolished. The bombers rendezvoused, with no sign of enemy fighters. Bill broke away as he got on the radio.

"Let's sweep the island before we go back."

We headed to the northwest.

The Japanese plane showed up on schedule, a twin-engine transport plane, flying on a course directly opposite to ours. It was about three thousand feet below us. All three of us spotted it but said nothing, waiting for Hutto. We waited and waited, but nothing happened. The big, red meatballs on the wings were visible as the plane passed under us; still, nothing. Finally, in desperation, Bill got on the radio.

"Hutto, did I just see something pass under your wing?"

Instantly we had to scatter as Hutto was all over the sky. "I see it, a plane," he said finally.

"You saw it first, she's all yours."

Hutto turned and got in position to start a run. He flew directly over the plane and went into an overhead run, that is, he dove straight down on the enemy. This is fine, except that it takes four thousand feet to recover.

Bill was on the radio. "Hutto, pull out, the mountains are thirteen thousand feet high, you'll go in."

Hutto immediately pulled out. "Sorry, fellows, forgot about the mountains."

Hutto got in position again and started a high-side run. The run was perfect, and we kept waiting for him to open fire, but he didn't. He flew right past the plane.

"I can't shoot it down. It's a DC-3. It must be one of ours."

Clint got on the radio. "I think it's a DC-2. We sold some of them to the Japs before the war. Besides, we don't have a base within three thousand miles of here."

Once again, Hutto got in position and made a run. Everything was perfect, and he set one engine on fire with the first burst. The

Jap plane immediately nosed over and headed straight down toward the mountains.

Hutto got on the radio. "Bill, I set him on fire, but he's climbing straight up. I can't get him. See if you can. Don't let him get away."

"You're upside down," Bill said as patiently as possible.

Hutto rolled his plane into the upright position. Everyone had at least one plane to his credit.

We headed back to the fleet. What we didn't know was that a Japanese formation of bombers was shadowing us and staying just twenty-five feet above the water. With our planes in the air showing up on the fleet's radar screens, the low-flying bombers would be invisible.

We landed just at dusk, and the combat air patrol followed us in. There was nothing on the ship's radar screen. After a quick debriefing, we took off our flight gear and headed to the wardroom for dinner. I had just reached the hangar deck when all hell broke loose. Every antiaircraft gun in the fleet opened fire. Looking out through the open doors on the side of the hangar deck, I saw Japanese planes everywhere.

Twelve Japanese twin-engine bombers codenamed "Betty" were flying between the ships, making torpedo runs. We had no fighter planes up and no time to launch any, but our antiaircraft fire blackened the sky. I had always been in the air on the receiving end of things when fire this heavy took place. I had no conception of the noise.

I felt I was about as safe where I was standing as anywhere else, so I stayed and watched the show. One Betty took a direct hit only a hundred yards from the carrier and blew up, then a second and a third. The hits seemed to rattle the other pilots, as their runs became erratic. They had a perfect setup. The fleet was steaming in a straight line, and we were caught completely by surprise. They should have gotten twelve hits, which might have crippled the fleet. Instead, they made wild runs and lost their advantage. They flew blindly between our ships and risked midair collisions, forcing them to abort their runs.

Meantime, our antiaircraft guns kept knocking them down. The remaining planes dropped their torpedoes and got out of there. They failed to get a single hit.

Standing for a moment, I couldn't believe what had just happened. The air had been filled with incredible violence only moments before, but now I stood there admiring a beautiful sunset.

Knobby Felt walked up. "Ready for dinner?"

"Sure," I answered. Moments ago we might have been sunk and in the process of abandoning ship. Instead, we were going to dinner where it would be served on white linen tablecloths by stewards. What an incredibly strange way to fight a war.

The following day was a wild one. Another fighter sweep was scheduled, but I drew CAP, so I remained over the fleet. Since Jap planes had slipped in the day before under our radar, the staff requested a volunteer to fly figure-eights fifty miles in front of the fleet at thirty feet to intercept any planes that evaded our radar. Bob Blakeslee volunteered. The fighter sweep, the CAP, and Bob took off simultaneously and went off on their assignments.

Halfway through the CAP, Bob opened up on the radio: "Six enemy planes approaching at twenty-five feet: twin-engine Betties. Splash one."

We were immediately vectored to Bob's position and dove at full power to get there. "Splash two," he announced, and, moments later, "Splash three and four." That was Bob's last transmission. We arrived in the area moments later but could find nothing in the air. There was some wreckage on the water, but we could not identify the type of plane. The Jap bomber had a twin-20mm-powered turret on the top of the fuselage, and we could only assume that they had shot Bob down as he got the last of them.

The cruisers USS *Canberra* and USS *Houston* were hit by torpedoes later in the day. Although they were in no danger of sinking, they were leaving a trail of oil which would no doubt attract submarines and aircraft.

Skip Hensen stuck his head in the room that evening. "Come on over if you want to hear something interesting."

Pete and I followed him into his room. Skip had a radio in his room and had it tuned in to Tokyo Rose. That melodious Japanese voice came in loud and clear.

"You sorrowful Americans on your sinking ships," she began, "you should have stayed cozy and warm at home, taking your Sunday drives in your oversized automobiles. But no, you had to make war on us, and now your precious Third Fleet has been sunk."

I looked at Skip. "What's she talking about?"

"She's putting out the story that their planes have sunk the entire fleet."

"Two minor hits on cruisers?" I asked.

"I've been intercepting reports all day from their headquarters. They think they've done major damage."

"Do you think their pilots got confused, or outright lied about their hits?" I asked.

"Pilots exaggerate," Skip said in mock horror.

"Pilots never do anything like that."

Tokyo Rose went on to list the ships sunk, including the *Lexington*. I wondered if their high command really believed it.

I was assigned to the CAP that was sent up to cover the two damaged ships the following day, but we sighted no enemy planes.

We steamed away from Formosa to refuel, then back to the Philippines.

# THIRTY-ONE

# ZEKE PARKER, BOY HERO

Once again we hit the airfields of southern Luzon. There was no air opposition, but the antiaircraft fire was heavier than ever. The number of planes parked on the fields was small, but I managed to find one and blow it up. Then, it was on to the docks, where sampans were waiting. I caught one tied up to the dock and blew it up, taking the dock along with it.

We passed another field on our return, and Smiley led us in a dive on the aircraft on the field. I was flying behind and slightly to the right of him when he took a hit. His plane headed for the ground as I held my breath. Smiley disappeared under my wing, but I was surprised to see him still in the air when he reappeared. Then it hit me: the part of his plane forward of the cockpit was skewed twenty degrees to one side. He'd already hit the ground and bounced back up. I hoped he might make it, but it wasn't to be. The plane nosed over and crashed in a giant fireball. We were losing skippers at an alarming rate.

I lined up on another plane and started to fire as I caught a glimpse of Masoner's plane taking a hit. I broke off my run and pulled over next to him. He gave me a thumbs-up as we rendezvoused and headed back to the fleet. As it turned out, all was not well with Bill. He almost made it to the ship but went into the ocean. He was quickly picked up and was back aboard before nightfall.

The next day was memorable. Weather was building to the west, which was where we were going. Shortly after takeoff, we ran into a front that seemed to slope down to the sea. We couldn't get underneath it, so we had to climb through it. With the dive-bombers and torpedo planes, we numbered forty aircraft. Flying formation in clouds is not recommended for long life. You could go one of two ways: The first was to fly very tight formation so that you could see your leader, but someone competent had to be on instruments, or the whole flight would go in. The other choice was to spread out, but now you couldn't see another plane, and you had to fly instruments, and there was always the chance of a midair collision. I elected to stay tight and was flying blind a few feet from the next plane.

We continued to climb for what seemed an eternity and were still in thick clouds. Suddenly, at fifteen thousand feet, we broke out—right in the middle of a flight of Japanese planes rendezvousing for an attack on our fleet. In some cases our planes were within two feet of a Japanese plane. I didn't have to aim; I just pressed the trigger and shot down a twin-engine bomber only twenty-five feet away. We were so close that if the plane had blown up, it would have taken me with him.

We were all so stunned that it took a few moments to realize the situation. There were airplanes everywhere. I flew past a Zero and could see the Japanese pilot in the cockpit, but we were so close we couldn't get a shot at each other. I slid in behind another bomber and fired a blast, and the plane started down, but I couldn't follow it, as I was lined up on another plane and started to fire. This plane also started toward the ground, but again I couldn't stay with it, as there were others immediately ahead of me. The result was that I shot down a number of planes, but I broke off before they blew up. Therefore, they only counted as probables at the time but were later confirmed kills. I stayed with the next two until they blew up and I was sure they were on my gun-camera film.

Once again, the sky was filled with columns of smoke as one Jap plane after another bit the dust. Having cleared the air, we proceeded to Lingayen Gulf and bombed the shipping in the bay. Pulling out of my dive, I spotted another twin-engine bomber out over the sea.

Calling it out, I pulled in front and headed for the enemy plane. We flew for quite some distance until someone in the group came on the radio. "Does anyone else see a plane out there?" he asked. No one answered. By this time I could see the meatballs on the wings. This was also the first time I realized that I had considerably better than twenty-twenty vision.

"Stick with me another thirty seconds, and if you don't see it by then, we'll give it up," I replied. By this time, I could see the pilot. We continued a short time, and I made a run on the plane, splashing it.

We turned back toward land with my section leader flying as my wingman. We crossed the beach, and I spotted another twin-engine bomber, no doubt left from the big fight, trying to sneak away at very low altitude. I called him out.

Masoner replied, "Go get him. I'll cover you."

I slipped down to find that the guy was flying about five feet above the ground down a dirt road that was tree lined and just wide enough for him to stay between the trees. There was no way to get a shot at him. In addition, the plane had the twin-20mm gun turret on the top. He was roaring away at me, and I couldn't get a shot.

I couldn't let him get away, so I sideslipped down behind him and yawed the plane to try to get a burst into the wing and engine, then eased back to knock out the gunner. The run was successful, in that the return fire stopped, and I could see gasoline streaming from the wing. One tracer in that gasoline, and he was finished.

I slid down, being very careful not to hit a tree, and pulled the trigger. Only one gun fired, and only three shots, when it jammed. I pulled out, charged the gun, and slid in again. The same thing happened again, only one gun firing, and only three rounds. I couldn't light up that gasoline.

In total disgust, I called Bill. "I've only got one gun firing, and only three-bullet bursts. She's all yours."

Masoner slid down into firing position, but nothing happened. He pulled back up. "What's wrong?" I asked.

"I'm completely out of ammunition," Bill replied. "Let's get out of here."

We hugged the ground as we found our way across Luzon. There were a number of Japanese fighters above us, but none saw us. We held our breaths as we neared the ocean on the eastern side of the island. Once again, we were in low clouds but broke out into the clear every so often.

We climbed to five thousand feet, as we didn't want to approach the fleet at low altitude. They fired on anything that came in low. As we were nearing the fleet, a Japanese plane approached us at the same altitude but going in the opposite direction. Since we were out of ammunition, we did nothing and flew past each other. Once we had our carrier in sight, we also discovered the carrier *Princeton* burning fiercely. The plane we passed had come out of the clouds, dropped one 500-kilo bomb on the carrier, and set it on fire.

The moment we landed, we checked out the information on the *Princeton*. It was not good. They were refueling planes when the Jap plane appeared, which meant they had gasoline pumped up to the flight deck. Once that fuel was set on fire, it was almost impossible to put out. A cruiser pulled up next to the *Princeton* and took the crew off. Not long after, it sank.

The fighter squadron had shot down sixty planes in one day. However, the air group had destroyed sixty-one. One of our dive-bomber pilots had shot down a Zero. When we broke out of the clouds, he found himself directly behind the Jap fighter and let go with his two forward-firing .50-caliber machine guns and downed him immediately. We didn't know what to do with this turn of events, and after much thought we decided to make a sitcom out of it. How else can you explain a bomber shooting down a fighter?

I enlisted the help of both Bruce Williams, who had been a journalism major in college, and the Associated Press correspondent who was aboard. In addition to his experience, he had a typewriter and knew how to type. The dive-bomber pilot who shot down the Zero was named Parker, so we named the series *Zeke Parker, Boy Hero*, Zeke being the code name for the Jap fighter. We worked up a theme song,

"Let Me Get One Of Those Yellow Bellies, I'll Beat Him Red, White, And Blue".

As the story unfolded, the pilot he shot down parachuted, and we recovered him. His name was Ensign Noki Moto, and this was his solo flight. He spoke perfect English, as he'd attended "UCRA." We put the series on over the ship's intercom to mixed reviews, but the number of episodes was limited due to the war.

That evening, word went around that contact reports had been received from several American submarines that units of the Japanese fleet were at sea. We were going on extended searches the next day.

THIRTY-TWO

# BATTLE OF THE SIBUYAN SEA

The procedure for searching for the Japanese Fleet was quite simple: We'd go out in two-plane sections made up of one dive-bomber and one fighter. The dive-bomber, being a two-man plane, was better equipped to do the navigation, and it had a larger radio that could cover the distance we were going. The fighter was for protection.

I took off, only to be advised that the dive-bomber I was to escort had engine trouble, and I was to go on alone. I headed north for 375 miles, which took me within 60 miles of the southernmost island of Japan. I expected to run into the entire Japanese air force, but as luck would have it, I saw nothing but blue sea. At the end of that leg I headed east for 75 miles, then south and hopefully back to the carrier.

Harry Bensen, a dive-bomber pilot, had the exact reverse happen to him. His fighter escort had engine trouble, and he went on the search alone. However, he had unexpected luck. He was to search the area two sectors west of me, and near the end of his first leg he spotted a Japanese fleet coming down from the home islands. The fleet was protected with a swarm of Japanese fighters.

Fortunately, there was cloud cover, and Harry quickly pulled up into the clouds to make his report. He did this so if he were shot down, our command would know there were Jap ships coming down on them.

"Contact, contact, this is Mohawk Twelve, Japanese fleet, approximately twelve ships." Harry gave the distance and direction in code. He waited for an acknowledgement but didn't receive one.

Circling in the cloud for a few minutes, Harry dove from a different direction and took a longer look at the ships, pulling back up before the fighters arrived. Harry got on the radio again.

"Amplifying report, confirm twelve ships including four carriers, two battleships, two cruisers and four destroyers. Course 180 degrees, estimated speed twenty knots. Acknowledge."

Again, there was no acknowledgement from the American fleet. Harry sent one more message and finished it with the words, "I am now going to attack."

Breaking out of the clouds over the Japanese fleet, Harry opened his dive brakes as well as his bomb-bay doors and armed the bomb. He headed straight for one of the carriers, with Zeros on his tail. Nearing the carrier, he released his bomb, closed the dive brakes, and pushed the throttle against the stop to try to outrun the Zeros. They chased him for fifty miles, but gave up. His rear-seat man saw smoke rising from the carrier.

Returning from the longest flight I had ever made from the carrier, I arrived at the rendezvous point, only to realize the worst fear of a naval pilot: the carrier wasn't there. One of the search planes had spotted another Japanese fleet west of the Philippines, and our fleet had already turned west to close with it. Fortunately, I didn't have to search long, and landed aboard. I caught a wire and let the plane roll backwards so the crew could disconnect the hook from the wire. Once my plane was free, the signalman gave me the sign for full power. I opened the throttle and the engine quit; I was out of gas. Crewmen had to push my plane past the barrier.

The moment Harry Bensen came aboard, the admiral sent word to report to the bridge immediately. Harry presented himself to the admiral, who addressed him:

"Lieutenant, I want to congratulate you on your action. It is above and beyond the call of duty."

"Thank you, sir," Harry replied.

"You got off a very quick contact report," the admiral continued. "I imagine you were in some peril at the time."

"There were Zeros hounding us, yes sir."

"Then you sent an amplifying report, then a further report."

"Yes sir."

"You never indicated you received our acknowledgement of any of these reports."

"That's right, sir," Harry answered.

The admiral continued. "You realize that if we hadn't received your reports and you got shot down, we wouldn't know the Japanese were out there. Since you didn't know we'd received your reports, your first duty was to get away and get the information to us." Harry just stood there, not knowing what to say. The admiral looked Harry in the eye. "You know we did receive your contact reports. If you tell me you received our acknowledgements, I'm going to recommend you for the Congressional Medal of Honor for attacking the Japanese fleet single-handedly. Did you receive our acknowledgement?"

Harry didn't hesitate. "No, sir."

The admiral stood for quite a while before putting his hand out and shaking Harry's.

"I admire your guts, and I sure as hell admire your honesty." The admiral awarded Harry the Silver Star anyway.

While Harry was going through his session with the admiral, the rest of us grabbed a quick bite as the crew prepared our planes for the Jap fleet that had been sighted west of the Philippines, heading for Leyte Gulf. Somewhere up the line, the brass made a terrible decision that both the dive-bombers and torpedo-bombers would be armed with general-purpose bombs. They felt the waters in the straits might be too shallow for torpedoes. We never heard a reason the dive-bombers weren't armed with armor-piercing bombs.

Flying west, we found the Jap fleet headed through the Sibuyan Sea. There were no aircraft carriers, but a number of battleships and cruisers, as well as escorting destroyers. The moment we came into view, they started to turn and throw up intense antiaircraft fire. We carried out a coordinated attack on battleships and cruisers, and both of our bomber squadrons scored a number of hits, but since the bombs were general purpose, all they did was burn the paint off the ships. A few of the cruisers sustained minor damage, but the fleet was still battleworthy.

Our photo planes took pictures of the hits, and as we were leaving the scene of what came to be known as the Battle of the Sibuyan Sea, the Japanese fleet was still in a turn and heading west. Once the staff on our carrier had made an intelligence appraisal, they decided the Japanese were seriously damaged and were heading back to Hong Kong. We told Jack Wheeler, our intelligence officer, that this wasn't the case, but the staff didn't take our comments seriously. That night, after dark, the Japanese fleet turned east again and headed for MacArthur's landing beaches on Leyte.

Admiral Halsey, feeling there was no threat from that fleet, took the fast carriers and the six newest battleships and headed north to attack the Japanese fleet that Harry had spotted. Although Admiral Halsey wore wings on his uniform, having gone through flight school at an advanced age, he was still a battleship admiral and wanted nothing more than to close with the Jap fleet and slug it out, ship to ship. He had saved the gun barrels of the battleships for just such an action. He wanted them to be perfect. That night as we slept, we could feel the pulse of the engines as the carrier drove north at full speed against the relentless sea. Tomorrow would be a big day.

THIRTY-THREE

# THE BATTLE OFF CAPE ENGAÑO

At breakfast at three o'clock a.m. on October 25, 1944, you could feel the difference and the tension. There was no small talk. We'd been in a lot of combat by this time, but we knew this would be different. We were going against a major unit of the Japanese fleet.

"Did you hear they revised the number of Jap ships?" Hutto asked.

"How many?" someone inquired.

"Four carriers, two battleships, two cruisers, and ten destroyers," Hutto answered. "Know how many antiaircraft guns that means?" No one answered. "More than four hundred," Hutto threw out. Somehow the powdered eggs lost their taste.

The dull, red glow of the night-vision lights in the ready room seemed eerier than usual. Hugh Winters, the air group commander came in.

"Listen up, fellows, I'm going to be the target coordinator. I'll be up above you and pick your target. Since you're now the senior group out here, you'll get first shot. Any questions? Good luck." He started to leave then hesitated for a moment. "One of the Jap carriers out there took part in the attack on Pearl Harbor. I'll assign it to you if I can."

We manned our planes in total darkness. I took a momentary glance at the five-hundred-pound bomb hanging under my wing and hoped I wouldn't have to dump it before we got to the enemy fleet. On the order, I cranked up my engine and waited to taxi to the catapult.

The catapult takeoff required the usual precarious balance between stalling and diving into the sea, but once again luck was with me. I searched in the darkness for the turtleback light on the plane ahead of me and started to rendezvous. Once the entire air group was together, we climbed slowly toward the north. We hung in the night sky, unaware of speed. The noise of my engine had long since disappeared. The entire scene was unreal. We were each in our own universe, that tiny cockpit. It's the only world that was real.

I was strangely calm; in fact, I was totally relaxed. I had never felt real fear despite the danger of the action I'd been in. Why was that? I certainly wasn't particularly brave, and I certainly didn't want to die. Could pure hatred drive someone to do the unimaginable? Did everyone in the squadron feel the same way? There were many questions but no answers.

Two hours of this, and suddenly the sun spread its light and brought me back to reality. The sea was still dark and invisible, but in only a matter of moments it appeared. "Contact, ships' wakes visible, thirty miles ahead," came over the radio. The Japanese fleet was exactly where it was supposed to be. I could make out the white wakes of eighteen ships dead ahead.

Automatically, I took my guns off safe and fired a few rounds as everyone else did the same. I took the plane off automatic lean and increased the rpm of the engine as I vented the gas tanks and opened my Eustachian tubes. I was at twenty-two thousand feet, and I didn't want trouble with my ears when I dove.

We continued toward the target, picking up speed as we went. We were still twenty miles from the fleet when we saw a tremendous explosion on one of the battleships. Some other groups must have been attacking, although I thought we were to go first. Moments later an antiaircraft shell exploded in the center of our formation, fortunately missing everyone. The Japanese were firing antiaircraft shells from their 16-inch guns and laid it right on target—not a welcome greeting. We continued toward the enemy, still circling the formation and watching for Zeros.

Our division happened to be on the side of the formation closest to the Japanese when the order came over the radio from Hugh to attack. Bill Masoner never hesitated; he turned toward the Jap fleet and nosed over. The problem was, we were so far away that our dive was too flat. We were going to come in fast and low without much chance of getting a hit. The surest way was coming straight down, but then you'd pick up too much speed. Our fighter planes didn't have dive brakes like the dive-bombers to keep our speed within reason, but we were on our way.

Diving from twenty-two thousand feet to eight thousand feet, we picked up speed and kept going in our flat approach. I'd come too far, and now that I had a chance to do something, I wasn't going to let this go by default. This was a chance to avenge Pearl Harbor, and I wasn't going to miss. I searched the sky and saw no Zeros near us. I pulled up. The other three continued in their dive.

I throttled back and let the plane coast up to thirteen thousand feet. It was relatively quiet, and I took a few moments to survey the Japanese fleet. A feeling of calm came over me as I slowed almost to stalling speed. I was directly over the carrier that was our target. The three planes of my section dropped their bombs short and were already out of there, and the rest of the air group was still approaching. I was going in alone, which would make me the only target of all of those antiaircraft guns.

I allowed the plane to stall and let the nose drop. All I could see was the deck of that aircraft carrier. I cracked the throttle slightly so the engine wouldn't stall, and let the plane fall. The response was instantaneous, as all of the antiaircraft guns in the Japanese fleet opened up. They knew where I was going, and they didn't have to lead me. They fired directly up over the carrier.

In moments, at ten thousand feet there was a black cloud of bursting shells from the 40mm and 5-inch guns. It was so thick I couldn't see through it. I knew I'd be dead in the next thirty seconds, but I also knew that if I had it to do over again, with all of the other alternatives I had, I'd be here now.

I flashed through the cloud, knowing it was filled with screaming metal from the explosions. I expected to feel the plane jolted any second, but I continued on. A second deadly cloud was forming at four thousand feet from the exploding 20mm shells. It was directly over the carrier, I had no choice but to fly through it.

Once again my luck held as I screamed down on the carrier, which now completely filled my gunsight. I rested my finger on the bomb-release button. I kept going. I wanted to make absolutely sure I got a hit. When it seemed I was going to hit the ship, I pushed the release and pulled out. I had not looked at my altimeter or air speed. I was way over the red line of the aircraft, and of course blacked out from the G forces on the pullout.

After a moment, I was conscious but couldn't see. I heard a slight change in the pitch of the noise and eased forward on the stick. Blood instantly returned to my brain, and I could see again, and what I saw scared me to death. I was so low I was clipping the spray from the waves. I was also forty knots over the maximum speed for the plane. But the main thing was, I made it—until I looked up ahead. I was flying right into the side of the *Oyodo*, a Japanese heavy cruiser. I pulled back on the stick, and nothing happened. I couldn't gain altitude. The elevator control must have been frozen due to the speed. Putting both hands on the stick and bracing myself against the rudder pedals, I pulled with all of my strength. The nose rose slightly, enough to clear the hull, but not enough to clear the superstructure. I was going to hit the ship. At the last moment I tried the aileron. It responded, and in that instant I rolled the plane on its right side and flew between the cruiser's second gun turret and the bridge.

I was perhaps three feet from the windows on the bridge and could see the Japanese officers and enlisted men commanding the ship. There was an admiral in dress whites, complete with sword. The other officers and men were also in dress whites. I was going 530 miles an hour, and I only got a glimpse, but that image is impressed on my mind forever.

I quickly distanced myself from the ship and slowed to a reasonable speed. I made no effort to take evasive action, as I knew no one was paying special attention to me any longer. Somehow, my subconscious alerted me that I shouldn't be flying in a straight line, regardless. At the speed I was going, it was painful to make a sharp turn, but I did. Moments later, there was a gigantic explosion where I would have been. That cruiser had turned one of its 8-inch gun turrets and fired at me. If I hadn't taken evasive action, they would have hit me. I made another turn, with the same results. They were really determined. One more shot and I pulled up into a cloud, where I circled, then came down in another direction.

We had barely rendezvoused when Hugh called on the radio. "The carrier's sinking, and they're trying to take the admiral's staff off on a cruiser. Go down and strafe it."

We didn't need a second invitation. We peeled off and dove on the *Oyodo*, which had pulled up at the stern of the carrier. Officers were jumping from the carrier to the forward deck of the cruiser. They were huddled together. We tore them to pieces. No one could have survived the fire from our machine guns. I only hoped this was the same staff that was aboard when they attacked Pearl Harbor. When that attack took place and I was a student in college, I never in my wildest imagination thought that I would have the chance to avenge that attack. I felt the greatest satisfaction I'd ever felt in my life.

Flying back to our carrier from the Battle off Cape Engaño, I thought of the way I'd struggled to take those cans of peas to school to feed the Japanese. What if some of the Japanese I fed were on that ship? I cursed the fact that my mother wasn't the ordnance officer on the carrier. I wouldn't have had a five-hundred-pound bomb; it would have been at least one thousand pounds or maybe two thousand pounds, even if I could barely fly with it.

We had sunk the *Zuikaku*. Her sister ship, the *Shokaku*, had been sunk in the Battle of the Coral Sea. They were the two largest operational carriers the Japanese ever had. The *Zuikaku* was the last Japanese aircraft carrier afloat that had taken part in the raid on Pearl Harbor, and assisting in her sinking was beyond my wildest expectations.

The *Zuikaku* had been commissioned on September 25, 1941, and was the flagship of the Imperial Japanese Navy as well as the flagship of Admiral Ozawa. She displaced thirty thousand tons and could carry eighty-four aircraft. Her antiaircraft guns numbered sixteen 5-inch and ninety-six 20mm cannons.

We had a number of hits on the carrier: five-hundred-pound bombs from the fighter planes, two-thousand-pound bombs from our dive-bombers, and several torpedo hits from the torpedo squadron. We lost one torpedo plane and a crew of three. The Japanese lost 843 officers and men when she went down. They and other countries were learning the consequences of a sneak attack on the United States.

THIRTY-FOUR

# DITCHING AND RESCUE IN A TYPHOON

While we were attacking the Japanese fleet to the north, the Japanese fleet we had attacked the day before, coming through the Sibuyan Sea, had returned during the night and attacked the American fleet, supporting the landing on Leyte. Admiral Halsey and his battleships headed back to Leyte, never having gotten into range of the Japanese battleships up north.

Halsey did not make it back in time to help the supporting American fleet. They were completely at the mercy of the Japanese, but at a critical moment the Japanese turned and pulled out of the battle, retreating toward Hong Kong. Skip Hensen, our Japanese interpreter, who monitored the Japanese communications for the staff, told us later that when the American admiral in command of the jeep carriers and destroyer escorts got on the radio, imploring Halsey in non-coded language to come immediately, the Japanese commander thought this was the signal for Halsey to appear over the horizon and annihilate his fleet. Rather than lose the fleet, the Japs fled. In reality, Halsey was hundreds of miles to the north, and the Japanese could have sunk hundreds of ships in our invasion fleet at their leisure. It might have defeated our invasion of Leyte and the Philippines.

The following morning we were back in the waters off Leyte, and it was determined that in the battle, a Japanese heavy cruiser had been damaged and was unaccounted for. Once more we were going on a search. I drew the island of Samar for my search.

Samar is quite sizeable and had many stretches of shoreline where a large ship could be brought right up against cliffs and covered with camouflage netting. As a result, I flew at low speed, at an altitude of ten feet above the water's edge all the way around the island. The beauty was breathtaking, with magnificent beaches, hidden coves, and jungle coming right down to the water. It appeared a tropical paradise, but I found no Japanese cruiser. I returned to the carrier empty handed.

While I was gone, a strike was launched against docks at Manila. The strike force arrived at the target, and there, big as life, anchored in the middle of Manila Bay, was the Japanese cruiser. Back on the carrier, all hell broke loose. Another typhoon was expected, and they wanted to get that cruiser before weather made it impossible. Hugh Winters was to be target coordinator once again, and I was to fly his wing.

This time, armor-piercing bombs were loaded on the dive-bombers and torpedoes on the torpedo planes. We arrived over Manila without opposition, and antiaircraft fire was spotty. We took up a position high over the cruiser as Hugh ordered our planes to attack. It was a perfectly coordinated attack. I watched the ship, the size of a battleship. One moment it was twenty-five thousand tons of metal, then a tremendous explosion, and when the smoke cleared, nothing. It had simply disappeared in one great flash.

Several Zeros came out of the clouds, and we turned toward them, but before we got close enough to fire, they flew back into the clouds. The four of us had ventured to the south end of Manila Bay. The air suddenly filled with bursting shells from antiaircraft fire. I felt my plane rock slightly, but everything seemed to be under control. Then I noticed I was losing fuel. I called Hugh.

"You have a choice," he replied. "You can fly out past Corregidor, where the rescue sub is waiting, or try to make it back to the ship."

I knew that if I had to bail out over Manila, the odds were ten to one that the Japanese would get me. On the other hand, if I went down over the countryside, the odds were in my favor that friendly Philippine guerrillas would get to me first. Barney Garbow became my wingman, as I elected to try to make it back to the carrier.

Flying unopposed, the two of us made it to the east coast of Luzon, and things were looking up for my chances to make the carrier. I kept one eye on the fuel gauge and hoped for the best. Once over water, I was permitted to break radio silence and turn my IFF set to the emergency channel. This would show as a special blip on the carrier's radar screen, indicating that I was in trouble and my location. I put a call in to the ship. "Mohawk base, this is Mohawk Four, losing fuel fast; request permission to make a straight-in approach when I have you in sight." The answer was disheartening. "Negative, Mohawk Four, we are under attack and can't take you aboard."

With that, my engine cut out. I placed one more call to the carrier. "Mohawk base, this is Mohawk four, you and I are through." I fired my guns until I was out of ammunition, to lose as much weight as possible, and nosed over toward the ocean. The winds were mounting, as the typhoon was approaching. This was both good and bad: good, in that it reduced my landing speed, but bad, as it had whipped the waves up to forty feet and I was going into them.

I unlatched my parachute harness but tightened up on my shoulder straps as much as I could, and dropped my flaps. Slowing almost to stalling speed, I headed for the next wave and flew straight into it. Momentarily, the plane went under the water then bobbed up. Disconnecting the seat belt and shoulder harness, I scrambled out onto the wing and pulled my parachute with the survival pack attached out of the plane. In seconds I inflated the boat, threw everything in, and pushed off. My plane sank out of sight. Barney was circling me, and I waved that I was alright. My practice in getting out of a plane in an emergency had paid off. It took me only ten seconds.

Quickly taking the short lines provided in the survival pack, I tied myself to the boat and meticulously tied each piece of the equipment as well. In a wind such as this, it is easy to get thrown out of the boat, and it would blow away before you could swim for it.

I was now riding the one-man life raft up and down the forty-foot waves like a ride at an amusement park. The winds had also risen to forty knots. I was alone, sixty miles from Luzon and perhaps thirty miles from the fleet. I decided to put up the small sail and try to sail back to Luzon although the weather was going to be a problem. I could only imagine what it would be like out there at night if the waves got to one hundred feet.

Looking out over that endless sea I wondered what my chances really were. I was at least sixty miles from land, and that was held by the Japanese. Right now, a prison camp almost looked good. I had water and some survival food, but I was alone; my God, *was* I alone! I remembered the stories of the navy pilots early in the war and their courage under similar circumstances. In addition, I had no other choice; I was going to sail to the Philippines.

Carefully slipping the sail out of its case, I debated how to put it up in this wind. While I was so occupied, I glanced around the area as I hit the crest of a wave, and there in the distance was a destroyer approaching me. They had spotted me, which in itself is unbelievable. The ship kept approaching until it was quite close. When I was at the top of a wave, I could almost reach over and touch it, but when I dropped to the bottom of the trough, I couldn't see the ship.

This destroyer had picked up a number of pilots, and they had rigged a boom, which they could swing out with a cargo net attached. They threw me a line and pulled me into the V between the hull and the cargo net. I kneeled in the raft until the cargo net was right on top of me, then grabbed it and climbed up to the deck of the destroyer.

Everyone topside congratulated me. Then, an ordnance man took my pistol to clean. Others led me to the room of one of the officers and lent me some clothes until my flight suit could be washed and dried. I was now about to learn what life on a destroyer was like—in a typhoon.

The captain invited me up to his quarters. He was six feet tall and had not let two years at sea dampen his sense of humor. He was everything the skipper of a destroyer should be and more. I asked what he was doing so far from the fleet, but he just smiled. I had the feeling the ship had been detached for some special duty, such as landing some agents in the Philippines, but he never explained. In any event, I was damn glad he was there. He informed me that the *Lexington* had been hit by a kamikaze and had sustained considerable damage. They couldn't transfer me back to the carrier in any event, due to the weather, which got worse by the minute. By dinner time the waves were over sixty feet high. I thought it was rough on the carrier during the previous typhoon, but that was relatively calm compared with this.

The wardroom on a destroyer is one room at deck level running across the width of the ship. There was one long table that could seat all of the officers at a meal. The ship was rolling violently by dinner time, so the mess stewards placed metal poles an inch thick at each place, slipping them in a slot in the ceiling and screwing them into the steel deck in threaded holes provided for that purpose.

The trick was to sit down with your arms around a pole on each side of you so that you could hold your plate and roll with the ship without sliding to one side or the other.

I sat down to dinner with most of the ship's officers and was introduced to those I hadn't already met. The skipper was not present, as he ate alone in his cabin. The executive officer was senior man at the mess. I hadn't met him, and he had yet to make an appearance.

I was tipped off that the exec had just arrived on the ship when we were last in Ulithi, having come from a desk job in Washington. I could feel that the rest of the officers were not too fond of him.

Fourteen of us sat down, seven on each side of the table, and immediately the stewards brought us soup. Each man took the bowl of soup from the steward and held it in his two hands, keeping it level as the ship rolled. As the last bowl of soup was served, the executive officer walked in.

"Attention," the next senior officer shouted.

We all put our soups down and snapped to attention as the exec took his seat at the head of the table. The ship rolled precariously in his direction, and before anyone could do anything about it, the fourteen soups slid down to his end of the table and one by one fell off the table into his lap. It looked like something out of a Bugs Bunny cartoon. The executive officer sat there with the contents of fourteen hot soups in his lap and never said a word. No one laughed. The exec got up and left and didn't eat at the mess for the rest of the time I was aboard.

The weather continued to deteriorate, and by the following morning it was almost a full-fledged typhoon. Despite this, there were indications that the Japanese might be active, so the captain suggested that I position myself on top of the bridge with field glasses and a headset and act as a spotter, since I was trained in recognition of Japanese planes. I got up there on that bobbing ship and held on for all I was worth. It seemed somewhat like being up in the rigging of a sailing ship.

There was one other thing that bothered me: In the event of an attack, carriers were allowed to fire at enemy planes even if destroyers were in the background. Destroyers, in turn, were not allowed to fire into the carriers. Fortunately, we weren't attacked.

The next two days were beyond description. The waves got as high as one hundred feet, with winds of 170 miles an hour. The ship was totally blind at night, and she held her position in the formation by radar. Sometime during the second night, two destroyers vanished from the radar screen.

While I was eating dinner with the captain the second night, he informed me that two-thirds of the crew were so seasick they couldn't respond to a general-quarters alarm. Only three men aboard were not seasick to some extent, the skipper, the doctor, and myself, and this crew had been out for two years.

The following day the seas subsided enough that the crew was going to try to transfer me back to the carrier. They pulled alongside and passed a line, then a breeches buoy attached to a hawser, in preparation for me to get in the tiny seat and be hauled over to the other ship. Before they would send me back, they demanded payment of twenty quarts of ice cream, since the destroyer didn't have the equipment to make it. At last I knew what I was worth: twenty quarts of ice cream.

I watched the ice cream coming over to the destroyer and watched the line go taut as the ships rolled apart, then almost go in the ocean when they rolled toward each other. If they lost you in those seas, there'd be no finding you.

I climbed into the breeches and was pulled off the destroyer. My feet were almost in the water one moment then I was high in the air the next. I made it and gave a big sigh of relief. Returning to my room, I found that my two roommates had drunk all of my liquor. They said they did it because they thought I'd been lost, and they were so broken up about it. Somehow I didn't believe them.

The following day we were standing on the aft part of the bridge watching the combat air patrol land. The four planes were in the landing pattern, the first one in the groove. "What's with the third plane?" Pete Sprinkle threw out.

We all focused on the third plane on its downwind leg.

"It's losing altitude," I answered.

The plane continued to fly toward the water. "That's Knobby," Pete said. We watched in horror as the plane continued down and smashed into the ocean. Knobby Felt didn't get out as the plane sank out of sight. Did his eyesight finally catch up with him? Did he push those prescription goggles up to make the landing? We'd never know. All we knew was that Knobby was gone.

Once again the fleet headed back to Ulithi for supplies and rest. We needed both.

THIRTY-FIVE

# THE NAVY CROSS

Following a day of throwing the football on the flight deck and a little volleyball, we headed for the bar on Mogmog island. I ran into Hugh Sommers, a cadet I'd trained with at Naval Air Station Willow Grove. We sat under one of the palm trees and caught up on our duty since then.

"I was on one of the jeep carriers off the coast at Leyte," he began.

"Were you attacked by the Jap fleet?" I asked.

"We didn't know anything was up. I was having an early breakfast, when suddenly there was a funny noise. I looked up, and there was an eight-inch hole in the wall on one side of the ward room and another on the other side. An armor-piercing shell from a Japanese cruiser had gone right through the carrier."

"My God, why were they firing armor piercing?" I asked.

"The only thing we could think of was they thought our carriers were armored. If they'd fired high-explosive shells I wouldn't be here, along with a lot of others."

"What happened?"

"I raced up to the ready room and put on my flight gear, but we couldn't launch planes, as the Japs were coming from the north and we were going full speed to the south. The wind was from the north, and we couldn't get enough wind over the deck to launch planes. We couldn't outrun the Japanese cruisers, and they were bearing down on us. In addition, we were headed for land and would soon run aground."

"I don't believe this," I threw in.

"Neither do I, but it gets better. The captain of the carrier got on the speaker and said, 'In ten minutes we'll run aground if this cruiser doesn't sink us first. I'm not going down without a fight. In five minutes I'm going to issue everyone a gun, and in seven minutes I'm going to reverse course and ram the cruiser. We'll all go over the side, board the cruiser, and try to take the ship. This will be the first boarding of an enemy ship by the United States Navy since the War of 1812. Good luck.'"

"What happened?" I asked, holding my breath.

"The crew were lined up to be issued weapons, when the Japanese fleet turned around and fled. We'll never know why."

I bought Hugh as many beers as he could drink.

The following day a basketball tournament was announced, and, of course, the squadron entered a team. We had one big advantage: pilots were limited in height to six feet two inches, but we had an engineering officer who was six-four and a half and had played college basketball at an eastern powerhouse before the war. We also had a group of pilots that were five-eight to -ten and were quick and could run the legs off most of the others. We alternated the two teams each quarter, and within less than a week we were in the finals. As luck would have it, we ended up playing a team from the admiral's staff on our carrier. They also had some name athletes and it was not going to be any shoo-in.

The best player on the staff was Byron "Whizzer" White, who had already earned a nickname, "the Dentist," so named as he was continually checking your teeth with his elbow. Naturally, I drew him to guard in the finals. I have been on a lot of athletic fields and courts in my life, but I'd never been on any court with anyone as dirty as this guy. The worst part was, he was so good at it. We only had one official, the executive officer of the carrier. It's the only game I've ever been in where you wouldn't get a technical foul; you'd get a court-martial.

The game was about half-over, and I'd spent a good part of the time down on the steel deck after being tripped and shoved at just the right moment. Finally, I'd had enough.

The next time we went behind the ref, I sprinted ahead of Whizzer and turned and waited for him. I caught him flush on the chin and sent him down. I waited for him to get up and come after me. Instead, he got up and ran right past me. The tripping and elbows to the ribs continued. The next time, he knew what was coming, and I really let him have it. Again, he went down, and I marveled at the fact he was going to get up. Again, I waited for him, but again he ran right past me.

As I caught up with him, he turned and sneered, "What the hell's the matter with you?" "Nothing," I replied, " but as long as you keep playing this dirty, I'm going to hit you." He never said another word, but all of the dirty stuff stopped instantly. He still played hard as hell, and he was tough, but not dirty. We won the game by two points.

The following day they held an award ceremony on the flight deck. The air group commander made the awards. I received the Navy Cross for being a part of the group that sank the *Zuikaku*. The Navy Cross is the highest decoration in the United States Navy, second only to the Congressional Medal of Honor. Never in my wildest dreams could I imagine such an honor. John Paul Jones had received the first one. It gave me a real sense of history and the honor of the navy.

The citation read: "Lieutenant (Junior Grade) William Edgar Davis, III, United States Naval Reserve. For distinguishing himself by extraordinary heroism in operations against the enemy while serving as pilot of a carrier based fighter aircraft on 25 October 1944. Flying through intense antiaircraft fire, he made an aggressive attack on a Japanese carrier, first strafing and then delivering a well placed bomb from low altitude. After this attack the carrier was left burning and subsequently sank. His courage and skill were at all times in keeping with the highest tradition of the United States Naval Service."

I lay awake that night. It all seemed like a dream, a sophomore's idea of a glamorous life. I thought of Maui, but I knew that was a dream. The most amazing part was, I was still alive; or was I? Had I actually been killed a long time ago and was merely dreaming the end? Were all of the squadron that had died still dreaming they were in it, going through the same daily routine? Was there any way of telling if you were still alive?

There was one way, and several of the officers noticed. We were anchored near a hospital ship, and this meant nurses. Such things are not for the lower ranks; this is restricted to officers with scrambled eggs on their visors. The seven full commanders on the ship held a meeting in the executive officer's quarters. It was decided that the air group commander was the smoothest of the bunch so he was selected to go to the hospital ship and try his luck, but first of all, he had to go to the captain of the ship and see if he could borrow his launch. What excuse he gave I don't know, but he got the launch. That afternoon, all decked out in a freshly starched uniform, he headed for the ship.

Two hours later he returned with seven navy nurses, all dressed in white uniforms. They quickly disappeared into the executive officer's quarters, that room guarded by two marine MPs at either end of the corridor. A movie was going to be shown that evening on the hangar deck. The entire crew was assembled when the order was given, "Attention." We all snapped to. While we were standing at attention, the seven commanders each with a nurse walked to the front row of seats and sat down. There was not a sound from the crew; you could have heard a pin drop. None of us in the air group had seen a woman for at least six months, but some of the ship's crew hadn't seen a woman for two years or longer. The movie ended, and once again we stood at attention as the officers and dates filed out.

That night we were all in our bunks, but no one was sleeping. There was a tension in the air. The walls of the rooms in officer's country did not go quite to the ceiling, for purposes of ventilation. As a result, you could hear everything that was going on in the area.

At midnight the sound of high heels striking steel deck could be heard. No one said a word. The nurse was being led through the labyrinth of passageways to one of the commander's cabins. Perfume filled the air. Suddenly a female voice wafted over us. "I'll bet I'm lost," she said.

A male voice from a junior officer's room responded from the blackness. "You sure are, baby."

We had rested for quite a time and had an instinctive feel that something was coming. The following evening after dinner we got the word. The air group commander came in the wardroom. "Gentlemen," he began, "tomorrow morning the fleet is heading north. We're going to hit the Japanese islands. This will be the first action against them since General Doolittle's raid two years ago. We can expect heavy opposition. You are now the senior group, so you will lead the attack."

It had to come sooner or later. The Japanese fleet was one thing, the main islands another. We congregated in Bill Masoner's room, but no one was saying much. Suddenly, Hutto burst into the room. "Hey, fellows, there's a carrier coming in." We all looked at each other, then jumped up as a man and ran to the flight deck. There she was, entering the lagoon.

Word came almost immediately. "She's carrying an air group, our relief. We're not going to Japan tomorrow, we're going home."

I took the quart of bourbon that I'd squeezed from my roommates and drank the whole thing in an hour. My God, was I drunk? I realized I was going to throw up and raced for the forecastle deck and headed for the side. In my drunken haze, I misjudged and hit the cable and went over.

Hanging desperately to the cable, I tried to pull myself back on the deck while throwing up. All I could think was, "After what I've been through, what a way to die." I finally succeeded and got back aboard.

The following morning we took off and landed on the *Enterprise*, the carrier that was going to take us to Pearl Harbor. We watched the fleet leave for Japan. I would have liked to have gone with them; on the other hand, there's nothing wrong with living.

We were the only air group aboard, so we kept a combat air patrol over the ship for the first two days. After that, it was nothing but basketball. Our stay in Pearl Harbor was so brief we didn't even have time to go into town, but I had time to race to a pay phone on the base. There was a line of enlisted men a mile long waiting for the phone. I thought of pulling rank but decided against it. I was about to leave when one of the enlisted men spoke up.

"Sir, did you just come in on the *Enterprise*?"

"Yes," I answered.

"We'd let you in line, sir." I couldn't resist.

"Thank you."

I entered the phone booth and called the exchange on Maui. A voice I didn't recognize answered. "Lucette, please," I said.

"Lucette doesn't work here anymore, not since she got married."

We were transferred to a jeep carrier for the trip to San Diego.

THIRTY-SIX

# THE SETTING SUN

We rounded Point Loma, and I can tell you San Diego never looked so good. We were home, we'd made it, and on top of everything else, it was December 17. We were going to be home for Christmas. Disembarking from the carrier, we found we were assigned quarters, as there were apparently some formalities before we went on thirty-day leave.

The party at the Del Coronado Hotel that night was a real screamer, until we ran into several pilots from the air group that had been relieved a month ahead of us. They were still at San Diego. We dragged them away to find out why they hadn't gone home.

"You don't stand a chance in the world of getting home before Christmas," one of the pilots began.

"Why in the hell not?" I asked.

He just laughed. "Each one of you has to go before a board, one at a time. It's made up of four officers, one of them a captain and one a psychiatrist."

"A psychiatrist," I exploded, "what's that for?"

"They want to find out if you're ready to go out for another tour."

"You mean go out and fight again?" Pete asked.

"That's right," the pilot answered.

"Hell," Joe threw in, "no one wants to go out again. The odds build up against you. You know sooner or later you're going to get killed."

"That's the point," the pilot continued. "If you don't want to go because you know you're going to get killed, that's not considered a sufficient reason."

"What is?" I asked.

"If you're suffering battle fatigue, or some such thing, then you'll stay stateside, as an instructor or something. That's why they have the psychiatrist; he's supposed to be able to tell such things."

"How long does this take?" I asked.

"They've talked with some of our guys for four days. You may be here for two months." The following morning we held a squadron meeting. We came up with a plan.

Lin, now being senior in the squadron, was the first to go in before the dreaded board. They sat on one side of the table and Lin alone on the other. The captain started the proceedings.

"Congratulations, lieutenant, you're the only reserve officer commanding a squadron," he began.

"Thank you sir," Lin answered.

"Your squadron has made quite a record for itself."

Lin smiled and nodded.

"What has impressed you most about being back home?"

"The fresh fruit," Lin answered without hesitation.

The psychiatrist sat forward. "The fresh fruit?"

"Yes sir, I'd almost forgotten how good it tasted."

The board looked from one to another momentarily at a loss. Finally another officer spoke up. "How did you feel in combat?"

"Loved every second of it," Lin answered.

Again a pause. The last officer leaned forward. "How do you feel about going out again for another tour?"

"I can't wait, I want to get out there and finish the job."

The officers sat there dumbfounded. The psychiatrist finally broke the silence. "You actually want to go back into combat?"

"That's right, that's what I trained for and that's what I want to do."

The captain finally looked around the table. "Any other questions?" They all shook their heads no. "In that case, next man."

Lin had taken only ten minutes. We got the entire squadron through in less than three days. This is the only squadron in which every man volunteered to go back into combat immediately. This caused such a stir in the navy that Hugh Winters was flown back to

Washington to explain how he'd developed this kind of fighting spirit in an entire squadron. The truth was that we knew we were all going back into combat anyway, so we might as well say yes and get home for Christmas. No one, including the psychiatrist, tumbled to the truth.

The squadron did have a wonderful record: 155 planes shot down, plus 16 probables; 190 destroyed on the ground, plus 127 damaged; and over 100,000 tons of shipping sunk.

The squadron received fifteen Navy Crosses, one of those to Hutto, the bravest of the whole bunch. His photographic flights at low altitude in a straight line, ignoring the ever-present antiaircraft fire, were an inspiration to all of us.

Home for Christmas meant more that year than any in my life.

I was shocked to see my father. My mother seemed to be in good health, but my father definitely was not. Nitroglycerin tablets were the order of the day when he became exhausted. His hair had turned from gray to white, and he no longer had the look of vitality in his face. I could tell he was proud of me, although he wouldn't put it into words. His only remark regarding the Navy Cross was, "Did you have to do something that brave?"

I had never asked in my letters about my dog Spec, and my family never mentioned him. I guess I knew that he'd died, and I really didn't want to know, but coming home to a house without him was the straw that broke the camel's back. I wanted to come home to that dog.

That Christmas I enjoyed the parties to the fullest. Everything seemed festive. I went to downtown Philadelphia to buy a few things and stopped by the Federal Reserve Bank to find out how my college friend Bill Davis was doing. When I arrived at his father's office, his secretary told me Mister Davis would want to see me but he was in an important meeting. She tiptoed into the meeting and came out in a few moments.

"He does want to see you and asked if you'd mind waiting for fifteen minutes. The meeting will be over, and he'd like you to have lunch with him."

I, of course, said yes. In fifteen minutes precisely, Mister Davis came out, accompanied by seven other men: the Senate Banking Committee. The nine of us went to lunch in the executive dining room. I wasn't prepared to discuss the economic situation in the United States, but the only thing they were interested in was my experiences in the war. It was a great lunch, and I got Bill's number in Washington.

The phone call to Bill was a joy, but all I heard from him was the mistake he had made by electing to go for an engineering job in the navy rather than volunteering for combat. It was the regret of his life. Once established in Washington in the Bureau of Ships, he put a request in every month through his commanding officer to be transferred to the fleet. His requests were routinely turned down. Bill had received a commendation for something he'd developed in his job, but this meant nothing to him. In his own eyes he was a slacker, and nothing I could say to him would change his mind.

I called on Duke's family, hoping I could lessen the sorrow of Duke's death. I didn't even come close. They were the most bitter people I'd ever met in my life. They didn't blame the Japanese, but rather the United States government and especially the navy. They were beyond consoling. Nothing I said got through. I've never felt such pain in a family, and I realized that this was being repeated in thousands of families across America. After a short time I beat a hasty retreat.

A merry Christmas came and went, and I was nearing the time that I would leave and rejoin the squadron for a brief period of training, then back into combat. I could see the strain on my father's and mother's faces. I could only imagine them facing what Duke's family had.

I was within days of leaving when the new orders arrived by wire. I was to report to the California Institute of Technology for two years of graduate work in aeronautical engineering. The navy was preparing for a long war, and they wanted men in the Bureau of Aeronautics who were both pilots and engineers. At last, being an engineer paid off. I could see the change in my father's face. A tremendous load had been taken off his shoulders.

My father had held out until I got home, but then I think he knew his time had come. Between worrying throughout the Depression and then worrying about me in combat, his heart gave out. I received the telephone call shortly after reporting to Cal Tech. He was only fifty-nine.

The class at Cal Tech was made up of low-ranking officers, but every one of us had been in combat. My old squadron, "Fighting Nineteen," reformed and eventually made it out to Maui on their way to the Pacific. They were there when the war with Japan was over. They never made it back into combat.

Just as the war ended, I received a note from the other Bill Davis that his request for active duty had finally been accepted. He was to join a cruiser in the Pacific and was part of the fleet that steamed into Hong Kong to accept the Japanese surrender there. The first night they had shore leave, Bill and several of the other ship's officers went ashore and found a restaurant up on the side of a mountain. After dinner and many sake martinis, four of them headed down the mountain in a jeep. They were all no doubt very drunk and drove off a cliff, killing all of them. Bill had avoided combat for the sake of his father and ended up a victim of a drunk driving accident. He was the finest friend I ever had. I tried many times to reach his family, but to no avail. I suspect they weren't taking calls, especially from someone that had the same name as their son.

Graduating from Cal Tech, I was offered a job with Bell Aircraft Company as a preliminary design engineer and test pilot, which I accepted. Shortly after my arrival, Bob Stanley, the vice president of engineering, asked me if I'd ever thought of flying the X-1, the first plane designed to fly through the sound barrier.

"It's the only thing I've thought about since I arrived here," I told him.

"You've got it," he replied.

We sent my qualifications to the Army Air Corps at Wright Field but never received an answer. Instead, the Air Corps announced that they were going to do the test flight, and it would be made by Captain Chuck Yeager. My chance for immortality vanished.

We held a squadron reunion twenty-five years later, and by this time, being the youngest in the squadron no longer mattered. Del Prater and I, the two youngest, asked the skipper, Hugh Winters, about Toby Cook, the original executive officer.

"I've never told anyone about this," he confided, "but I began to realize that he was a fine naval officer, but a poor pilot. I also knew that I was going to be promoted to air group commander and he'd become skipper of the fighter squadron. I called him into my room and told him I was recommending him for a job on another carrier as navigation officer. It would have been a career step up.

"He went through the roof and accused me of trying to deny him his rightful place as skipper. He said it was because his father had been a mustang, and if I went through with it, he'd go down to his room immediately and commit suicide. I backed down and told him he was all wrong and went ahead and recommended him for skipper of the squadron—a mistake I'll regret for the rest of my life."

I stayed in touch with Pete Sprinkle after the war. He'd gone to USC and taken architecture. Running out of money before he completed his work, he moved to the Miami area and worked as an architectural draftsman until the Cuban "invasion" of Florida. He had been making one hundred dollars a week, but a number of world-famous

Cuban architects, fleeing Castro, came to Miami and offered to work for fifty dollars a week. Pete was immediately out of work and couldn't find anything. Shortly thereafter he was diagnosed with cancer and died after a brief illness. The death certificate said he died of cancer, but I knew he died of a broken heart. He could no longer make a living in the country he'd volunteered to fight to protect, displaced by men who wouldn't fight for their country.

The last time we saw Joe Kelley he was floating in the harbor at Haha Jima. I assumed he was taken prisoner and spent the rest of the war in a Japanese prisoner of war camp. It wasn't until the second tier of war crimes trials in Tokyo that I found out what had happened to him.

After we left the area, the commander of the Japanese garrison on Chichi Jima, Major Sueo Matoba, also known as the Tiger of Chichi Jima, had Joe brought before him. The major thought all night about his next action. In the morning he had Joe killed, then instructed the army chef to cook him. The major had a table set on the parade field and assembled all of the troops in a formal parade and proceeded to eat Joe in front of them. He made a speech to the effect that he was doing this to show that the Japanese had more spirit than the Americans. He then had Joe served to the troops. He was found guilty of war crimes and hung.

Many men mentioned in this book or who served in the air group went on to positions of prominence. Ben Buttenweiser was appointed assistant high commissioner for Germany. Don Engen, of the dive-bombing squadron, stayed in the navy and made admiral, then after retirement headed the Federal Aviation Administration. Upon retiring from that, he became head of the Aerospace Division of the Smithsonian Institute. Unfortunately, he was killed flying an experimental glider over the Nevada desert in 1999. A number of the men became airline pilots. Ed Schock became a test pilot. Hutto was one of the first Blue Angels. Byron White was appointed a justice in the United States Supreme Court. A. Q. Jones resumed his career as an architect and became dean of the School of Architecture at the University of Southern California.

And there were many more. No one will ever know what the third of the squadron that were killed would have done, all lost because of that idiot on the white horse. Hirohito, the great war criminal of World War II, who remained as emperor but was advised that he was no longer a god.

The squadron shot down 155 enemy planes while losing only two in aerial combat. No torpedo-bomber or dive-bomber that we were protecting was shot down by an enemy plane.

It was a phenomenal experience; I only wish I had done more. I still have one piece of naval uniform, my officer's cap, complete with the sticker from the Stork Club on the hat band.